Solving the Productivity Puzzle

Solving the Productivity Puzzle

How to engage, motivate and develop employees to improve individual and business performance

Tim Ringo

Publisher's note

Every possible effort has been made to ensure that the information contained in this book is accurate at the time of going to press, and the publishers and author cannot accept responsibility for any errors or omissions, however caused. No responsibility for loss or damage occasioned to any person acting, or refraining from action, as a result of the material in this publication can be accepted by the editor, the publisher or the author.

First published in Great Britain and the United States in 2020 by Kogan Page Limited

Apart from any fair dealing for the purposes of research or private study, or criticism or review, as permitted under the Copyright, Designs and Patents Act 1988, this publication may only be reproduced, stored or transmitted, in any form or by any means, with the prior permission in writing of the publishers, or in the case of reprographic reproduction in accordance with the terms and licences issued by the CLA. Enquiries concerning reproduction outside these terms should be sent to the publishers at the undermentioned addresses:

2nd Floor, 45 Gee Street	122 W 27th St, 10th Floor	4737/23 Ansari Road
London	New York, NY 10001	Daryaganj
EC1V 3RS	USA	New Delhi 110002
United Kingdom		India
www.koganpage.com		

Kogan Page books are printed on paper from sustainable forests.

© Tim Ringo, 2020

The rights of Tim Ringo to be identified as the author of this work has been asserted by him in accordance with the Copyright, Designs and Patents Act 1988.

ISBNs

Hardback	978 1 78966 476 8
Paperback	978 1 78966 474 4
Ebook	978 1 78966 475 1

British Library Cataloguing-in-Publication Data

A CIP record for this book is available from the British Library.

Library of Congress Cataloging-in-Publication Data

Names: Ringo, Tim, author.
Title: Solving the productivity puzzle : how to engage, motivate and develop employees to improve individual and business performance / Tim Ringo.
Description: 1 Edition. | New York : Kogan Page Inc, 2020. | Includes bibliographical references and index.
Identifiers: LCCN 2020011670 (print) | LCCN 2020011671 (ebook) | ISBN 9781789664744 (paperback) | ISBN 9781789664768 (hardback) | ISBN 9781789664751 (ebook)
Subjects: LCSH: Employee motivation. | Employees–Training of. | Manpower planning. | Organizational change. | Organizational effectiveness.
Classification: LCC HF5549.5.M63 R56 2020 (print) | LCC HF5549.5.M63 (ebook) | DDC 658.3–dc23
LC record available at https://lccn.loc.gov/2020011670
LC ebook record available at https://lccn.loc.gov/2020011671

Typeset by Integra Software Services, Pondicherry
Print Managed by Jellyfish Solutions

To my father Charles Philip Sr, and my father-in-law P B Michael Handscomb, both of whom were thinking about and working to improve employee experience and people productivity decades before I took up the subject.
From the testimonials of those that worked with them, they both had a tremendous impact on the organizations and the people they led; I am grateful for this and for their input and inspiration, much of which I hope I have captured in this book.

CONTENTS

List of figures xi

Introduction 1

01 The future is more malleable than you think 7
    The emerging challenges facing organizations and people today 14
      The technology tsunami 17
      The shrinking workforce 18
      The stressed-out workforce 20
      The skills development treadmill (is speeding up!) 21
      The motivation and engagement gap 23
      The wrong people, wrong place, wrong time dilemma 25
      The avalanche of data dilemma 27
      The machines are coming (look busy!) 28
      The productivity paradox 31
    References 33

02 The productivity paradox: the peril and the promise 37
    The value of productive people 40
    Engaged people do more stuff, better 49
    Creating drive in the workforce 51
      Autonomy 52
      Mastery 56
      Purpose 59
    Rewards re-invented 62
    Workforce employee experience and well-being 66
    Innovation: the engine driving engaged people and greater productivity 71
    References 76

03 People engagement, innovation and performance – PEIP 81

Work smarter, not harder – it's OK, really 85
  Working smarter is doing more 86
  Working smarter is not working to the deadline 88
  Working harder can make you sick 89
  Smarter data can be more insights 90
The integrated human capital lifecycle is working uber-smart 92
PEIP: solving the productivity paradox for driving peak people performance 97
  HR operating model 97
  Tools and technology 101
  Mindset, behaviours and skills 104
PEIP unpacked 110
  Right people 110
  Right skills 114
  Skills forecasting – aka skills anticipation 117
  Right place, right time (strategic workforce planning) 124
  Right motivation 136
PEIP – bringing it all together 139
References 139

04 Turbo-charging the future 145

Five trends to ride, now 145
The ageing workforce is not ageing so fast anymore 147
Gender balancing and the power of female/male co-leadership 151
Create innovation with 'different brains' 154
Harness the intelligence of the machines 160
Digital at home, digital at work 168
  An (abbreviated) history of the human resource information system (HRIS) 172
  Fast forward to the modern HRIS of the 21st century 176
Digital at work, finally! 177
References 178

05 Making the case for change 181

The optimists' case: it's a strong one 181
What is an effective 'case for change'? 183

The human point of view 184
Technology 184
Economic viability 184
What do you want to do? Articulate your case for 'why now?' 184
What outcomes are you seeking? 185
What are the pros and cons? Risks, challenges, opportunities 185
What is the business case? Qualitative and quantitative benefits 186
Who are your stakeholders? The decision makers 186
What is the cost of doing nothing? The monetary and opportunity costs of no change 186
What is your roadmap for change? Proposed options and scenarios to get from here to there 187
Identifying the benefits of PEIP 187
Simplification and modernization 188
Actionable insights 189
Intelligent processes and technology 189
Employee engagement and experience 190
Total workforce management 190
Quantifying the value of PEIP: the business case 190
The PEIP business case: what does good look like? 191
Quantifying PEIP 195
Developing a roadmap: getting from here to there 198
Step 1: Programme vision 198
Step 2: The critical goals 198
Step 3: The implementation strategies 199
Step 4: The tactics 199
Step 5: Potential roadblocks 200
Step 6: The milestones 200
Step 7: Management and accountability 200
Beating the transformation odds: key success factors 202
References 203

06 A workplace revolution – are you an optimist or a pessimist? 205

Seize the moment – or let it pass? 205
The role of small to medium-sized organizations 206
The public sector role 209

Engage talent to join 'the mission' 210
PEIP for public sector roles 212
Political will to drive PEIP in society 213

The private sector role 215
Know 216
Plan 216
Engage 217
Invest 217
Measure 218

The human sector role 218
Optimist or pessimist? Your choice 220
References 224

Index 227

LIST OF FIGURES

Figure 0.1	People engagement, innovation and performance (PEIP) 4
Figure 0.2	Turbo-charge PEIP 4
Figure 1.1	The HR value model 8
Figure 1.2	Technological progress over time 15
Figure 1.3	Learning as a tool for retention 23
Figure 1.4	Talent shortfalls from poor planning 26
Figure 2.1	Projected average rate of growth in GDP 46
Figure 2.2	Engagement and business outcomes 50
Figure 3.1	Workforce analytics: predicting the future (not the past) 91
Figure 3.2	The integrated human capital lifecycle 92
Figure 4.1	The evolution of HR technology 173
Figure 5.1	The high-level benefits of PEIP 188
Figure 5.2	Main areas of business value of PEIP 193
Figure 5.3	The PEIP value tree 196
Figure 5.4	A typical return on investment summary 197
Figure 5.5	HR transformation roadmap – an example 201

Introduction

All of us are born with a desire to contribute; we are hard-wired to be useful to each other and to society as a whole. If you think about it, there are few things more satisfying than a job well done. Having a sense of purpose, mastering a task and having others approve of, or even admire what we achieve is highly motivating. It feels good.

Problem is, as we grow older and our experiences build over time, many of us become disillusioned, disappointed or just plain bored by the work we do – we get in a rut. The joy diminishes from the day-to-day piling up of things to do that do not align with personal values, personal motivations, aspirations and/or the types of skills we wish to master. There are few things more demotivating than this.

Of course, this happens to everyone at some point; however, when dissatisfaction lasts months, and months turn into years, something has gone wrong. Why continue doing something that does not align to one's personal motivations and desires?

There comes a time when you ought to start doing what you want. Take a job that you love. You will jump out of bed in the morning. I think you are out of your mind if you keep taking jobs that you don't like because you think it will look good on your resume. Isn't that a little like saving up sex for your old age?

WARREN BUFFETT, INVESTMENT GURU, CHAIRMAN
AND CHIEF EXECUTIVE OFFICER OF BERKSHIRE HATHAWAY

There is a certain truth to what Warren Buffet says here; however, when one must worry about a mortgage, school fees, a car payment or a student loan to pay back, the mind becomes focused on this at the expense of aspiration and desire. The real reason that so many of today's workforce end up in a rut is far more complex than just pulling up your bootstraps and going out to find that perfect job. In fact, many of the reasons people fall into uninspiring work are outside of their control.

If you think about the economic realities the vast majority of people face on a day-to-day basis it's no wonder that we sometimes fall into a trap of taking what is on offer at any given point. Often the dilemma starts from a young age: Do we go to university? Can we afford it? Can we make the grade? Or do we skip further education and go for an entry-level position and work our way up? This is a profound decision for a 17- to 18-year-old. However, this is where most of us start our quest for that perfect job, the ultimate career. To add to the daunting task, perfect jobs do not grow on trees, so even if a teenager has a clear view about what they want to do, how do they find that job? And what do they do to support themselves until that job is discovered? After all, it can take years to get where we want to be.

Additionally, if you think about the current state of the world of work, the method by which people find careers and careers find people is largely unchanged since the beginning of the Industrial Revolution. True, today we have LinkedIn and some digital job posting boards, but largely the process is the same as it has always been: employer posts job, prospective employee finds posting (mainly online, these days) and applies. From there, the process of interview and assessment, selecting candidates and getting them onboarded is also largely unchanged. It's a very two-dimensional world controlled by supply and demand, navigated with a bit of luck (for both employee and employer). It's highly inefficient, time consuming, and rarely gets the right person, with the right skills and the right motivations in the right job at the right time. Throw in the whims of the normal business cycle – growing economy followed by shrinking economy (supply and demand) – and the complexities multiply. This traditional way of finding and deploying the workforce in constantly changing market conditions, I would argue, is the fundamental reason why so many people find themselves doing uninspiring work and feeling trapped in it. Pull up your bootstraps and go find that job! Good luck with that.

The other challenge today's workforce deals with is how to get stuff done while living at the centre of a maelstrom of data and technological change. With all the 'amazing' technology that we have, one would think we must be significantly more productive than we were, say, 20 years ago. Unfortunately, this is not the case. It is true, studies show, that technology and gadgets have made us more productive at home, but when we get to work, it's like 1997 all over again. We sit at a desk with a PC, a mouse and most of us still use Windows or Mac as our interface to the organization. Additionally, most organizations are constantly throwing new systems and processes at the workforce, with very little training or explanation of what they are supposed to do with the latest system. So, it's no wonder that most economists are finding that increases in human productivity levelled off around 2004 and are now heading downward (Guillemette and Turner, 2018).

Everyone has been made for some particular work and the desire for that work has been put in every heart.

RUMI, ANCIENT PERSIAN POET PHILOSOPHER

What would the world of work be like if we could turn technology and technological change to our advantage and use it to match the perfect person to the perfect job; a job that gives purpose, the opportunity to master new things, and the opportunity to be left to get on with that work without too much interference by others? What if we change the mindset (and processes) to think differently about bringing in new talent and deploying it at the right time and right place with the right skills and right motivations. Most would say this is impossible in today's workplace – the tools we have are very one-dimensional, and do not help us to think and do differently. And you can add to this today's economic realities, where there is a complete focus on quarterly results, profits, cutting costs, growing the top line, and saving the taxpayer money (in the public sector) that override many people's desires and motivations: just get on with the work! Produce *more* with *less*, meet objectives, meet the deadline, and at all costs, deliver! Most of us get caught up in these whirlwinds and we put our heads down and plod through, quarter after quarter – a treadmill.

But does the world of work have to be this way? Is there a different way to do things, a different way to look at things? Maybe the simple 'equation' given in Figure 0.1 can illustrate a way forward.

What if we created a workforce 'marketplace' that not only balances supply and demand of resources, but also maps people's skills, motivations, and aspirations to the right job at the right time (PEIP)? If we can achieve

FIGURE 0.1 People engagement, innovation and performance (PEIP)

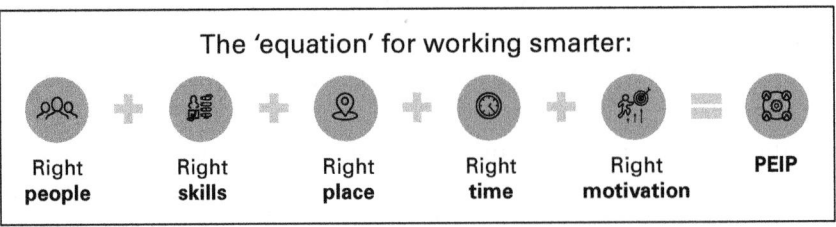

FIGURE 0.2 Turbo-charge PEIP

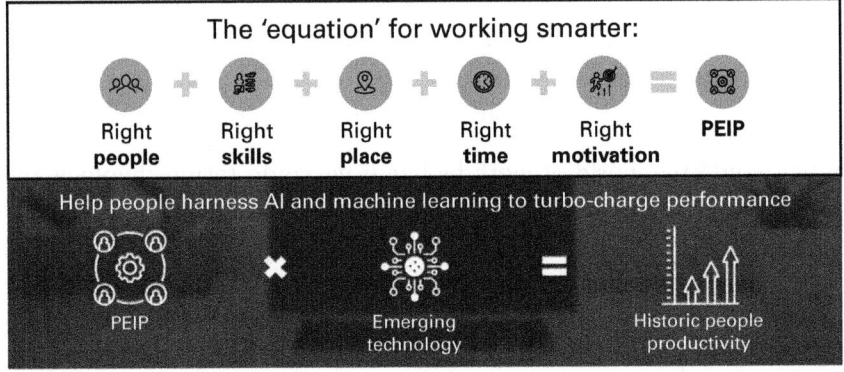

this, then (as postulated by Rumi) the chances that people 'made for some particular work and the desire for that work' find and succeed in that work go up dramatically. The benefits for individuals, and society at large, would be tremendous – even miraculous.

Imagine, then, if we 'turbo-charged' this equation with emerging 'intelligent' technology, as pictured in Figure 0.2, using artificial intelligence (AI) and machine learning to further maximize the efficiencies of PEIP – a new way of working where individuals and organizations use smart technology to find each other, to get the right people in the right role. People doing jobs they love for organizations they love will be highly engaged and create great places to work. Imagine that, once PEIP is in place, people could leverage smart technology to help them be even more productive than they are today; robots working for us, and with us, to make work more fun and fulfilling. Let the robots do the mundane work and free up the humans to do higher-order work. Sounds like science fiction, but it's not – the technology to make this happen is available today, and the time for this to happen is here and now. Demographic and other trends in the work environment are rapidly emerging alongside the latest technology trends and are creating a 'perfect storm' of challenge, but also *opportunity*.

Consider trends such as the elongation of human life-span, the realization that people on the autistic spectrum bring incredibly innovative ideas, there are more senior and experienced women in work, and the fact that we have a much better scientific understanding of the workings of the human brain and what truly motivates people. These trends, combined with PEIP, demonstrate that we may be on the cusp of a truly transformative time in the world of work. One where 'everyone has been made for some particular work and the desire for that work' can be realized.

There is no doubt that the challenges that organizations and the workforce face today are myriad and growing in scale and complexity. It is easy to get overwhelmed and feel buffeted by the workplace transformation that is well underway; it feels like we are barely maintaining control of the day-to-day, let alone the future. However, in this book we are going to be pragmatic and open about the challenges we face, while at the same time combining new ideas with concrete, proven solutions to address the challenges; to harness them to our advantage. As we unpack PEIP and other concepts throughout the six chapters of this book, new ways of thinking and doing will emerge and the fog will begin to clear. True, some of the new ways of thinking and doing will require some fundamental, even radical, change in how we operate today. However, others will be more a matter of tweaks in our approach to work.

We will unpack each component of PEIP in turn, building on each section, while also presenting real examples of what many successful organizations are doing today to leverage the concept. This is not a theoretical book of 'what-ifs' and 'wouldn't it be nice?'; the ideas here will be grounded in the art of the possible. Additionally, we will focus on the *value* of improved people and organizational performance. Making change work requires investment of significant amounts of scarce resources and funds. It's no good coming up with new ways of thinking and doing if the resources required to make it happen cannot be justified by concrete returns. Demonstrating clear value and a realistic roadmap for how to make change happen are critical in taking the ideas here and making them a reality. Success will be dependent on two key things: first, the courage and commitment to embrace new ways of thinking and doing; and, second, grounding programmes of change in what humans can realistically absorb as well as in the fiscal realities of our age. It may seem like these are two very big asks, so let's put them in the context of some modern, Irish wisdom to lighten the load:

The world is more malleable than you think, and it's waiting for you to hammer it into shape.

BONO, MUSICIAN

Reference

Guillemette, Y and Turner, D (2018) The long view: scenarios for the world economy to 2060, OECD Economic Policy Papers, 22, OECD Publishing, Paris. Available from: https://doi.org/10.1787/b4f4e03e-en (archived at https://perma.cc/AE5Y-4969)

01

The future is more malleable than you think

In talks I deliver across Europe, the Middle East, Asia and North America, I like to start with a seemingly simple question to the audience: 'How many of you know exactly how many employees you have as of today? Please raise your hand.' Surprisingly, on average, only about 35–40 per cent raise their hands. I then ask those who have their hands up to keep them up for the follow-on question: 'How many of you know exactly how many employees you will need 18 months from now, and what type of skills they will require?' Almost all the hands go down, followed by some nervous laughter.

This story is illustrative of where we are today. Most leaders in most organizations do not have a basic grasp of the make-up of their workforces, both now and in the near future. Yet few would argue against the fact that this is a fundamental aspect of running a business effectively. In fact, many would argue that as a result, they feel like pilots at the helm of an aircraft, in a fog, with faulty navigation systems. A very uncomfortable position to be in while the turbulent winds of a highly unpredictable global economy buffet us around.

Yet when we think about it, it should not be a surprise that we struggle to get to grips with such a basic understanding of the people who make up our workforces. The answer can be found squarely in how we measure success in human resources (HR) organizations; we expect HR to stay focused on the back office of people operations, spending their time refining and optimizing areas like payroll, benefits, shared services and clunky HR systems. Of course, all of these things are important; however, they tend to suck up all of the oxygen, leaving little room or time to focus on what really

FIGURE 1.1 The HR value model

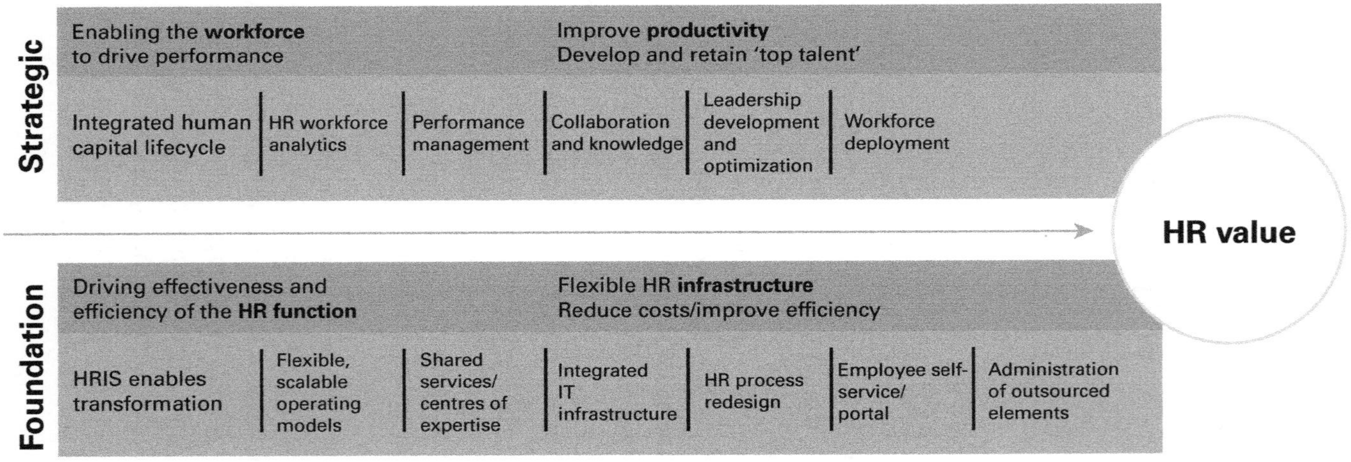

Strategic

Enabling the **workforce** to drive performance

Improve **productivity**
Develop and retain 'top talent'

| Integrated human capital lifecycle | HR workforce analytics | Performance management | Collaboration and knowledge | Leadership development and optimization | Workforce deployment |

Foundation

Driving effectiveness and efficiency of the **HR function**

Flexible HR infrastructure
Reduce costs/improve efficiency

| HRIS enables transformation | Flexible, scalable operating models | Shared services/ centres of expertise | Integrated IT infrastructure | HR process redesign | Employee self-service/ portal | Administration of outsourced elements |

→ **HR value**

matters and drives the most benefit: getting the right people, right skills, right place, right time, with the right motivation – people engagement, innovation and performance (PEIP).

As a result, HR organizations end up trying to balance two 'value agendas': 1. running an effective and efficient HR back office – saving money; 2. enabling people productivity and engagement – making money (see Figure 1.1). The key thing to note is that these two value agendas are not equal. The top part of the model – people productivity – has been extensively studied and found to be worth significantly more dollars than the bottom part of the model – HR efficiency and effectiveness. McKinsey Global Institute (Bucy *et al*, 2016) found that engaging the workforce in improving productivity is worth up to 10 times the value of saving money through efficient HR services. This point is not to diminish the bottom part of the model at all. In fact, it is not possible to engage the workforce in driving more productivity if there is not an effective and efficient HR organization, underpinned by a best practice operating model, with processes and a technology platform to facilitate performance. As most HR leaders will confess, they end up spending the vast majority of their time in the bottom part of the model. Problem is, no HR organization will win medals from the chief executive officer (CEO) or the management board for an efficient HR back office. It is just expected that this happens, and the only time it gets noticed is when something goes awry. However, give the CEO a more productive workforce that produces more with less, drives more top-line revenue, greater customer satisfaction and more profit (or uses less taxpayer funding) and you are on to a winner. So, the question becomes how to balance these two agendas and become heroes – a daunting task. Let's use a real-life story to illustrate.

CASE STUDY
Global telecom company

A short time ago, I was the strategic adviser to the HR Leadership team of a large global telecom – a company that had been in the midst of a very acquisitive phase, buying up smaller telecoms all around the globe, and growing rapidly as a result.

The chief human resource officer (CHRO) was attending a regular company board meeting, where the first question from one of the board came his way: 'How many employees do we have as of today?' After flipping through numerous briefing notes, he had to admit that he did not have that figure. The follow-on question was even more pointed (and problematic): 'Do we have any figures for how many people we will need in 18 months from now, and what types of skills will be required?' Again, the CHRO, flustered, had to admit that he did not have those figures either. He was told, in no uncertain terms, not to return to the board until he had these basic facts about the company workforce.

Minutes after this HR executive was summarily dismissed from the board meeting, I got a call from the director of HR Strategy, sounding somewhat rattled: 'Tim, we need to get the HR Leadership team together and figure out how many employees we have today, and how many we will need in 18 months; as well as a picture of the types of skills we will require in the future.' My answer was probably not what he was expecting: I told him that this would be a pointless exercise and would not give us the data or insights that we needed. Taken aback, he asked why; my response was to point out that there were over 40 different HR systems across the entire company, with just about as many different HR operating models. As a result, there was not 'one version of the truth' and therefore no way to get to a validated number on either question.

I reminded him that the week before we had discussed with the HR Leadership team the importance of addressing the problem where there was no consistency across the business in how HR operations were conducted. I also pointed out that this was not the fault of the HR Leadership as it was no surprise, given how many companies had been acquired and were still being assimilated into the group company. Each of those companies came with their own HR operating model, processes and legacy HR systems. Nonetheless, the situation needed immediate addressing as the company strategy of rapid growth through acquisition was at risk of failing if the HR operating model, processes and technology were not aligned to the business objectives.

The Strategy director noted that the chief information officer (CIO) and the IT department were well down the path of choosing a new human resource information system (HRIS): the decision had been taken to replace all legacy on-premise systems with a Cloud-based HRIS. This new system would be quickly implemented across the Group and would give 'one version of the truth' of HR data. I agreed that this was an important step but without defining the HR operating model and the HR IT landscape for the entire Group, the new system would reflect the current state of the organization: a chaotic mix of different ways of working in HR. We needed to define 'HR's reason for being'.

The key for them was to step back for a moment and define who they were as an HR organization today and how they would set up in the future to support business strategy while engaging the workforce in this strategy. Define who and what they wanted to be as an HR organization; what will best support the business in achieving its goals and how to get there.

I recommended we get the HR Leadership team together to work on this first, then let the decisions from this work drive the effort to answer the board's key questions about the workforce. We pulled the entire team together from all regions to spend two days at headquarters, where we put any discussions about a new HR system on hold and asked ourselves two basic questions:

1 **Where does the centre of HR management and operations sit?** At head office, in the local regions/offices, or a hybrid of both? In other words, is HR a 'federated' model – where the local regions and business units each have their own HR organization and operating model that is customized for each region – or a centralized HR organization at HQ – where one model is applied across the entire business (with minimal localization) – or a combination of both models?

2 **Who does talent management in the organization?** Does HR own the end-to-end talent management lifecycle, or is talent management pushed out into the business where it is mainly done by direct line managers? Are people managed by teams of HR business partners or are managers responsible for leading teams: recruiting, personal objectives, learning, workforce deployment, succession, etc; or again, a hybrid model of both?

As I pointed out to the team at the time, it's important to keep in mind that there is no overall right answer to these questions, other than what is right for a particular organization. The choices completely depend on the business strategy and culture of that organization.

Throughout my work across organizations large and small, answering these two questions is a very effective place to start. In the case of this particular organization's HR Leadership team, after a few days of debating the different options, it was decided that a 'federated' model was the best fit for a company that had mainly been built by acquisition across a wide geographic footprint. The second question was where the most heated debate took place: who was responsible for talent management?

There were two camps, roughly spilt down the middle, in terms of numbers: Group One felt the right model for managing talent was for HR to be mainly responsible in coordination with local leadership; Group Two felt the right model was to push the majority of responsibility for managing talent out to the business and the local management. Group One, I sensed, was concerned that to give up control of the talent management lifecycle was to put HR in a diminished role in the organization – and besides, who knew better how to manage talent than HR and the HR business partners? Group Two's main concern was one of giving managers 'a pass' on managing their teams' objectives, development and performance. That the best model was one where people were directly managed and developed by their direct supervisor, effectively pushing the centre of gravity for people performance out to the managers themselves, with support from an HR business partner.

Group Two, to my mind, had a more confident outlook on where HR could provide more value: being strategic talent advisers, rather than direct talent managers of the workforce. Group One had less confidence that the organization could be effective talent managers: that it was HR's traditional role to lead on the subject. So, it was a rather heated debate, which was taking the shape of a religious debate where both sides had fervent faith in their outlook on the question. As facilitator of this discussion, it was like being the agnostic among the believers! Both groups put together very cogent and strong arguments for their positions, and it was difficult to find much fault with either argument.

To break the deadlock, I proposed that we bring in senior HR leaders from some similar companies that had addressed this divide, to hear what they found in deciding and implementing the chosen model. Additionally, I recommended that once their stories were heard, and taken in, that we take the arguments to the CEO and CHRO as the final arbiters; both groups would have to make their case the top two stakeholders.

The result of these discussions with other organizations who had been down this path was to first delay the procurement of a new Cloud-based HRIS and second, conduct a companywide leadership discussion around the two questions posed. This effort took about three weeks and was very enlightening to all involved. In fact, what we found across the Group was somewhat unexpected; there was more consistency across the organization in terms of HR operating model and processes than was initially thought. Additionally, a few of the operating units had implemented, to varying degrees, a Cloud-based HRIS to support back-office and talent management efforts, and measured good results in terms of cost savings, productivity and people engagement. The effort to get to 'one version of the truth' did not look as daunting as was initially thought.

Following this brief review, it was agreed that a Group 'HR Transformation Programme' was required to stitch the various best practices and systems together into a group-wide approach to HR underpinned by the latest Cloud-based HRIS technology. So, the HR Leadership formed a team for a brief 'Phase 0' project, with a remit to answer three key questions:

1 Where does the centre of HR management and operations sit?
2 Who does talent management in the organization?
3 What HR technology is required to underpin the HR transformation?

The project had as its ultimate goal producing a comprehensive 'case for change' including a value case describing the financial and other benefits of this programme and a 'roadmap' on how to implement the transformation programme should it be approved for investment.

The Phase 0 project kicked off immediately, with a cross-functional team of HR, Finance and IT senior managers selected from each of the major regions of the company. This early key decision to create a cross-functional team was critical. HR working with Group Operations, Finance (support on the value case) and IT (support on the technology landscape) ensured that the key stakeholders were part of the analysis and would own the joint conclusions of the analysis. Each brought specific skills and experience to the table to make sure the findings were based on solid data, and fully vetted and agreed.

Over the six-week duration of the programme, this cross-functional team looked into every corner of the HR organization, looking for HR best practice, value drivers and effective technology that each of the business units were utilizing. All of the data collected was reviewed centrally each week, with key findings and key areas of potential value logged for use in the final analysis and conclusions. Although initially the programme was seen as somewhat suspicious in the local business units, the fact that each region and business unit had a highly regarded local senior manager representing them calmed the waters somewhat and encouraged participation.

It became clearer as time went on that the back office of the HR organization was where the HR teams spent most of their time. One participant made the observation that, generally, 'HR is good at keeping the lights on,' but lamented that there was little time left to focus on building workforce performance and engagement. The vast amount of resource and effort went into 'keeping the lights on' by focusing on the HR back office almost entirely. Additionally, a couple of key value drivers emerged early on: the business units that had a central repository of 'real time' accurate people data to make decisions were much more agile, spent less time taking decisions and created better outcomes, and teams where the manager was responsible for all aspects of talent management (performance management, learning, compensation and rewards, succession, etc) were, in the vast majority of cases, the highest-performing, most engaged teams in the company. These managers – talent managers – were also provided with simple-to-use online tools to conduct talent management in their teams.

A picture was emerging of what the future might look like. However, this was only the beginning. In the external world, a maelstrom of complex and confounding trends was emerging that also needed addressing, and all the findings needed to be looked at through the prism of the whims of the external business environment. Let's take a look at them next.

The emerging challenges facing organizations and people today

Part of what gets many people up and going in the morning is the fact that there is stuff to get done. Of course, there are always the hum-drum routines of the day to deal with, but also very often more exciting things that require us to dig deep into our reservoir of energy, experience and skills – the things that challenge us mentally (and sometimes physically); the challenges that, when successfully tackled, make a tangible difference to the people around us and the organization as a whole. It is very satisfying to meet a challenge as an individual and, many would say, even more satisfying to do so as a team; to make something happen where the outcome is never assured but benefits are clear and unambiguous to all. These are usually challenges that, when broken down into their component parts and divvied up to the right people in the team, are within our 'circle of influence' and our capabilities to address. These challenges are usually seen as each of us doing our part – our daily contribution.

However, there are other challenges that are more nebulous and, in many ways, out of our control. They may seem beyond our current capabilities and are largely outside of our 'circle of influence' – usually described as 'external factors'. These challenges can be vexing and often spoil best-laid plans. The trick is to be aware of and identify these external challenges in the context of our organizational objectives and try to put actions in place to mitigate them – even better, turn them to our advantage and treat them as an opportunity. For example, when faced with stiff competition for top talent, many organizations today are investing in better defining and codifying their employer brand. Defining what are they all about, creating a clear purpose, to attract people who buy into this purpose and want to be a part of it – a win/win. These are the kinds of challenges which, when anticipated and met with a plan, can become a clear competitive advantage.

We are living in a unique period in human history here in the early part of the 21st century when technological change is occurring at such a depth, breadth and speed – people everywhere are impacted almost simultaneously and struggle to keep up. Sure, the 20th century ushered in electricity, the automobile, the telephone, and even space flight to other worlds; the 20th century saw such great leaps of technology and scientific understanding as had never been witnessed before. However, these changes occurred over decades, and took many years to reach all regions of the globe. Going back even further, from 10,000 BC to 1750 AD, there was relatively little technological achievement. The arc of human technological progress was actually an almost entirely horizontal line, plotted over millennia; merely a series of incremental discoveries building on each other over a very long period of time. Then came the Industrial Revolution, which set the stage for an exponential explosion of technology in the latter parts of the 19th century that accelerated (and is still accelerating) into the 20th and 21st centuries. Suddenly that very long, nearly flat line on the graph plotted over the 'time' axis and the 'technological and scientific achievement' axis went almost vertical (see Figure 1.2).

It's astonishing the progress made in such a short period of time: 1750s to 1901. A minuscule sliver of time compared to the thousands of years that went before. Of course, computers, PCs and the internet were mid- to late-20th century inventions; however, arguably it has really been the 21st century that has seen these technologies combine to completely transform our lives. In the early 2000s the smartphone put these technologies, literally, in the palm of our hands. Add to this the rapidly increasing speed at which hand-held devices can process very, very large amounts of data, connected to vast networks of wires and signals like a biological nervous system, and the entire world bristles with electronic and digital life. My son was born in 1997. Today he is attending university in a very different world from the one I attended in the 1980s. In less than 20 years we went from class papers written on an electric typewriter, lecture notes taken on a legal pad with a number two pencil, to lectures given over the internet to a tablet (notes provided digitally!), 'papers' written on a device many times more powerful than all the computers used aboard the Apollo 11 lunar landing module to safely land on the moon. Students today have unimaginably quick and easy

FIGURE 1.2 Technological progress over time

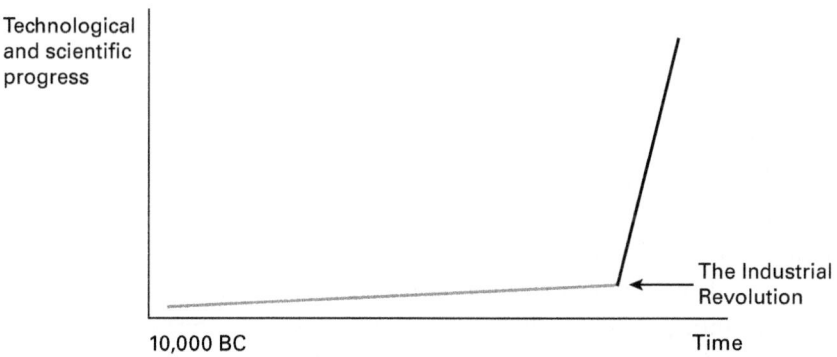

access to terabytes of data, a worldwide knowledge pool. The global nervous system of the Internet of Things (IoT) has us and 'things' connected to this network almost all the time and in almost all places around the globe.

Another 21st-century technological explosion has been in the medical sciences. Our understanding of the human body, and in particular the brain and how it works so magnificently, has increased exponentially. The human genome was almost entirely decoded in the late 1990s and this knowledge has completely transformed our capabilities to fight diseases and chronic conditions, and even begin to grow new organs that we can then use to replace worn out ones. Though the brain is still a mystery on many levels, our increasing understanding of how it works is allowing scientists to map the brain down to the cellular and even molecular and quantum level, much as the DNA scientists did at the end of last century. For example, we understand autism and similar conditions much better these days and increasingly recognize the unique capabilities and talents that people with 'different brains' can bring. More and more companies are recognizing the power of 'neurodiversity' in their workforce and are actively recruiting people, for example, on the autistic spectrum, as this pool of talent often successfully solve knotty challenges that the majority of people cannot do. For example, the mathematician and early computer scientist, Alan Turing is widely considered to be the father of computer science and artificial intelligence. During the Second World War, he was recruited by Britain's intelligence agencies to crack the German Enigma Coder machines. He is generally regarded as being autistic and it is thought his autism was a major contributor to his ability to come up with a solution to crack the Enigma code. As a result, the UK's Government Communications Headquarters (GCHQ) agency, to this day, is a major recruiter of people on the autistic spectrum, as they have found this is a pool of talent that has unique capabilities that are an ideal fit for the type of complex, and deeply analytical work the agency undertakes.

So, all the above is amazing and spectacular and jaw-droppingly interesting; however, it all comes with a 'health warning'. This technological and scientific progress combined with some unusual (at least in recent history) demographic realities – an overpopulated world dealing with diminishing resources and global warming – has produced some profound challenges in the external environment that are impacting all of us. We need to be aware of these, anticipate these challenges, develop some creative solutions and, where possible, turn them into opportunities. Below are a number of challenges (or are they opportunities?) that I have seen emerge and observed affecting organizations today. Let's get them out on the table, and then we can spend the rest of the book exploring how to turn these to our advantage.

The technology tsunami

Significant investment in IT and ever more effective (and intelligent) software and hardware continues at a pace; however, it outstrips the ability of the workforce and organizations to absorb it. Currently, governments and companies are ill-prepared to close this capability gap and ride the IT wave to greater productivity; they are not structurally organized to take advantage of the Technology Tsunami, as many are still structured and run according to 1950s (and older) management models. Many organizations have 'digital transformation' projects, to design and implement new software and hardware; however, true 'transformation' to a digital world is more about a mindset as well as developing a set of skills, especially digital leadership skills. As we saw in the case study above, 'transformation' very often is a project focused on the software and hardware, when the real value is in changing the organization structure and culture to adopt these new tools most effectively.

Organizations were expected to invest US$1.3 trillion (*Business Wire*, 2017) in 2018 in digital transformation initiatives to apply digital capabilities to improve efficiencies, increase customer value and create new monetization opportunities. Unfortunately, research tells us that 70 per cent (Bucy *et al*, 2016) of these initiatives will not reach their stated goals. That equates to over $900 billion worth of spend that will miss the mark. As technology leaders, we have a tremendous challenge before us. Peter Drucker framed this challenge very well when he said (Drucker, 1999):

> The most important, and indeed the truly unique, contribution of management in the 20th century was the fifty-fold increase in the productivity of the manual worker in manufacturing. The most important contribution management needs to make in the 21st century is similarly to increase the productivity of knowledge work and knowledge workers.

To meet this challenge, we need to rethink how our teams work together across the enterprise and apply a modern approach to work with new systems and models, enabled by the right tools. Only then can we fully exploit the massive investment in digital transformation and get the expected return on the $900 billion off-target spend. Then we can finally enable our teams to focus on what we actually hired them to do: dream, create and innovate (ZoBell, 2018). Additionally, it's not just about spending money on stuff, it's also about spending money on creating a culture change. Many organizations have a 'digital transformation project'; however, the investment funds go almost entirely to hardware and software, when what is really needed is a change in the 'human software' – how we think about digital is as important as using digital. Being digital is an attitude, a culture, a way of doing things (or not doing things). It's less about the gadgets.

The shrinking workforce

Between 2010 and 2060, OECD country populations are expected to increase by 17 per cent, but the working age population (age 15–70 years) is projected to fall by up to 7 per cent globally (Guillemette and Turner, 2018). This illustrates the obvious problem that there will be fewer people in work yet more people on the planet – not a sustainable situation. In order to maintain world productivity and economic growth, we will need to find a way to plug this emerging gap. We need to find willing, able and capable workers to fill the gap.

The good news is, one key demographic is already stepping up: the 70+ age group – the fastest-growing workforce demographic globally. In the United States, for example, according to a report from the Society for Human Resource Management (SHRM) (Wilkie, 2018), the senior segment is projected by the Bureau of Labor Statistics (Evans, 2017) to be the fastest-growing group in the workforce through 2024 (Toossi, 2015). While in 2011, 6.6 million Americans age 70 or older were working in the United States, by 2016 that number had risen to 8.9 million people – an increase of nearly 35 per cent.

The US nonprofit organization, AARP, has found that among people aged 65 to 74 who are currently working or looking for work, 35 per cent cite the need for money as the most important factor in their decision to work. Finances are therefore likely a key factor for many women working later in life. Approximately 19 per cent of people aged 65 to 74 say that the most important factor in their decision to work is that they enjoy working (Schramm, 2018). Whatever happened to retirement? Frankly, money and longevity. 'Several factors influence how long people stay in the labour force,' Jen Schramm, SHRM-SCP, senior strategic policy adviser for labour market issues at the AARP Public Policy Institute, states in their report. Schramm elaborates, 'Increasing longevity means that people need to finance a longer period of retirement. Many people have not saved enough money for retirement and are facing increased costs of living – particularly burdensome are housing costs and medical expenses.'

Another beneficial part of working into one's later years, shown by a number of recent studies, is that those who maintain a meaningful profession into their early 70s have a much longer life span. In the UK, a report published in 2018 suggests that people who remain in paid employment past retirement age or involved in community and voluntary work improve their chances of staying healthier for longer (Davis, 2018). The chief medical officer, Professor Dame Sally Davies, says those aged 50 to 70 are better off staying in work, or else taking up new hobbies to keep physically and mentally active in retirement. Dame Sally, who is 67, said she had no plans to retire, and she urged others to follow suit. Her annual report on the state of the public's health urged people not to slow down their pace of life as they hit their 60s. Dame Sally says: 'People are living longer than ever and so retirement presents a real opportunity for baby boomers to be more active than ever before. For many people it is a chance to take on new challenges, it is certainly not the start of a slower pace of life it once was.' So, work longer, live longer?

Clearly, there is great potential in leveraging the senior population to plug the emerging gap in the shrinking workforce numbers. However, there are other populations with great potential as well. For example, more and more women are coming into work. The population of male workers is forecast to decline slightly in coming decades; however, the female number is forecast to increase. In the United States, which mirrors global trends, the share of women in the labour force is projected to increase from 46.8 per cent in 2014 to 47.2 per cent in 2024. Over the same period, the number of men in the labour force is projected to grow at an average annual rate of 0.4 per cent, a rate slower than that of the previous decade. Men's share of the labour force is expected to decrease from 53.2 per cent in 2014 to 52.8 per cent in 2024 (Toossi, 2015).

Another potential source of talent (and innovation) that is being left out of the workforce comes from those with 'different brains' – those on the autistic spectrum. Recently, the term Autistic Spectrum Disorder (ASD) has become the accepted umbrella term for the condition which includes autism, Asperger's syndrome and other pervasive developmental disorders. Studies in Asia, Europe and North America have identified individuals with ASD with an average prevalence of between 1 per cent and 2 per cent (CDC, 2016); however, the unemployment rate for university graduates with ASD has been measured in the 85 per cent range (Lyn Pesce, 2019). If you agree with PayPal founder Peter Thiel, who has long been a proponent of hiring staff with autism to avoid what he describes as 'herd-like thinking and behaviour', this group is a great source of innovative thinking. In his book, *Zero to One* (Thiel, 2014), Thiel says people with ASD have a single-mindedness that gives startups and other organizations a unique advantage. In the United States it is estimated that those with ASD number about 3.5 million and in countries like the UK, around 700,000 – a vast pool of talented resource to pull from. We will go deeper on this subject later in Chapter 4 of this book.

The bottom line is: those companies that learn to acquire diverse talent and deploy that talent most effectively develop a significant competitive advantage. The challenge faced by both organizations and the workforce is that the current structure of work is not optimized for bringing in and retaining older workers. As we will see throughout this book, this development is key for plugging not only the workforce numbers gap, but also the workforce productivity gap.

The stressed-out workforce

The Great Recession of 2008 drove a relentless focus in organizations to 'do more with less'. Organizations were 'streamlined' and 'right-sized' to achieve this and those workers that remained in their jobs were asked to pick up the rather substantial slack. In my travels and work with companies around the world during this period, I heard stories from innumerable employees and managers that the workload increased suddenly and to an unmanageable level, but many felt powerless to push back and demand more realistic objectives. After all, if they couldn't handle the workload there were literally thousands of people out of work who would be happy to be brought in to replace them!

Unfortunately, during the lengthy recovery period from that recession, the mantra of 'do more with less' has persevered. For example, in 2013 over 70 per cent of respondents to an Everest College survey felt their companies demanded an unrealistic workload (GlobeNewswire, 2013); worse, 43 per cent of respondents reported that their company 'never' or 'rarely' had realistic workload expectations. So, not surprisingly, here we are, some years later and 40 per cent of US workers say they are overly stressed from their workload (GlobeNewswire, 2013). The same number, 40 per cent, of Italian workers say that they are so stressed by their job that they would like a new one; the figure is the highest in Europe, which sits at 30 per cent for the rest of the continent according to the WorkForce Europe 2018 survey, conducted by ADP on over 10,000 workers on the continent including 1,300 employees in Italy (ANSA, 2018). In fact, the majority of mental health issues people experience these days come from a combination of both work and home pressures. In most cases, one informs the other: either people take their work stress home or take their home stress to work. And we know that stress leads to absenteeism, health problems like fatigue, headaches and depression, and decreased productivity.

This growing issue is a major challenge for organizations big and small. The good news is, some organizations are putting in place programmes to help the workforce deal with stress. Additionally, it is becoming more acceptable for people to share with their employer and even their colleagues their mental health challenges. However, there is some way to go on these issues. The ADP WorkForce Europe 2018 survey shows just 14 per cent of respondents believe their company has no interest in their mental well-being at all, with just over a third (34 per cent) saying they have a low level of interest (ranked between one and four on a ten-point scale.) That compares to nearly half (46 per cent) who say that their employer does take an interest (a score of between six and ten), while just 6 per cent say their employer is 'most interested' (ANSA, 2018). Very similar numbers are also found in the United States.

The skills development treadmill (is speeding up!)

Skills needs are constantly shifting as innovative technologies, new ideas and modern strategies change the face of work. The degree to which this is taking place now is unprecedented in the history of work. This creates constant gaps in our workforces' capabilities. The speed with which new jobs, new roles and whole new industries pop up or fade away is astonishing. To stay in demand, employers and employees must continuously update their skills, in preparation for the needs of the future. Yet research shows this may not be happening fast enough, with only 83 per cent of workers feeling confident that they have the skills to succeed in their role – a one percentage point drop since 2018, and a worrying 6 percentage points fall since 2016 (ANSA, 2018). The workforce feels under constant pressure to keep their skills relevant, and many organizations are not very well structured to help their workforce develop new skills. Therefore, online universities and other online vocational training companies are seeing a boom in business since 2008. The good news is that effective and easily accessible learning is becoming more and more available as the long promised 'e-learning revolution' seems to finally be coming to fruition. After years of low growth, the global online education market is projected to witness a compound annual growth rate of 10.26 per cent during the forecast period 2017 to 2023, to reach a total market size of US $286.62 billion by 2023 – a significant increase from US $159.52 billion in 2017 (Business Wire, 2018). In 2018, 65 per cent of US millennials said they chose their jobs because of personal and professional development opportunities (eLearning Infographics, 2018). In 2017, approximately 77 per cent of US corporations used online learning (eLearning Industry, 2017); however, 98 per cent planned to incorporate it in their programme by 2020 (Bose, 2017).

However, a *Harvard Business Review* study from 2018 found that in the United States the proportion of people who received employer-funded training decreased from 21 per cent in 2001 to 15 per cent in 2009 (the most recent data available) and business cycles weren't to blame; the decline was steeper in boom periods than during recessions (Hamori, 2018). In fact, even in the middle of a relative boom in 2018, these numbers did not return to pre-2009 levels (Hamori, 2018). This gap illustrates the emerging trend of individuals taking control and seeking their own development programmes. This is a real missed opportunity for organizations as the data shows that those which provide development for their employees have more highly skilled employees and employees who are more likely to stay longer. Studies show that providing world-class learning opportunities, leveraging assets like MOOCs (massive open online courses), which are usually open source and readily available, has very positive effects (see Figure 1.3).

For years, we heard 'e-learning' is going to change everything! Particularly in the late 1990s and early 2000s. However, this did not turn out to be true – until more recently. The combination of innovative assets, like MOOCs and social networks, for collaboration have seen technology finally start to change the way people seek and consume development assets. In fact, the combination of these types of tools best matches how humans actually learn (more on this in Chapter 5). So, we finally see this technology improve the efficacy of learning and help people keep up with the constantly changing work landscape. The challenge for organizations is to first understand the challenges people are facing on the skills treadmill, and second, leverage the emerging tools and approaches while changing their learning organizations to support this new wave of effective development. It's an exciting time in the learning and development world, so time to move into the 21st century.

FIGURE 1.3 Learning as a tool for retention

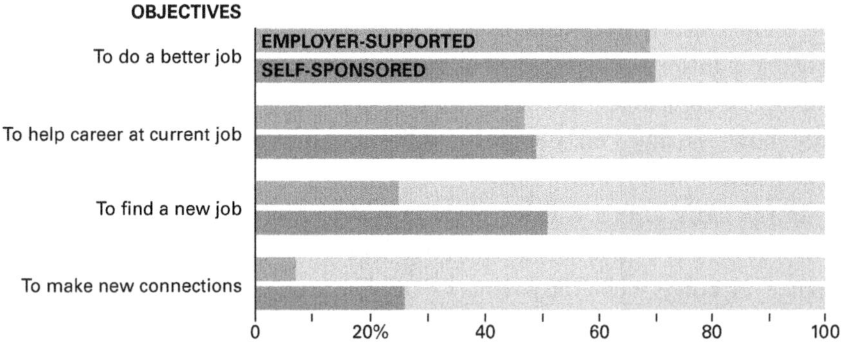

OBJECTIVES

- To do a better job
- To help career at current job
- To find a new job
- To make new connections

EMPLOYER-SUPPORTED
SELF-SPONSORED

0 20% 40 60 80 100

SOURCE Hamori, 2018

The motivation and engagement gap

Believe it or not, 18th-century Industrial Revolution 'motivational' techniques are very much still in use today: the carrot and stick. Pay people more and it is thought they will work harder and produce more; punish 'bad' behaviour and they will stop this behaviour. The mounting evidence shows this dated approach does not work and actually has the complete opposite effect, creating a demotivated and disengaged workforce that produces less, takes more risks and does not collaborate with colleagues. Unlike the 18th- and 19th-century workforces, which were mostly agrarian or factory workers, the 21st-century workforce is increasingly made up of 'knowledge workers' who have very different motivations and reasons for taking a particular job and staying in that job: intrinsic motivation (internal – thinking about why I come to work for you in the morning, the purpose imperative) and extrinsic motivation (external rewards – money for my output).

The challenge is getting the balance between these two motivations. It is critical to improving people engagement and output and for retaining top people in your workforce. However, most organizations cling to the carrot and stick, the command-and-control structure, sub-optimizing people productivity and engagement. The best work on this subject, in my experience, is Daniel Pink's book *Drive* (2011). It is a seminal (and entertaining) book that really takes everything we thought we knew about how people are motivated and turns those beliefs on their head. Pink has lifted the subject of motivation out of the self-help books and into the forefront of people's minds. As he says: 'There is a mismatch between what science knows and business does.' A great number of companies have learned the lessons of this thinking from experience, however, and Pink's book has influenced and *motivated* (sorry), many organizations to try a new tack.

In the early 2000s I was a partner in Accenture (during its transition from Andersen Consulting), where we had the dreaded February 'performance' meetings when the partners would hole up in a windowless meeting room in a hotel somewhere and spend two days debating (it felt more like arguing) the merits of our particular individuals and teams of people to try to get them the best bonus possible from a limited pool of funds. We used forced distributions (some people *had* to be at the bottom!) and we used an approach that seemed to be more about finding faults with people to get the distribution curves to the correct numbers instead of celebrating performance. All of which was soul-destroying for all involved. No one enjoyed it, and no one looked forward to it. And worse, our people did not look forward to it either. Invariably, mainly because of the forced distribution, it was inevitable that the majority of people were unsatisfied with their assigned ranking, and even less satisfied with their bonus. People were very conscious of their ranking relative to others, how much this ranking was worth, and their focus was on this, not on performance and even less on collaborating with their colleagues who were 'the competition'. It was a mess, to say the least. It usually took about two months to get our teams refocused on the job after performance reviews. Not surprisingly, Accenture were one of the first to revamp their 'performance management' approach a few years back, which got rid of rankings and forced distributions and reconfigured compensation and rewards accordingly. This has worked well for Accenture, who continue to grow the top line, the bottom line and the number of employees, and are considered one of the best places to work for top talent. So the good news is that many organizations are starting to take a hard look at how they performance manage and incentivize their employees (compensation) to greater engagement and performance (motivation). It's one of the 'true' revolutions in the workforce of the 21st century.

The wrong people, wrong place, wrong time dilemma

Take a look around your organization. Would you say the right people are in the right place at the right time? Would you conclude that there is a world-class capability to do this? Probably not. However, you would be in good company; in my time working with some of the most successful companies, both big and small, very few organizations have an effective capability to do this. Yet, when I speak with senior executives of these organizations, the value they place on having this capability is very high. Unfortunately, most just accept, or assume that the complexity (and chaos) of running an organization day-to-day makes it very difficult to do. While senior management often talks about the importance of the development of a workforce planning strategy, the challenge is moving from talk to action and making this a compelling issue for the organization. Attention should be brought to the risks associated with failure to plan and to workforce planning's crucial role in the overall corporate strategic plan. A glaring example of a company being caught with their trousers down on workforce planning is Ryanair in late 2017. In 2018, the CEO of Ryanair, Michael O'Leary, blamed a big part of a full-year earnings drop on what he called a pilot 'shortage'. In September 2017, Ryanair had to cancel 20,000 flights, stranding 400,000 passengers when they experienced a pilot holiday rota 'boo-boo' (Robinson and Dinham, 2017). In fact, this situation was merely a symptom of a much bigger problem that Ryanair had. First, Ryanair was famous for having a very poor and antagonistic relationship with the pilot's union, which caused pilot work stoppages on a somewhat regular basis. Second, many pilots were being recruited away to other airlines (due to point number one, above). And third, they had a very manual and primitive scheduling rota – mostly paper-based. All of this was a time-bomb waiting to go off, which it did in that fateful September, when Ryanair had to withstand embarrassing headlines and angry customers appearing on 24-hour news channels on constant rotation. You may think this is a rather extreme example, but I have seen this situation over and over again inside of some of the world's most famous companies. The only difference is that Ryanair's situation became public, because of the news reports from airports all around Europe. Most other companies suffer in a silence that does not get glaring headlines.

Ryanair are not alone, by any stretch of the imagination. In a 2015 *Harvard Business Review* survey of corporate executives, 73 per cent said that poor workforce planning resulted in talent shortfalls that caused an inability to meet business objectives (see Figure 1.4) as well as financial impacts (Visier, 2015).

FIGURE 1.4 Talent shortfalls from poor planning

TALENT SHORTFALLS HAMPER CORPORATE GOALS
Percentage of respondents who say poor workforce planning leads to staffing gaps and hurts business results. *(Choose all that apply)*

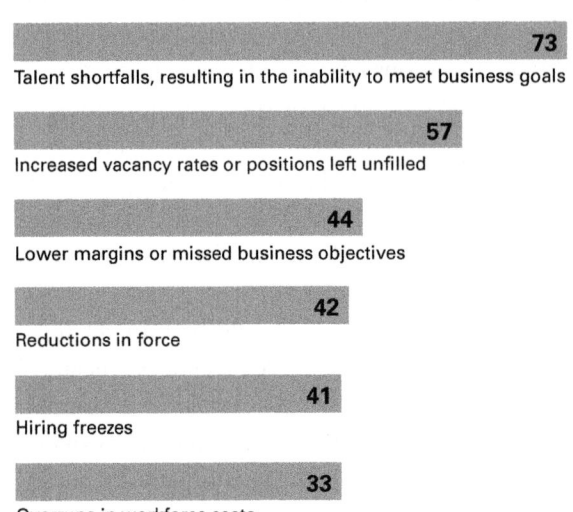

Category	%
Talent shortfalls, resulting in the inability to meet business goals	73
Increased vacancy rates or positions left unfilled	57
Lower margins or missed business objectives	44
Reductions in force	42
Hiring freezes	41
Overruns in workforce costs	33

Visier (2015b) Tackling Talent Strategically: Winning with workforce planning, *Harvard Business Review*. Available from: https://hello.visier.com/hbr-tackling-strategically-workforce-planning/

SOURCE Visier, 2015

An entire crowdsourced network has emerged by and for people to help them find the right roles themselves: LinkedIn. Nearly 500 million subscribers use this network to find roles and collaborate with colleagues. LinkedIn has dramatically changed the multi-billion-dollar recruitment industry as well. What does it say about the current state of things that people became so fed up they took matters into their own hands? This is also where you can end up, without changes in the organization approach, with what I call 'hiring and firing binges'. A form of organizational bulimia, where during the good times companies will bring in lots of people and in bad times they will show lots of people out, which, when done consecutively through business cycles, can start to destroy business value. Hiring and firing binges can create a situation where organizations get into a death spiral of talent coming in and out, bringing with it disruption and reduced productivity.

As we can see the costs are high and the downsides rather large. The good news is that as technology becomes more sophisticated and intelligent, many organizations are starting to apply this technology to the problem. In addition, a number of the world's top universities are creating entire degree programmes around the subject of workforce planning. In fact, I would argue that those who are getting bachelor, and even master's degrees in the subject are going to be the future 'rock stars' of forward-thinking organizations.

The avalanche of data dilemma

There are '2.5 quintillion bytes of data' (a factor of 10^{18}) created each day, which is accelerating with the growth of IoT devices exponentially, increasing the amount of data that is coursing through the internet (Marr, 2018). The numbers start to become mind-boggling large, where we will soon need a new numeric vocabulary to describe them.

Another data point: from 1836 to January 2016, it is estimated that there were 2.7 trillion images captured. Between January 2016 and January 2018, it is estimated that 3.4 trillion images have been taken and stored – in just TWO years we have captured 50 per cent more images than all of those taken across all of photographic history. We are getting closer to the day when we will have to invent new words to describe the size of data in the world – currently a 'googolplex' is the largest number we have a name for: which is a 1 followed by a googol zeros, where a 'googol' is a 1 followed by 100 zeros.

Very soon, the size of all the world's data will be larger than the human brain can imagine or process. And let's not stop there. When you also add in the *speed* with which this massive data can be processed, relative to even only a few years ago, the mind truly boggles. For example, the first computer processor was the Intel 4004, which was only a 740 kHz processor and capable of processing approximately 92,000 instructions per second. Today's processors are multi-core multi-GHz processors (a move in speed from *kilo 103* to *giga 109*) capable of processing over 100 billion instructions per second. That is not a typo – 100 BILLION per second. Again, the mind boggles and when the mind boggles, we have a challenge in understanding.

We have all heard the term 'big data' constantly bandied about to the point where it has lost its meaning; it is often attributed with being 'a good thing', but the poor results of the 'data revolution' are very telling. Fact is, big data is *everything* and *anything* and when something is 'everything and anything,' it is actually as good as having *nothing*. It's impossible to gain insights that have optimal value when there are few limits on the inputs involved. The cliché 'can't see the wood for the trees' really could not be more apt. In a previous book that I co-wrote, *Calculating Success* (Hoffman *et al*, 2012), we took a detailed look at companies that had the most successful workforce analytics programs, and found that all of them had one key success factor in common: they only had a handful (five or six) of specific workforce analytics that they focused on.

Lastly, another emerging challenge in the workforce analytics space is one where employees have become very wary of what organizations do with people data, particularly when there is a lot of it sloshing around on various systems. With data breaches of major proportions being reported on an almost weekly basis, it is no wonder employees are concerned. Moreover, employees are also beginning to worry about what data the organization collects on them and what they plan to do with this information, particularly the data collected on employees' health and well-being. In the United States for example, there are increasing concerns about employers using internal and external data about their workers' health habits to predict who is likely to be unhealthy and therefore a cost burden, and then using this information to terminate employees to cut down on healthcare costs. These concerns need to be addressed now so as not to fester and alienate the workforce of the future. We will look at this in more detail in Chapter 4.

The machines are coming (look busy!)

There are a number of economists who say we are in the midst of a 'Second Machine Age' (Brynjolfsson and McAfee, 2014). A transformative time like the first machine age (the Industrial Revolution), which saw the steam engine and the mechanization of the textiles industry completely transform the number of outputs that could be manufactured and the manner in which those outputs were produced. Today's machine age is one where digital bytes and bits are driving clever machines and devices to once again transform our economy and how we live life on a daily basis; transforming what and how we produce things, as well as how we *do* things. Like the first machine age, we are seeing large-scale disruption of entire industries and individual jobs on a scale and speed not previously known. True, we are not seeing the rise of a violent movement like the Luddites, who, for five years from 1811 to 1816 fought back against changes brought about by the mechanization of the textiles industry. However, one could argue that parts of the recent political ructions and unrest we see in many regions of the world have as a root cause the disruption caused by both the Great Recession of 2008 and the disappearance of jobs and whole industries brought about by new technologies. People everywhere have felt both the benefits and the disruption brought about by these new machines and the intelligent software that runs them. It is a disconcerting, and in some ways a difficult time for human capital in the workplace.

Organizations are all faced with a challenge of how to adapt to and take full advantage of the benefits of new technology – to reduce costs and improve customer experience, for example – to help humans partner with and harness the power of these new machines to be more productive and engaged with their work. In many ways technology can help humans do more, but also do things that are more *interesting*, more value added. Take for example grocery stores. Over the last 10 years, most grocery stores have implemented automated, self-serve check-out kiosks. The job of ringing up customer shopping must be one of the most mundane and mind-numbing ever created (I am reminded of my teenage days working on a grocery till). However, today, the machines let customers do their own ringing up, freeing up the former check-out clerks to focus more on helping customers. The grocery chains that have made the most of this technology did not see it as a way to replace workers, but a way to change the way they look after customers. Walmart recently introduced shelf-scanning robots in 50 locations around the United States. The robots check inventory, prices and misplaced items to help each individual store's inventory practices. Additionally, these robots will be collecting data – data that Walmart claims will help them improve inventory practices across the nation (Robotics Online Marketing Team, 2017). As Massachusetts Institute of Technology (MIT) economist Andrew McAfee, co-author of *The Second Machine Age* (Brynjolfsson and McAfee, 2014), observed in a recent interview:

> Let's be clear about one thing: digital technologies are doing for human brain power what the steam engine and related technologies did for human muscle power during the Industrial Revolution. They're allowing us to overcome many limitations rapidly and to open up new frontiers with unprecedented speed. It's a very big deal.

The key point here is that throughout history inflection points in technology created the opportunity for humans to harness this technology to make them better and more productive. I, and a number of others, argue that smart machines will take some of our tasks, but overall they will make us *more* human. By giving the machines the boring repetitive tasks, which they are exceptional at, we can go do the things that humans do really well: be creative, use intuition and judgement, and sell (convince others of a particular viewpoint). Yes, we will be freed up to do the 'cool stuff'. What history shows us is that during each inflection point we had to (and did) rethink work and how we approach it. It's the crux of the challenge we have today, which is to rethink how we harness these smart machines to make us better. As I stated above, many organizations have 'digital transformation' programmes; however, they tend to focus on software and hardware and do not focus on the truly hard work of changing how we *think* and *do*. We will look at this in more detail in Chapters 4 and 5.

As we think through how we will change the way we work, there are two key differences today from past technology inflections that add to the challenge of humans harnessing technology:

1 the *speed* with which the changes are coming (and going);
2 the downward pressure on people's incomes created by technology.

We covered earlier the speed (and scale) of change. However, one of the things we need to do differently in the future is treat change as a constant and put in place a discipline around becoming more forward thinking in anticipating change (not just waiting for it to come), as well as becoming perpetually agile. Don't treat 'agile' as a transaction, but as a constant in the way we work and plan. The other great challenge that has very little precedent in recent history (since the beginning of the Industrial Revolution) is the emerging and very real crisis in people's ages. From the end of the Great Depression in the late 1930s until the late 1970s the growth in median income increased year on year in industrialized economies. However, in the 1980s the increase in wages began to sputter. In the past 15 years it's turned negative; once you adjust for inflation, a US household at the 50th percentile of income distribution earns less today than it did in 1998, even after accounting for changes in household size. Job growth in the private sector has also slowed – and not just because of the 2008 recession. Job gains were anaemic throughout the 2000s, even when the economy was expanding. This phenomenon is what Brynolfsson and McAfee call 'the Great Decoupling' (2014). The two halves of the cycle of prosperity are no longer married; economic abundance, as exemplified by gross domestic product (GDP) has remained on an upward trajectory, but the income and future earnings prospects for typical workers have failed to keep up. This situation has, rightly, created significant anxiety in the workforce, which has bled over into the challenges that organizations face in keeping their people engaged and feeling valued in their work. We will cover more on this in Chapters 2 and 4, but this situation cannot be underestimated in the amount of disengagement, productivity disruption and social unrest created.

True, the challenges are significant, and a few of them have no precedence; however, the point to keep in mind as we go forth and take on these challenges around technology and how we will work in the future is: humans are more intelligent than we think, and machines are not as smart as we think. We can be simpatico, if we are 'smart' about it.

The productivity paradox

For the global economy to grow, and for people to become more prosperous, there must be consistent growth in human productivity year on year. In other words, the output of goods or services from given inputs of labour must increase over time for people to have any expectation of rising wages and abundant job opportunities – and therefore better standards of living. It is, similar to the theory of general relativity in physics, a universal law of economics. There is little debate on this point as the theory has been proven repeatedly throughout the 20th and so far in the 21st century. Where there is significant debate is around the idea of the 'productivity paradox', which generally holds that over the last 40–50 years we have not seen a consistent uplift in human productivity in line with the rapid development of information communications technology (ICT) – computers and the internet. Professor Robert Solow earned a Nobel Prize in 1987 for demonstrating that economic growth and productivity no longer come from people working *harder*, but people working *smarter* (Solow, 2019). This observation created a sea-change in thinking of how organizations leverage technology, and ignited further the already simmering debate about the future and how technology could (or could not) produce a golden age of human productivity and prosperity. Professor Solow famously observed to the *New York Times* that 'you can see the computer age everywhere but in the productivity statistics' (Lohr, 1999). At the time, economists measured slowly declining human productivity rates during the late 1960s into the 1970s, which were coming off the productivity highs created from the post-war boom. Rates began to tick back up in the 1980s and by the time the early to mid-1990s rolled around there was an unprecedented boom in human productivity, and therefore GDP, particularly in the United States. This was largely attributed to the emergence and implementation of ICT in the workplace, and the focus on aligning people to these new technologies to help them 'work smarter'. This boom lasted into the early 2000s, when it then ran out of steam, from both geopolitical shocks (9/11 terror attacks and subsequent wars) and from the significant and sudden decrease in investment in aligning human capital to emerging technologies. Since 2004, economists have measured a significant softening in the rate of consistent human productivity increases, which have had the follow-on impact of reducing the rate of increase in GDP. The Great Recession of 2008 significantly exacerbated the trend which had started a few years earlier.

So, the question that is currently under intense debate is why have we seen consistently poor rates of human productivity growth, for a relatively long period of time, when we are in an age of 'amazing technology' advances? Given the revolution in clever devices, apps, machine learning and AI, one would think that we would be seeing a golden age of people engagement, innovation and productivity at work. Instead we see, at minimum, a 'flattening' in productivity growth (some have measured significant drops in productivity). So, the question has reignited the discussion around the productivity paradox. What is going on?

There are several different camps with different viewpoints on this paradox, which can be summarized, broadly, as:

1 We are not measuring productivity correctly in the digital age.
2 We are experiencing a natural occurrence of diminishing returns from the ICT revolution.
3 Our latest technology is not as clever as we think it is.
4 There is a lag between emergence of new technology and its adoption in society.
5 Organizations are not investing in people and restructuring/rethinking work to take full advantage of technology.

Fact is, probably all these things are playing some part in the current challenges we face in reversing the trend of decreasing rates of human productivity. However, not all of these suspects are equal in my experience. Having spent significant time advising organizations, big and small, private and governmental, over the span of nearly 30 years, one thing has become abundantly clear: when organizations implement innovative technologies and invest significantly in aligning human capital to this technology, they thrive. For those that restructure the organization around how, who, when and where work is done, people become more engaged, drive new ways of doing things and significantly improve productivity. I saw this in the 1990s in the first wave of ICT revolution, and I see it today in those organizations that are once again completely rethinking, reorganizing and reinvigorating how work is done in the digital age and are seeing a transformation in their abilities to compete and win. The challenge is encouraging everyone in industry, everyone in government to do the same so that we *all* can benefit from rising productivity, rising GDP and rising prosperity for all.

This is the core focus of this book: to challenge you and to give you the tools and techniques that can help you and your organization solve the productivity paradox, so we see a rising tide that 'floats all boats' in society at large.

Let's get after it!

References

ANSA (2018) 40% of Italian workers stressed out [blog] *ANSA General News*, 22 March. Available from: http://www.ansa.it/english/news/general_news/2018/03/22/40-of-italian-workers-stressed-out_a85fac16-78e8-4524-bb4a-1fde117c9793.html (archived at https://perma.cc/7WER-69J6)

Bose, S (2017) 98% of all companies plan to use e-learning by 2020 with opportunities for small biz, Small Business Trends. Available from: https://smallbiztrends.com/2017/12/2018-e-learning-trends.html (archived at https://perma.cc/2WMJ-MU4E)

Brynjolfsson, E and McAfee, A (2014) *The Second Machine Age: Work, progress, and prosperity in a time of brilliant technologies*, W W Norton & Co, New York and London

Bucy, M, Finlayson, A, Kelly, G and Moye, C (2016) The 'how' of transformation [blog] *McKinsey Insights*, May. Available from: https://www.mckinsey.com/industries/retail/our-insights/the-how-of-transformation (archived at https://perma.cc/793Q-FD22)

Business Wire (2017) IDC forecasts worldwide spending on digital transformation technologies in 2018 to reach $1.3 trillion in 2018 [blog] *Business Wire News*, December. Available from: https://www.businesswire.com/news/home/20171215005055/en/IDC-Forecasts-Worldwide-Spending-Digital-Transformation-Technologies (archived at https://perma.cc/LA4B-3SU3)

Business Wire (2018) The global online education market forecasts from 2018 to 2023. Available from: https://www.businesswire.com/news/home/20180226006458/en/Global-Online-Education-Market-2018-2023-Type-Technology (archived at https://perma.cc/UE99-NQ5P)

CDC (2016) Summary of Autism Spectrum Disorder (ASD) prevalence studies, *Centers for Disease Control*. Available from: https://www.cdc.gov/ncbddd/autism/documents/ASDPrevalenceDataTable2016.pdf (archived at https://perma.cc/Q79X-DBMU)

Davis, S C (2018) Annual Report of the Chief Medical Officer, 2018: Health 2040 – better health within reach. Department of Health and Social Care, London. Available from: https://assets.publishing.service.gov.uk/government/uploads/system/uploads/attachment_data/file/767549/Annual_report_of_the_Chief_Medical_Officer_2018_-_health_2040_-_better_health_within_reach.pdf (archived at https://perma.cc/VG5Y-2QK8)

Drucker, P (1999) Knowledge-worker productivity: The biggest challenge, *California Management Review*, **41**, pp 79–94. Available from: https://doi.org/10.2307/41165987 (archived at https://perma.cc/Y646-RVNF)

eLearning Industry (2017) Online learning statistics and trends. Available from: https://elearningindustry.com/online-learning-statistics-and-trends (archived at https://perma.cc/FG9H-67TY)

eLearning Infographics (2018) 7 statistics that prove elearning is super important for your organization. Available from: https://elearninginfographics.com/elearning-super-important-organisation-7-statistics-prove-infographic/ (archived at https://perma.cc/CJ4N-PPXZ)

Evans, S (2017) Building better benefit experiences for a multi-generational workforce [blog] *Benefits Pro*, 13 December. Available from: http://www.benefitspro.com/2017/12/13/building-better-benefit-experiences-for-a-multi-ge (archived at https://perma.cc/M7Z9-R5AW)

GlobeNewswire (2013) Workplace stress on the rise with 83% of Americans frazzled by something at work [blog] *GlobalNewswire*, April. Available from: https://www.globenewswire.com/news-release/2013/04/09/536945/10027728/en/Workplace-Stress-on-the-Rise-With-83-of-Americans-Frazzled-by-Something-at-Work.html (archived at https://perma.cc/HLB2-6VV9)

Guillemette, Y and Turner, D (2018) The long view: Scenarios for the world economy to 2060, OECD Economic Policy Papers, 22. OECD Publishing, Paris. Available from: https://doi.org/10.1787/b4f4e03e-en (archived at https://perma.cc/TV2T-NW3T)

Hamori, M (2018) Can MOOCs solve your training problem? *Harvard Business Review*, Jan/Feb. Available from: https://hbr.org/2018/01/can-moocs-solve-your-training-problem (archived at https://perma.cc/WN9Q-FGUS)

Hoffmann, C, Lesser, E and Ringo, T (2012) *Calculating Success: How the new workplace analytics will revitalize your organization*, Harvard Business Review Press, Boston, MA

Lohr, S (1999) Computer Age gains respect of economists, *New York Times*, 14 April. Available from: https://www.nytimes.com/1999/04/14/business/computer-age-gains-respect-of-economists.html (archived at https://perma.cc/VKJ8-R8ZP)

Lyn Pesce, N (2019) Most college grads with autism can't find jobs: This group is fixing that, *Market Watch*, April. Available from: https://www.marketwatch.com/story/most-college-grads-with-autism-cant-find-jobs-this-group-is-fixing-that-2017-04-10-5881421 (archived at https://perma.cc/UM4G-YJCF)

Marr, B (2018) How much data do we create every day? The mind-blowing stats everyone should read, *Forbes*, 21 May. Available from: https://www.forbes.com/sites/bernardmarr/2018/05/21/how-much-data-do-we-create-every-day-the-mind-blowing-stats-everyone-should-read/ (archived at https://perma.cc/4RKB-G7VL)

Pink, D H (2011) *Drive: The surprising truth about what motivates us*, Canongate Books, Edinburgh

Robinson, M and Dinham, P (2017) The pilots' revolt: Ryanair staff across Europe join forces to stand up to O'Leary and say they will take their holidays after he threatened to replace anyone who defied him, *Mail Online*, 21 September. Available from: https://www.dailymail.co.uk/news/article-4905876/Ryanair-boss-Michael-O-Leary-faces-shareholders.html (archived at https://perma.cc/9G4Y-JHZ8)

Robotics Online Marketing Team (2017) Robots in retail stores are making a big Impact [blog] *Robotic Industries*, 26 December. Available from: http://www.robotics.org/blog-article.cfm/Robots-in-Retail-Stores-are-Making-a-Big-Impact/76 (archived at https://perma.cc/WX2Y-GKFP)

Schramm, J (2018) Older workers and part-time employment, Fact Sheet 640, AARP Public Policy Institute, Washington DC. Available from: https://www.aarp.org/content/dam/aarp/ppi/2018/part-time-older-workers.pdf (archived at https://perma.cc/H9CW-6KFG)

Solow, R M (2019) Prize Lecture: Lecture to the memory of Alfred Nobel, December 8, 1987, NobelPrize.org, Nobel Media AB. Available from: https://www.nobelprize.org/prizes/economic-sciences/1987/solow/lecture/ (archived at https://perma.cc/SG8R-XDCF)

Thiel, P (2014) *Zero to One: Notes on startups, or how to build the future*, Crown Publishing, New York

Toossi, M (2015) Labor force projections to 2024: The labor force is growing, but slowly, Monthly Labor Review, U.S. Bureau of Labor Statistics, December. Available from: https://doi.org/10.21916/mlr.2015.48 (archived at https://perma.cc/JV44-D8ZS)

Visier (2015) Nearly three-quarters of businesses have missed objectives due to inadequate workforce planning, Harvard Business Review Analytic Services report reveals [blog] *Visier*, 21 September. Available from: https://www.visier.com/press-release/nearly-three-quarters-of-businesses-have-missed-objectives-due-to-inadequate-workforce-planning-harvard-business-review-analytic-services-report-reveals/ (archived at https://perma.cc/2RXH-7WHH)

Wilkie, D (2018) Number of older Americans at work has grown 35 percent [blog] *SHRM*, 2 February. Available from: https://www.shrm.org/resourcesandtools/hr-topics/employee-relations/pages/older-workers-.aspx (archived at https://perma.cc/H4LJ-PQL3)

ZoBell, S (2018) Why digital transformations fail: Closing the $900 billion hole in enterprise strategy, *Forbes CommunityVoice*, 13 March. Available from: https://www.forbes.com/sites/forbestechcouncil/2018/03/13/why-digital-transformations-fail-closing-the-900-billion-hole-in-enterprise-strategy/ (archived at https://perma.cc/CT7S-Y5EQ)

02

The productivity paradox: the peril and the promise

Productivity isn't everything, but in the long run it is almost everything.
PAUL KRUGMAN, NOBEL PRIZE-WINNING ECONOMIST

Let me start this chapter by saying I completely agree with you on something you may already be thinking. The word 'productivity' is not a very attractive word. It puts us in a position of thinking about humans as if we are some kind of a machine, mechanically producing widgets in a factory somewhere or sitting in a cubicle processing words or data. Nothing could be further from the truth. Humans are complex multi-dimensional beings that can do amazing, remarkable things. However, if you just bear with me for a moment, I think we can address this. It's true we could use a different word, like 'performance', but this word on its own does not work either. It's very 'consultant-like' (as a management consultant, I can confirm this to be the case) and is kind of a meaningless and over-used term. What may help us here is if I define what I mean in this book by the term *productivity* – very simply it is:

> Getting stuff done that measurably improves the economic and human interests of organizations and society at large.

This, I propose, is complementary to the classical definition of 'productivity' defined by economists as: 'Various measures of the efficiency of production; a productivity measure is expressed as the ratio of output to inputs used in a production process, i.e. output per unit of input' (Sickles and Zelenyuk, 2019). In this chapter, I want to marry the classical definition of the word with a broader definition, to make it more meaningful and more impactful, to challenge ourselves to think and do differently at work. Therefore, I settled on using this unattractive word, but with a more comprehensive definition, which I think makes a lot more sense. I hope you will agree.

Given the broader definition we are going to use, I break down productivity into three components:

1 **Value** – the fiscal side of productivity: inputs, outputs, labour, which drives GDP.
2 **Engagement** – workplace that is purpose driven, gives employees the opportunity to flourish.
3 **Innovation** – more productivity leads to more innovation, and vice versa; a virtuous cycle.

To illustrate the point, a compelling study produced by Bain & Company in 2017 is worth outlining for context. Companies like Apple, Netflix, Google, and Dell are 40 per cent more productive than the average company, according to their study. You might think that it's because these companies attract top-tier employees – high performers who are naturally gifted at producing more – but that's not the case, according to Bain & Company partner, Michael Mankins (Mankins, 2017):

> Our research found that these companies have 16 per cent star players, while other companies have 15 per cent... They start with about the same mix of star players, but they are able to produce dramatically more output.

So why is this? There are a number of factors that allow these organizations to do much more with the same or less human capital. Companies like these put their employees in the best possible position to get more stuff done. Some say that by 10 am, the Googles or Netflixes of the world 'get more done and with higher value outputs, than most companies can do in a week', companies with the same or even *more* human capital (Sickles and Zelenyuk, 2019).

For example, Spotify was, until 2012, organized in a traditional company structure like any other non-digital company. However, when they suddenly found themselves in a life-or-death struggle with the up-and-comer Apple Music, the founder and CEO, Daniel Ek, made some radical changes to free up the organization to compete effectively against the Apple behemoth. He looked at the organization carefully and realized that they were not organized in a way that put people in the best position to succeed: to be innovative and agile. There was too much 'organizational drag' – wasteful processes and procedures – which was preventing them from moving fast and unlocking the talent and innovation in his teams. Ek saw that a change of direction was needed, and fast. Two things Ek addressed immediately: culture and organization structure.

On culture, he learned that what people needed to be motivated, to be engaged and productive was: *autonomy* to do what needed to be done; the freedom to be *innovative* and try new things; and lastly, have *respect* for individuals in taking risks, taking decisions, even when they weren't successful.

On the organization structure, Ek blew it up. He didn't need to be inside of every decision, every twist and turn of the daily work. The company was, at over 2,000 employees, too big for that. The centre of gravity of decision making had to be where the work was being done.

The outcome was transformational. Not only were they able to compete effectively with Apple and other streaming services, they made the company a better place to work, a magnet for talent, and in 2018 they conducted an **Initial public offering (IPO)** of shares on the New York Stock Exchange which valued the company at nearly $26bn. They cracked the code of 'getting stuff done that measurably improves the economic and human interests of organizations and society at large'. They were economically productive, but also innovated the workplace, which then innovated how we as consumers – society at large – consume musical content. They changed the world *and* the world of work!

The key things that these companies do differently from others are:

1 Know the make-up of the workforce (who are the top contributors) and seek to understand individuals' motivations and ambitions and what drives them in their day-to-day work.
2 Create rewards that match to the contribution of an individual (and teams); creative approaches to compensation, opportunities to earn equity or other non-cash rewards.
3 Create 'mission-critical' or 'purpose-driven' cultures where people completely buy into what the organization does/produces and its contribution to society.
4 Create a 'frictionless' employee experience, one where the structure of how work is done reduces or eliminates 'organizational drag': remove processes, policies and/or management layers that waste time and energy.

5 Focus on the well-being of the workforce: mental and physical wellness of employees.

6 Group top performers into teams that are assigned to the most mission-critical jobs (also known as 'pivotal' jobs).

7 Have a highly efficient HR organization that has successfully implemented an *integrated human capital lifecycle*; from recruitment, to performance and goals, to learning, collaboration, succession, and workforce deployment it is all a seamless process supported by digital technologies that put this lifecycle into the palm of the hand – literally – of employees and managers.

We will spend the rest of this chapter expanding on the topics of value, engagement and innovation in the context of our broader definition of productivity.

The value of productive people

Over longer periods, however, years of comparatively steady TFP growth tend to be followed by rather abrupt transitions to years with steady but substantially different growth. For example, estimated trend growth in TFP remained relatively strong in the 1950s and 1960s, slowed considerably from the early 1970s to the mid-1990s, and resurged in the late 1990s and early 2000s. Around 2005, a few years before the recession and financial crisis that began in 2007, TFP growth again slowed in many industries and throughout the international economy. In CBO's estimate, TFP growth in the domestic non-farm business sector was only about one-third as rapid during the 2006–2017 period as it had been from 1996 to 2005.

THE CONGRESSIONAL BUDGET OFFICE (CBO), CITED IN TAYLOR (2019)

In 1964, a commission of scientists and social theorists sent an open letter to President Lyndon Johnson (Pauling *et al*, 1964) arguing that:

A new area of production has begun. Its principles of organization are different from those of the industrial era as those of the industrial era were different from agricultural. This cyber-nation revolution has been brought about by the combination of the computer and the automated self-regulating machine. This results in a system of almost unlimited productive capacity…

It's an astonishing statement on several levels. First, the fact that it was made over 50 years ago, yet sounds very prescient here in the 21st century, is uncanny. It must have been one of the first uses of the word *cyber* – which comes from the Greek word *kubernētēs*, meaning pilot or governor – specifically referencing computer technology. Second, it presages a move to different principles of organization and production that would have a major impact on the laws of economics as we understood them in the mid-20th century. Third, it clearly and accurately recognizes that the coming age will be as big a change as was experienced in moving from the agricultural age to the industrial age. And lastly, it touches on a profound aspect of the digital age: we are on the verge of living in a world where scarcity will be replaced by abundance, referenced here as 'an almost unlimited productive capacity'. Fast forward into 2020, and this is exactly what we see today. The economics of productivity, and in fact, human productivity, have changed dramatically.

From the late 1970s until the early 2000s, we watched human productivity mostly move in an upward trajectory with more and more machines helping humans improve the quantity, the quality, and the speed of their of outputs, which saw the cost of manufacturing products and services reduced dramatically as a result. Services can be provided at a fraction of the cost and with a speed unimagined in say, the early 1970s. The progress made in more efficiently utilizing new organizational models, new machines and new technologies to produce goods and services accelerated an evolution in changes to economic models that have stood for centuries. Humans combined with machines continually drive down the per unit production costs of products and services to a point where in the digital world some goods and services costs approach zero and the amount of products produced can approach infinity. Think about the ones and zeros that make up the applications that you use on your smartphone; the cost of these apps is virtually zero while the number of people that can use this product is practically unlimited. A couple of high school best friends can produce the latest 'must-have' app in a very short period of time and get it out to millions, if not billions, of people in an even shorter period of time. The value of this app can be in the millions and billions also in a very short period of time.

Looking back at history, say the 400 years before the start of the Industrial Revolution (and possibly going back millennia), there was almost no global economic growth. The global economy was built on trade in scarce natural resources, and/or pilfering someone else's by invasion and acquisition. However, over the last 135 years, starting with the development of the steam engine, we have seen population growth, international social development and standards of living skyrocket relative to those in previous centuries. It is not a coincidence that this one piece of new technology opened up an entirely new era of human productivity (and disruption) that probably eclipses all that happened before added together. And here we stand, yet again, at another technological inflection point as profound as the introduction of the steam engine. However, the economics of this revolution are going to be almost entirely driven by people power – rather than steam. People harnessing amazing new technologies will drive an era of prosperity not seen before.

For a recent example of the point, let's look at South Korea. Not every country has natural resources to exploit to create wealth, and the Korean Peninsula is an excellent example of this. The Peninsula, overall, is quite barren and has an extreme climate which makes it very difficult to create a sustainable agriculture-based economy. It also has virtually no valuable minerals or oil deposits or any other type of worthwhile natural resource. As a result, the country has been almost entirely dependent on brain power and technological innovation to drive their economy and produce wealth. It's a remarkable success story. I was speaking at a conference in 2009 in Seoul, South Korea, where former UN ambassador Richard Holbrooke was the keynote speaker. In the 1970s and 1980s he was Assistant Secretary of State for East Asian and Pacific Affairs, based in Seoul. He told a fascinating story of his early years living and working in Seoul; how, only a couple of decades after the horrendous Korean War, the South Koreans looked to be a centre of innovation and technology to overcome the challenges they had in rebuilding their society, with the goal to make their economy one of the powerhouses of Asia. The government made its sole focus development of human capital and put great incentives on the start-up of new companies that were developing new gadgets, appliances and innovative technologies. Mr Holbrooke went on to describe how in only 10 years, he watched South Korea very quickly become a powerhouse of technology, bringing to the fore of the world economy what were then quite small firms, like Samsung and LG, developing new products and services that no one had really thought of to that point. He put at the core of his story the remarkable foresight and focus the country's leaders put on human capital, with what little investment funds they had for education, skills development and high-tech industries. At the time it seemed like, at best, a long-shot hope. However, Koreans are an industrious, hard-working people who take great pride in educational attainment, innovation, and entrepreneurship. So, the bet paid off – very handsomely. Mr Holbrooke went on to describe the South Korea of today, compared to the backwater it was in the late 1950s.

In June 2019, Caleb Silver, Editor-in-Chief of *Investopedia*, wrote about what many call the 'miracle on the Han River' (Silver, 2019):

> The South Korean economy, known for conglomerates such as Samsung and Hyundai, is the 11th largest economy in the world with a nominal GDP of $1.53 trillion. The country has made incredible progress in the past couple of decades to establish itself as a high-tech industrialized nation.
>
> South Korea over the past four decades has demonstrated incredible economic growth and global integration to become a high-tech industrialized economy. During the 1960s its GDP per capita was among the poorer countries in the world which is now at the 29th spot with $29,981. Its GDP (PPP) is at $2.02 trillion. South Korea entered the trillion-dollar club in 2004 propelled by international trade and industrialization. It is among the top exporters in the world and presents great investment opportunities reflected in its ease of doing business ranking.

Koreans have created a high-tech economy that is a producer (and innovator) of high-value, relatively low production cost, products and services. For three decades now, they have benefited massively from the new economics of the digital age, effectively creating huge leverage from a constrained workforce pool and almost no natural resources. A very different model than at the turn of the 20th century when wealth was created mostly from natural resources (or from taking someone else's). It's a remarkable story in what has been the most competitive environment for international trade in all of human history. But it illustrates perfectly how the power of human capital, when focused, given a clear goal, and then unleashed, can achieve miracles of wealth and prosperity. It would be easy to say that South Korea is just a 'one-off', and a lucky bet paying off. However, when we look at the world economy since World War II, we find example after example of similar spurts of amazing human productivity that produce vast wealth and prosperity for a nation, or even a single organization. The problem is that, for a number of reasons we will cover in this book, nations, trading blocs and individual companies find it difficult to create consistency in execution; they struggle to create a sustained focus on delivering on the power of right people + right skills + right place + right time + right motivation: *PEIP*.

As we have seen, there are numerous challenges to creating an engaged and highly productive workforce. However, what does 'good' look like when we get PEIP in balance? Where has this been done before and what did we learn from it? The good news is there are a few key data points in recent times that give us some indication of the power of PEIP.

For example, in the 1990s the United States became a lasting case study for the approach. From 1994 to 2001, the US experienced a startling and sustained uptick in people productivity, GDP and GDP per capita. Numerous studies have shown that during this period, US companies and the US government were investing heavily in new hardware and software to take advantage of the new opportunities the internet created to improve efficiencies, reduce costs and reach new customers. As well as investing in and implementing new technologies, a concerted effort was put in place to re-skill and educate people in using these new technologies to make them more productive. The striking acceleration in output and productivity growth in the United States in the early 1990s has been much discussed and a consensus has emerged that this incremental growth can be traced at least in part to the effects of the ICT revolution (Liao et al, 2016) and the investment in aligning the workforce to these technologies was key. These effects can occur through three transmission channels. First, rapid technological progress in the production of ICT goods raises 'total factor productivity growth' in ICT manufacturing industries. Second, falling prices of ICT goods induce a technology investment boom. This adds to the capital available to workers, making them more productive. The accelerating progress in semi-conductor manufacturing technology sustains this substitution of ICT capital for other input types (Jorgenson, 2001). Third, as argued by Jorgenson, ICT typically is a general-purpose technology, which is pervasive and will spread with a time lag. It facilitates and induces firms to introduce more efficient organizational forms. It will eventually boost productivity growth across the economy following significant reorganizations of business processes around ICT capital (Brynjolfsson and Hitt, 2000; OECD, 2004).

There is plenty of consensus among the world's economists on this point: more innovation creates more productivity, and this creates more wealth. It can seem like an obscure economic concept, but it is quite simple. If you view the overall economy as a pie in which countries and individuals have their particular slice, the way to higher wages and more prosperity in an economy, in a country, is really down to steadily growing the economic pie every year. Don't just take your slice and be happy with it. The more productivity produced, the more the pie grows, and the more a country and its citizens can take from this expanding pie. Currently, the economic pie is growing at a slower rate, compared to the recent past, which means that individuals feel the negative impact of it in their pay packet and in wages that either stay the same or grow at a slower rate, and in some cases, go in reverse. This has been the case since about 2008 and the Great Recession. In 2019, we are beginning to see this trend reversed somewhat, and there are signs that this trend may continue into the near future. More on this and the reasons why in Chapter 5.

Output per hour of employee is two-thirds of the total of economic output, or GDP in the world economy. This is well understood. However, there is little consensus on why we see a global stagnation in total output by workers. The OECD view on key economic trends and policy (Braconier *et al*, 2014) outlining the challenges (and opportunities) is a good place to start when considering what may be going on. The paper identifies and analyses the key challenges that OECD and partner economies will face over the coming 50 years if underlying global trends relating to growth, trade, income inequality, and environmental pressures, to name a few, prevail. Unlike the 20th century, it is not going to be just a matter of throwing more people into work and working harder – this will not be enough. Global growth is going to become increasingly integrated, complex and – most critically – dependent on all of us working *smarter*, not *harder*. Growth will have to come from better use of human capital, knowledge and technology to increase human productivity and economic growth – and consequently, standards of living.

Currently, economists that make these long-range forecasts assume the 20th-century status quo in how we align human capital to emerging technology. They assume we will not be able to develop and adopt new organization models, adopt new technologies or expand the pool of talent at a rate which will have the impact on productivity that is required in the 21st century. Looking at how we work today, they cannot see a route forward that creates a fundamental transformation in how we leverage human capital, so assume the status quo. This is the fundamental assumption that leads the OECD to forecast steadily slowing growth for the next 50 years, both in advanced and emerging economies.

Let's take a look at the macro-economic picture out to 2060. Slowing global productivity growth is going to impact global growth overall, although at different rates in different regions, as depicted in Figure 2.1. There are a number of factors at play here with somewhat different challenges based on where a nation's economy lies on the maturity curve.

FIGURE 2.1 Projected average rate of growth in GDP

A. Trend real GDP growth by area, %

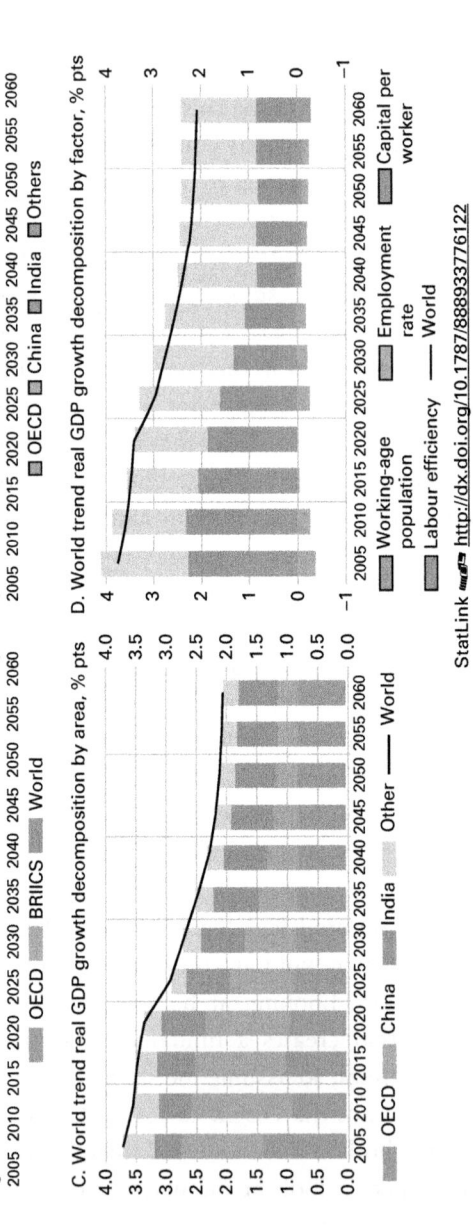

B. Composition of world output, in USD at 2010 PPPs

C. World trend real GDP growth decomposition by area, % pts

D. World trend real GDP growth decomposition by factor, % pts

StatLink ⇗ http://dx.doi.org/10.1787/888933776122

SOURCE Guillemette and Turner, 2018 (p. 8 fig 1)

We will look at these in-depth; however, let's first take a look at how we arrived at where we are today.

The period of the 1950s through to the late 1980s saw dramatic growth in GDP across developed economies. This was mainly due to a post-war manufacturing boom, but also down to technological and process improvements that helped labour – human capital – become more efficient and effective globally. This trend continued until the beginning of the 1990s for the OECD as a whole, but started a decline in both the actual and average trend GDP growth figures in the 1990s compared with the previous three decades. However, there was an interesting exception: during the 1990s the US economy created rapid GDP and people productivity growth. We will come back to this anomaly later in this chapter, but it is worth stating here that studies have consistently shown that during this period in the 1990s, US companies and the US government made unprecedented investments in ICT, and also invested heavily in building the skills of the workforce to adopt and align with technology to improve productivity. This anomaly is a good example which we will come back to in Chapter 3, in order to illustrate the power of PEIP.

Since 2000, the OECD has tracked significant volatility in global economic growth (real GDP). However, the overall average trend for all economies (emerging and advanced) during this period has been flat growth, although recent dates predict real GDP as falling gradually from 2018 onwards to 2060 – from 3.5 per cent average GDP growth in 2005 to 2.0 per cent by 2050 (Guillemette and Turner, 2018). Both emerging economies and advanced economies continue to see a downward trend during the period, with emerging economies seeing the greatest year-on-year decreases in GDP, where advanced economies will see a long, slow downward trend. This despite the regular innovation and implementation of ever more innovative technologies to support the workforce. Essentially, economists fall into two different camps – optimists and pessimists – when looking to forecast the rate of GDP growth, with two different scenarios that could play out.

1 **The optimists' view.** The optimistic view posits that we will identify and develop new organizational structures/systems and that processes will be redesigned to exploit the full potential of emerging technologies – creating cascading growth in complementary technology and innovations and thus steadily improving rates of productivity. This would drive what

economists call the 'the pace of change at the technological frontier' (Braconier, 2015), where the rate of adoption by humans of rapidly emerging technologies is efficient and keeps pace with the rate of emerging innovations. The speed of adoption moves forward at an equal or faster pace relative to history (eg Brynjolfsson and McAfee, 2011). Advocates for this position point to the significant lag between the discovery of other general-purpose technologies in history (eg electricity) and the burst of innovation that their discovery facilitated (eg the light bulb or the telegraph).

2 **The pessimists' view.** The pessimistic view argues that the main impact of the late-1990s ICT revolution has gradually diminished and future inventions that derive from ICT are unlikely to fundamentally change trend productivity. Such a view is consistent with the recent slowdown in productivity in many OECD countries, and slowing changes in the pace of discovery at the technological frontier. This view essentially is one where the assumption is that people cannot adopt emerging technologies at a rate that will positively impact human productivity. They assume that the status quo of the last years of the 20th century and the first years of the 21st century will prevail, and will not make the process or structural changes required to better align people to technology at a rate to change the trend of slowing growth.

Currently, the vogue is towards the pessimists' view – thus, the OECD forecasts and the challenge, or opportunity, depending on how one sees it. In this book, we will be taking the optimists' view (with an eye towards the pessimists' valid arguments).

Over the past 15 years or so, we have been able to paper over the slowing engine of growth by leaning heavily on emerging economies to keep the engine humming along. However, those days are rapidly coming to the end as – at the time of writing – we are already seeing the cracks emerge in China and India as their economies start to meet the forces of economic gravity: what goes up *will* come down. The days of emerging economies picking up the pace, plugging the gap for the stagnant economies in the US and Europe are over. So it is urgent that we act now, in order to reverse this trend, and find the next engine(s) of growth so that the increases in our prosperity we all bank on will come to fruition. We can and, in fact, must prove the expert economists wrong. There is too much at stake.

Engaged people do more stuff, better

In my travels over the years, one thing stands out as a constant, regardless of culture or geography: the key to engaging any human being is to know what drives an individual; to understand what their motivations are in life. It's a practice that I try to enlist in my daily interactions with my teams. I want to know what drives them both in work and personally. At an event I attended, I heard the explorer, Sir Ranulph Fiennes, say in a speech that when he is choosing the teams that work with him on his often-dangerous expeditions, he does not have a long list of characteristics by which he assesses who is in and who is out. He goes by one simple metric to assess an individual's fitness: what motivates a person in life and work. Once he understands this he can, first of all, make a selection and, second, use this knowledge while on the expedition to get the most of his team. As he says, once motivation is understood, 'it's pretty straightforward to engage and motivate people in their work.'

Everyone likes to be listened to, and a big part of understanding what motivates someone is 'putting on the big plastic ears' and just listening to them as they tell you their story. It helps the individual articulate their values and principles in the context of what they spend at least one-third of their day doing: their job. It's amazing how much this simple principle means to people, and the impact it can have on their engagement with their work. Fact is, no one can spend 100 per cent of their day doing exactly what they want to do in perfect alignment with goals, ambitions and principles. So, as a manager, I see it as my job to try to maximize the fit of the job and the tasks I ask them to do to a person's values and goals – their motivations. Right person, right place, right time, right skills, right motivations – PEIP – constantly an *aspirational goal*, one that is never 100 per cent in alignment. Therein lies the rub: it's the managing through the times when PEIP is not in balance, to engage someone even when the current tasks at hand are not perfectly aligned, but still necessary to overall success. However, when an individual understands that their manager, the organization they work for, is making the effort and mostly succeeding in putting an individual in the best position to perform, they will engage positively and give best efforts. This is core to engaging an individual in my experience. The results of engagement are extensively measured these days. A 2016 Gallup study (see Figure 2.2) drew the connection between consistently low-engagement team performance and suggested that when an employee's engagement needs are not met, there is a higher likelihood of turnover – which can cost an employer

FIGURE 2.2 Engagement and business outcomes

Engagement's Effect on Key Business Outcomes

When compared with business units in the bottom quartile of engagement, those in the top quartile realize improvements in the following areas:

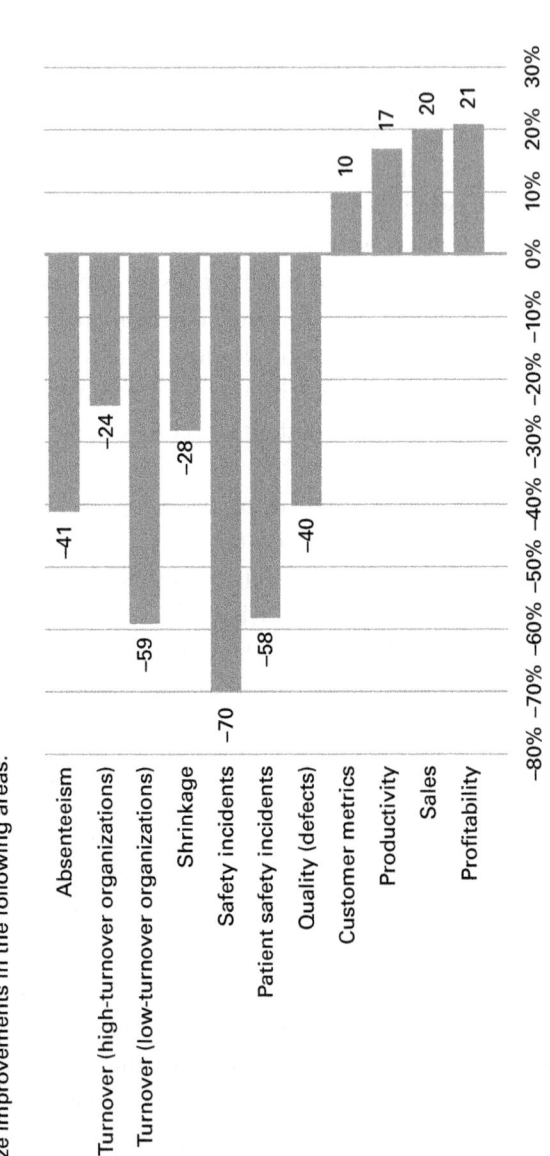

Area	% Change
Absenteeism	−41
Turnover (high-turnover organizations)	−24
Turnover (low-turnover organizations)	−59
Shrinkage	−28
Safety incidents	−70
Patient safety incidents	−58
Quality (defects)	−40
Customer metrics	10
Productivity	17
Sales	20
Profitability	21

SOURCE Reilly, 2016

1.5 times the employee's original salary. The study also found that engaged teams have lower turnover, 21 per cent greater profitability, 17 per cent higher productivity and 10 per cent higher customer ratings than disengaged teams.

There are a number of success factors emerging among organizations that are exceptional in creating workforces that engage with work to produce more with less, and with greater quality:

1 drive: autonomy, mastery, purpose;
2 rewards reinvented;
3 employee experience and well-being.

Creating drive in the workforce

As covered previously, Daniel Pink's book, *Drive* (2011), has been a mini-revolution in how organizations are changing the way they view and interact with their workforces on the subject of performance – he calls it 'Motivation 3.0'. It has upended the old order of traditional Industrial Revolution managing people – the carrot and stick – (Motivation 2.0) and replaced it with new ways of thinking and doing. Pink's book has influenced numerous organizations to relook at employee motivation and engagement across three distinct dimensions: *autonomy*, *mastery*, and *purpose*. He makes a very strong case that humans are wired to react positively to a work environment that gives them the space to take ownership of the means by which work gets done (autonomy), the opportunity to develop new skills and capabilities (mastery) and to work for a company that aligns with their personal values (purpose).

He asserts, and backs it up with data, that organizations that structure themselves to balance an individual's *intrinsic* motivation (why they work for you) with their *extrinsic* motivation (money/rewards) get better results. In other words, they align the reasons a person comes to work for specific organizations (personal values – intrinsic motivations) with meaningful remuneration for individual (and team) contribution. Additionally, these organizations are very effective in creating a shared sense of purpose among the workforce – people not only buy into the goods and/or services that the organization provides, they are inspired by the contribution that the organization makes to society at large. The most visible change that has come from Pink's work is that many organizations have transformed their performance management approach and processes to do away with the 'annual performance review' and forced rankings of individuals along bell curve principles. Many organizations have moved to 'continuous feedback' models of reviewing performance and development with individuals. Managers have regular 'check-ins' with their employees not only to discuss progress against objectives, but also to review development opportunities.

Additionally, many have moved from ranking people's performance against other employees according to outdated bell curves. That model essentially says that we will have a small number of very high performers and an equivalent number of very low performers, with the bulk of our people clustered near the average. This practice has been called, rather accurately, 'rank and yank'. It's the 1980s General Electric (GE) Jack Welch approach to distributing raises and performance ratings by this curve, which assumes that real performance is distributed across a bell curve. To avoid 'grade inflation', companies force managers to have a certain percentage at the top, a certain percentage at the bottom, and a large swath in the middle. The fact is, when studied carefully, it turns out that the bell curve is nowhere near describing how performance and, more importantly, *contribution* occurs in the organization. In 2011 and 2012, Ernest O'Boyle Jr and Herman Aguinis studied 633,263 researchers, entertainers, politicians, and athletes (in a total of 198 samples), and they found that performance in 94 per cent of these groups did not follow a normal distribution; rather, these groups fall into what is called a 'Power Law' distribution. This distribution takes into account the extremes of 'hyper-performers': individuals whose contribution is so profound that if they were to disappear it would turn a high-performing company into one that would be in danger of going out of business (O'Boyle and Aguinis, 2012). We will spend more time on this later; however, it is a fundamental shift in thinking on the subject of performance, contribution and rewards. Let's take a further look at the principles of autonomy, mastery and purpose in engaging the workforce.

Autonomy

When people are trusted, and indeed encouraged, to take ownership of their own work and development, they tend to value themselves and the organization more. When you think about it, when you are in control of your life, what you do and how you do it is very satisfying and takes a lot of stress out of life. There are few situations that cause more stress on human beings than when they feel they are not in control of their day-to-day life. It's one of the top reasons people develop mental illnesses. So, it's no surprise that when people are given the scope to control the levers of what they do and how they do it, they relax and, Pink argues (2011), as a result of relaxing, they become more productive, creative and innovative. Some argue that if an organization reduces the need to conform to strict workplace rules – regular office hours, dress codes, numerical targets, and so on – it can increase autonomy, build trust, and improve productivity.

But what exactly is autonomy? Autonomy in the workplace is usually defined by organizations across four principles (Wheatley, 2017):

1 the extent to which employees have the freedom to organize how work is done (task autonomy);
2 the extent to which employees are allowed to set their own schedules (time autonomy);
3 the relaxation of workplace rules around dress code, etc (rule autonomy);
4 the setting of targets and objectives (goal autonomy).

These factors are not mutually exclusive, and many organizations mix and match according to what areas work best for them.

The other dimension of autonomy is defining both individual and team responsibility. Members of a group are all interdependent on their team, each other and the entire cycle of operations. Individuals have shared responsibility in meeting goals and the demands of the work they are doing, all while contributing to the development of work on an individual and intergroup level (Enehaug, 2017).

In addition to these factors, another key element to keep in mind when designing autonomy programmes is company culture. I have had the good fortune to hold senior roles across three major global companies: Accenture, IBM and SAP. I found that each company and each team within a company had different levels of 'tolerance' for autonomy. Early on in my career as a manager in Accenture, I learned that my teams were very comfortable with and embraced having the autonomy to get on with their day-to-day work on projects. The leadership style that I developed in the late 1990s was one of a 'coach'. I gave my teams their 'game plan' and targets and let them get on with it – organize their work and execute it in line with client expectations. I was there if needed and would keep an eye on the outputs and the quality of the outputs. If I saw someone struggling or in difficult situations, then I would step in to help. My teams appreciated this freedom and it was clear in their day-to-day interactions. I recall one particular dinner with my manager, a senior executive in Accenture, after a team meeting. He commented on how engaged and 'happy' the project teams were, having organized themselves around the work to be done. He asked me how I became so comfortable letting the teams operate in this way. When I paused to think about it, I explained that they were all bright, experienced people, that our client trusted them and it seemed the natural way to manage and organize to get stuff done. Additionally, I explained that the team had their own expectations that they did not need or want to be micro-managed, so I went with it. He expressed some amazement at the idea but decided that it was something other teams should consider. In 2006, I was recruited to IBM to lead the global human capital consulting business. I brought the same approach of autonomy to my new teams, but quickly noticed something: many were not quite as comfortable with having as high a level of autonomy as I had employed at Accenture. It was variable across different individuals and teams, but largely people wanted more direction on a more regular basis. It was important that I adjust my approach and take into account people's expectations. I was happy to do this, and made a point to work on my own style to make sure it matched the team's comfort level. Similarly, when I joined SAP, I found an even lower tolerance for autonomy, so again adjusted my approach. However, in both the IBM and SAP roles, over time, people became more and more comfortable with having more autonomy, so the tolerance increased. Eventually the right balance was achieved, and team engagement and productivity increased.

It's important to keep in mind that autonomy is not only different for each group of teams but also different for each area of the business. For instance, a salesperson has little interaction face to face with their manager; however, many times the manager gives the salesperson strict rules limiting their autonomy and this then reduces the ability for the salesperson to perform, losing sales productivity. A large majority of salespersons who are allowed to have full autonomy tend to be more productive and also raise the levels of customer service. Autonomy also gives internal entrepreneurs the ability to achieve results through the need to make important choices and the need to have resources to facilitate the creative process to improve the performance and exploit opportunities for the organization.

In the end, the ability for employees to craft and design their own jobs is at the heart of autonomy and achieving good results from the approach. Mobile workers in the UK find that they are 13 per cent more productive than the office-based employees. Working remotely promotes a self-managed atmosphere which drives higher productivity (Crunden, 2016). Autonomy and job crafting are one and the same; job crafting is a conceptualized view of the ability of one person to design their job in the most strategic way possible, which in turn should allow for the person to have better job performance (Demerouti et al, 2015). Getting the balance right across these key factors is important as the chances of success are dependent on having a clear understanding of your workforce and how they are best motivated through greater autonomy. Each organization should work backwards from the company's overall strategy and objectives and the individual's/team's desires to design a mix of autonomy factors that best suit the company and its workforce.

Motivation by autonomy is often associated with software companies, who are viewed as more 'modern and forward thinking'. However, it's not just software companies adopting these practices for autonomy. For example, the German company Agro Food (part of a holding which produces pet food) a few years ago had to go through a complete upheaval in order to stay competitive. The whole production process was modernized by introducing machines instead of craft-based production. The new production lines required new employee competencies. Employees were educated and trained to take over every task in the manufacturing process. Moreover, some unskilled workers were trained to do production jobs – every employee had the chance to upskill and take over a skilled worker's task. Thus, former unskilled workers were trained in robotics and are now machine operators. At the request of employee representatives and the works council, every employee was given the opportunity to develop and to implement a training and career plan, which led to more qualified employees taking over more demanding jobs. Now workers at the production site have leeway to organize their work as long as they meet the production deadlines given by the customers. For example, they can decide themselves to take a break, to have a meeting, or to watch a football championship game as long as they fulfil the production targets. All these measures helped the company stay competitive. Employees like the production flexibility and the chance to improve their skills and competences as well as their new jobs.

When a well-designed programme of autonomy is put in place, it can achieve substantial improvements in performance and build new wells of people productivity. In 2017 an expert trio of UK specialists in leadership, well-being and human resources, Allan Lee, Sara Willis and Amy Wei Tian, conducted meta-analysis of all available field experiments on leaders empowering subordinates. In their report, 'Empowering Leadership', they examined the results of 105 studies, which included data from more than

30,000 employees from 30 countries (Lee *et al*, 2018a). They looked at whether an empowering leadership style was positively linked to improved job performance, and tested whether this was true of different types of performance, such as routine task performance, organizational citizenship behaviour, and creativity. They also tested several mechanisms that might explain how this type of leadership improves job performance; for example, were these effects caused by increased feelings of empowerment, or by increased trust in one's leader, or both? Finally, they explored whether leaders who focused on empowering employees influenced employee job performance equally across different national cultures, industries and levels of employee experience (Lee *et al*, 2018b). Their results were remarkable, showing a strong statistical correlation across all of these domains, leading them to conclude that an empowering leadership style shows much promise in changing the workplace for the better, and for creating more productivity. The evidence was clear: the positive effects of empowering leadership on performance, organizational citizenship behaviour, and creativity at both the individual and team levels were real and measurable.

Mastery

Mastery is an innate human desire to get better at something. If you are motivated by mastery, you'll likely see your potential as being unlimited, and you'll constantly seek to improve your skills through learning and practice. People who seek mastery almost need to seek it and attain it for its own sake. It becomes a self-fulfilling prophecy. For example, an athlete who is motivated by mastery might want to run as fast as she possibly can. Any medals that she receives are less important than the process of continuous improvement. During my Accenture days we were fortunate to have an inspirational sporting figure as our brand champion, someone who is considered an 'all-time great' – Tiger Woods. He often joined us for small private events with clients, which for many was an amazing treat; an opportunity to meet 'a master' of his sport. I attended a number of these events and one particular theme he often employed when talking with people was describing his motivation for spending the massive amount of time required to become World Number One and win so many golf Major tournaments. For him, it was really simple: the search for mastery. As he used to put it, the reason he was 'so obsessed' with hitting a little white ball was the fact that he 'would never be able to completely master' the skill, to achieve perfection. That it would always 'master' him. He was motivated by becoming as good at golf as was humanly possible. This idea always stuck with me, emphasized by the look in his eye when he would tell this story for the umpteenth time. His eyes would sparkle and he would completely engage with the concept. As a concept, it was something everyone could understand and could take to heart – it was inspirational. Tiger Woods' attitude to mastery is summed up by three 'laws' Pink outlines (2011):

1 Mastery is a Pain
2 Mastery is a Mindset
3 Mastery is an Asymptote

Studies show it takes at least 10 years of hard work to even approach mastering a subject. There is a process of sacrifice, experiencing the pain of failure and pushing oneself to get back up and try again. Stanford Professor Dr Carol Dweck, in her 1999 paper 'Self-Theories: The Mindset of a Champion', wrote about the sacrifice of 'champions' who seemingly all have a deep well of passion to care about something enough that they are willing to work for it – at almost all costs (Dweck, 2014). A real master will tell you that mastery is an all-consuming effort that requires a steely mindset of perseverance and passion. The extent to which success is achieved is based to the extent to which we are willing to persevere, to have a mindset to deal with the pain. Additionally, as Woods says, he realized he will never master the art of golf, that it is beyond his grasp, but that is part of the fun. Pink (2011) says, 'The mastery asymptote is a source of frustration. Why reach for something you can never fully attain? But it's also a source of allure. Why not reach for it? The joy is in the pursuit more than the realization. In the end, mastery attracts precisely because mastery eludes.' This is why putting people in a position to attempt to master new skills and feel the benefit, the allure of the rewards, can be so addictive, which can turn into a fly-wheel of perpetual motion of motivation and effort, increasing people's productivity. Let's look at a compelling example to illustrate the concepts.

Paper mills are the largest continuous production facilities in the world, and pulp manufacturing as a work process is particularly complex (Leppänen, 2002). The efficient and effective manufacturing of paper relies heavily on the mastery of the production process by both individuals and teams of people. A study of 15 paper machines across five different mills in Finland was conducted to test the effectiveness of programmes that help workers master both the conceptual and physical process of producing paper. The study covered a personal development programme that was designed by employees to help improve production processes and quality as well as workplace well-being. A small group of employees that worked on the 15 paper machines were tasked with the creation of the development programme based on their collective and individual understanding of these complex processes. They were encouraged to identify and document improved techniques and processes and put this into a learning programme that allowed others to master the process. The development programmes were based on the analysis of production processes, machinery and the work itself. The analysis of these processes required taking into account the elements of human activity at work, tools and the division of labour. In addition, the modes of action of the tasks in different situations, the cooperation of subjects within the work process and associated tasks such as maintenance or quality control were also analysed. In developing the programme, participants needed to conduct a thorough analysis of production processes, machines and the work. The teams needed to verbalize and elaborate on the different models that could account for each of the parts constituting the working process. During a learning development process like this one, teams learn to master the knowledge available from the individuals in the group. The skills and expertise of the production manager, process engineer, chemical process experts, automated operation system experts and marketing agents can also be solicited (Leppänen, 2002).

The development of the programme and the significant work that went into identifying new ways of working and then turning these into a learning event for others to master had two significant results. First, the people involved in the development of the programme significantly improved their own mastery of the most efficient processes, as well those who entered the programme and utilized it to master these processes as well; the teachers learned as much as the pupils. Second, the emergence of connections between mastery of the work process and satisfaction with the programme (both developers and students) showed that new professional qualifications became a source of pride and well-being in the organization that valued skills and demonstrated this through continued adoption of the development of the work process and mastery of this process as an organizational feature. Lastly, it was recognized that no matter what was developed and learned, it could always be improved. There was a continuous cycle of designing new ways of thinking and working. In a regression analysis of job satisfaction, 72 per cent of the variance in job satisfaction was explained by improving the processes, reducing work disruptions, positive assessment of the challenge of mastery at work, and an active attitude towards the development of a better workplace. Given the opportunity to control and improve their work conditions and master new skills along the way, the paper mills drove significant new benefits in engagement, innovation and productivity.

Purpose

Some years ago a mentor of mine gave me a piece of advice that has stayed with me, which almost always proves to be true – it's uncanny. He said that you can tell everything you need to know about an organization by how their main reception looks and how you are treated by the staff that greet you. If the reception area is uninspiring and the staff treat you with indifference, then that is very likely exactly how the company operates, treats its employees and, most importantly, treats its customers. If on the other hand the reception area is engaging, exciting and the staff treat you like a long-lost friend, you can bet that on the inside of this organization you will find the same. Every time I visit a company I have not been to before I remember this piece of advice. It rarely lets me down as a principle. Think about this, then think about your company. What do people experience when they come into the main reception? Is this the 'coal face' of what is known as 'the purpose-led organization' – or not? Purpose-led companies have a strong reason for being – they are clear what they stand for, are authentic in how they live up to this purpose on a day-to-day basis and articulate this purpose clearly to their customers and employees. It's a very powerful concept that, if executed effectively, galvanizes people to ignite long-lasting positive change, driving growth, productivity and innovation. OK, so that all sounds very lofty; however, it is true that organizations that define what they are all about and get people to buy into it reap significant benefits. It's the old adage that if your employees are treated well and inspired by what they do, your customers will be treated well and inspired by what you do.

When Steve Jobs was in his second stint as Apple CEO, he had a simple mission statement for the company: 'To make a contribution to the world by making tools for the mind that advance humankind.'

He often said that his personal purpose in life was 'to make a ding in the universe'. People working at Apple found that inspiring and wanted to be a part of it. They were doing something that was not only bigger than themselves, the company, the country, or the world, but would have an impact on the *Universe*! Not many companies could make that bold a statement and live up to it. Most could argue that this is exactly what Apple products have done in the 21st century. I have posited in many of my talks that, in the recent past, Apple retail stores could probably ask people to work for free (or for some free product, on occasion) and they would still have a line out of the door of willing staff to work in their stores. Apple has a lot of fan-boys and fan-girls; they have developed an almost cultish following from those days, early in the 21st century, when Jobs came back and re-invigorated the company's fortunes.

However, if you look at Apple's current mission statement:

> Apple designs Macs, the best personal computers in the world, along with OS X, iLife, iWork and professional software. Apple leads the digital music revolution with its iPods and iTunes online store. Apple has reinvented the mobile phone with its revolutionary iPhone and App store, and is defining the future of mobile media and computing devices with iPad.

It doesn't exactly trip off the tongue and appears to lack any of the lofty sentiment that Jobs used to aspire to. It's very product and services focused and seems to be more of an advert for stuff than a rallying cry to get behind. But, perhaps, both the customer and employee brand are so strong these days that Apple does not need a version of Jobs' grand vision to inspire. Time will tell.

Regardless, those companies that have a clear reason for being are clear what they stand for, are authentic in how they live up to this purpose and they reap significant benefits. Global tax and financial consultants E&Y recently published a paper that summarizes the benefits organizations can reap from developing purpose-led connection with employees and customers (EYGM Ltd, 2016). E&Y found that purpose-led organizations find and keep the best employees, attract, retain and engage customers, and as a result, increase returns for shareholders. For example, companies that embody an inspirational purpose have 1.4 times more engaged people and 1.7 times more satisfied customers (Schwartz, 2013). About 90 per cent of customers believe a purpose-driven company will deliver the highest-quality products/services (Edelman, 2012); similarly, 72 per cent of global consumers would recommend a company that has clear purpose, which is a 39-point increase from 2008. It was also found that purpose-led companies outperformed the S&P 500 by more than 10 times between 1996 and 2016 (Sisodia *et al*, 2014).

Tesla is an emerging example of the power of purpose. The company has a simple mission: 'To accelerate the world's transition to sustainable energy'. Elon Musk, like Steve Jobs, sees the company as a force for good in the world, and bigger than that, sees its role as 'driving a revolution' in the car industry. Everything about Tesla, from the car's design, to its manufacture, to the way consumers choose and buy their car, has been re-imagined. Purchasing a Tesla is more akin to buying a PC, or a phone in an Apple store. There is no car showroom in the traditional sense. In fact, they are called Tesla 'stores' and have the look and feel of an Apple store. I recently decided to take a test drive in a Tesla, so stopped into one of their stores (with a booked appointment, online). There are no car salesmen in broad, loud suits lurking in the corners. Instead, your first interaction is with a 'product specialist' whose main role is to educate potential buyers about electric cars. Often they are young people in smart, fashionable casual clothing, who are not pushy or 'salesy'. The type of people you will encounter is best illustrated from a Tesla job posting on Glassdoor for a product specialist:

> You will provide a fun educational experience for customers who come into the Tesla retail store and educate the public about the electric drive experience. For you, it's a unique opportunity to help us revolutionize the way in which potential customers experience the Tesla brand.

The focus is on 'fun' and 'education', which is the complete opposite of what you would experience in a typical car showroom. In my case, young Graham showed me around a deconstructed chassis of a Model X, explaining the drive systems and how they work. The real treat, though, is when you are taken to a car for the test drive. From the moment I sit down and look around the space, it is clear this is no car like any that I've driven before. This is where Graham's passion for his job becomes clear. He clearly enjoys the reaction people have to their first experience with the product. He enthusiastically walks me through the basics and the unusual features of the car, the main one being there are no dials or buttons, just a rather large touch-screen device from which all of the features and functions of the car are accessed. We take the car out and he coaches me through various features, including using the auto-pilot function – a strange sensation to say the least! All the while, Graham is focused on making sure I am both having fun and being educated on the car and its capabilities. When we return to the store, the car is instructed to find a parking place and then parks itself, all while Graham and I chat about the different models available for purchase. This is then the end of the experience. Graham does not try to get me to meet a sales manager and sit down and go through financing options. He is more focused on leaving me with some final thoughts about how Tesla cars are going to change the world. His passion is contagious.

In many ways, having both employees and consumers totally buy into the mission and purpose of Tesla cars is essential. It is extraordinarily difficult to change an industry, and even more difficult to change the car industry, which has done things the same way for over 100 years. When you have to start by educating consumers about the basics of your product, one that is so different in every way, you start from way behind in competing with your rivals. When you look at Tesla's history, it has been a herculean struggle to manufacture, sell and out-perform the competition to the extent required to be a sustainable and profitable business. Tesla's struggles in becoming a sustainable and profitable business are well documented. This reality has required Musk to be a hyper-demanding boss, asking his employees to go way beyond what most CEOs would ask of their teams. Add on top of this the fact that Musk, much like Steve Jobs, is both a revered and reviled boss, known for his inspirational vision as much as for his perceived lack of compassion for the extraordinary demands he puts on those that work for him. In the end, people are so inspired by Musk's vision for changing the car industry and, more importantly, *accelerating* the world's transition to sustainable energy, that they will put in the extra hard work and effort to help him achieve it. This passion for the purpose of the company translates into financial success. If you speak to a Tesla owner, they are as ardent a supporter of the company's products as Apple aficionados have been for Apple products. The Tesla driver buys into the mission and purpose of the company and its products, just as the employees do. I believe it is safe to say that without this extraordinary combined employee and consumer desire for Tesla cars and what they stand for, the company would not have survived taking on the entrenched car industry and winning. In fact, at the time of writing, Tesla had its first-ever back-to-back quarters of profitability, after overcoming two years of production problems and bad public relations stories of customers disappointed by late delivery of cars. Despite all the challenges and near-disasters, Tesla made a $139 million profit in the fourth quarter of 2018, the first time the electric automaker has ever posted back-to-back profitable quarters in its 15-year history. It was also Tesla's fourth profitable quarter ever, as of January 2019. Tesla generated $7.2 billion in revenue in the quarter, a record for the company.

Rewards re-invented

Another big part of engaging the workforce is putting in place innovative rewards programmes to cover not just a person's extrinsic motivations, but also their intrinsic motivations in working for your organization. In my experience, it is largely true that the 21st-century workforce very often does not have money at the very top of the list as to why people do a particular job. Modern society is mostly not worried about basic shelter and food, so is some way up the pyramid of Maslow's Hierarchy. Most people have their basic needs covered and therefore have choices in what they do and where they work. I do not want to leave the impression that the problem of extreme poverty is resolved; however, over the past 100 years there has been significant progress in lifting large populations out of extreme poverty around the world. Nonetheless, rewards for work done remain a very powerful motivator and done correctly can have a significant impact on people productivity.

As fewer and fewer people work in factories or in agriculture, and more work in office-based services type organizations, employers are being forced to re-look at how they motivate the workforce when it comes to remuneration. It's no longer a transaction: a person works, produces outputs, and a company pays the market-level wage for that work. Rewards in the 21st century are more complex and are increasingly a combination of both cash and non-cash interactions designed to create engagement linked to better organization outcomes. This is why rewards are such an integral part of people engagement and are increasingly a combination of different aspects that includes, of course, money, but also other forms of compensation that are considered 'soft benefits', for example:

- experiences;
- recognition programmes;
- office perks;
- learning and degree programmes;
- equity award programmes;
- paid sabbaticals.

A combination of these, together with an appropriate salary/hourly rate, are powerful motivators, as well as key to retaining top talent. When looking at reward programmes it's worthwhile thinking about them in three buckets:

- pay the bills;
- reap the reward;
- make them whole.

The first is fairly obvious: pay people a fair wage for their daily time and effort, which ideally should be enough that they are covering their bills and not worrying about the rent or mortgage. Second, real-time rewards for having done something or created something special that goes beyond the day-to-day contribution. This can be individual or team-based, or both, depending on how the organization gets work done. Third is a focus on the more long-term reward, where people are earning significant and meaningful long-term investment either in financial equity of the organization or, if in the public sector, investment in giving people time back or time for intellectual/spiritual improvement.

- **Pay the bills: a fair wage, a living wage**
  There is an emerging school of thought that is gaining currency among many in policy-making spheres as well as private company strategy: pay people enough so that they are not worrying about the mortgage/rent, food, medical and children's school/college expenses and are completely focused on their work. Take the idea of money off the table. A number of studies have shown that when people are making 'a living wage', their work production increases and their behaviours change among their fellow workers. More collaboration and teamwork are found when people are focused on the work to hand, and not the cash side of things.

- **Reap the reward: experiences, recognition programmes, office perks**
  There are literally hundreds of real-time rewards that an organization can provide to their employees that usually don't cost tons of money, but do have outsized meaning to people. They typically come in three areas – experiences, recognition and office perks – and the sky is the limit for the things that you can invent to provide people with rewards based on extra performance. One of the favourites with 'millennials' is giving them experiences when recognizing a job well done: a dinner for two, or bungee jumping (may want to think that one through!), or concert tickets, etc. More tenured employees often prefer perks like a primo parking spot, a new office (or a cubicle with a view), or lunch with the boss. Some recognition programmes are as simple as allowing employees to send a 'thank you' with a link download to a small monetary award (Amazon vouchers) or other meaningful gift. These are very popular across the spectrum of generations in work. Everyone likes being personally and meaningfully thanked for that extra effort.

- **Make them whole: equity awards, degree or other courses, paid sabbaticals**
These are more future-looking rewards that are often designed to create long-term engagement and retention of key employees. Significant and meaningful investments in top talent can literally change their lives and create long-term loyalty and commitment. Over the past 15 to 20 years there has been a steady move towards new ways of using compensation and rewards to engage and retain employees, particularly in the private sector, where more and more companies are offering employees ownership of the enterprise (shares in publicly traded companies and internal shares in private companies). I have seen the power of this approach up close. During my time as a partner in Accenture, we took the company public in July 2001. This was an exciting and bold move that completely changed the future of the company and created a significant amount of wealth, on paper, to the executive (partner) level. For the first time in the company's history, the IPO created a pool of equity (ownership) that could be shared with employees. Previously, as a partnership, the ownership of the company had been in the hands of the partners, which was a relatively small group of top executives. Now came the opportunity to share this ownership with employees. There was concern that much of the top talent that was just below the partner level felt like they were left out of the lucrative IPO and would leave for other companies because the 'partner carrot', as it was called, was now gone. A programme was set up to address this with the main goal focused on retention of top talent during this major transition in the company. Largely this programme worked, retaining some of the best project managers – the lifeblood of the consulting business. But surprisingly it had an unexpected benefit: gaining ownership of a growing firm changed the way people behaved. They began to think like owners and took decisions based on this principle. People became even more focused on delivering quality work for clients to gain their loyalty to help maintain consistent revenue while also watching internal costs carefully. For the share price to thrive (a new focus for employees) people knew how important it would be to deliver predictable revenues and keep costs down, which ultimately increases profit and earnings per share. The programme was so successful, it was gradually rolled out to all staff over time, with many of the same results.

Obviously public-sector organizations cannot award ownership of the enterprise, as it is already owned by the public. However, there are a number of powerful ways that these organizations can also invest in the long-term prospects of their top employees: time off and/or personal development. Many public-sector organizations offer time off to long-serving and high-performing talent. Significant time off – sabbaticals, as they are commonly known – is usually a period of paid leave granted for study or travel, which is traditionally one year for every seven years or so worked. This time off is prized as it is significant time away from the day job that allows people to do something completely different for a while. Many people travel, some do missionary or charity work, some go and learn a new skill unrelated to work. More time off is awarded for longer tenure and top performance, so increases in attractiveness (and value) over time. Another benefit often offered by public-sector organizations is development opportunities such as degree courses or specific courses related to current role or future aspirations. Government pay schemes mean that incentives are difficult to offer in competing with private-sector organizations. Therefore, it is common for public organizations to sponsor their own staff to be part-time students. Ambitious young people put a high value on development and those who want to work as graduates for the big local public sector organizations can take advantage of national schemes to improve their skills. For example, in the UK, over 250 local councils sponsor members of staff to undertake Open University degrees. Much of the Open University is made up of online courses and degrees that are highly flexible and have the same status as a degree from any top UK university. Having these courses paid for by the organization is a powerful development and retention tool and allows the public sector to compete for top talent.

Workforce employee experience and well-being

CEOs increasingly understand the power of employee well-being; not just talking about it, but putting in place programmes to improve employee mental health, and letting them know that it is imperative to use them.

In 2019, SAP CEO Bill McDermott asked employees to focus on *mental and emotional health*, to improve quality of life and job satisfaction. He encouraged employees to beware of the 24/7 'always on' world, where these things can become 'too much of a good thing'. He urged the company to focus on *resetting this balance* by, for example, joining other SAP employees who had already participated in mindfulness training programmes. His view was that none of us can do good work for the company if we don't keep ourselves well.

People look for retreats for themselves, in the country, by the coast, or in the hills ... There is nowhere that a person can find a more peaceful and trouble-free retreat than in his own mind. ... So constantly give yourself this retreat, and renew yourself.

MARCUS AURELIUS

One trend that has emerged slowly over the past 20 years, but is now coming on quickly, is a focus on 'employee well-being', It started out in the late 1990s as a focus on what most called 'health and safety' and has now morphed into a more broad-based people strategy focusing on individual 'wellness' – employee health. Health and safety used to be looked upon as something that was immeasurable in terms of benefits to the organization and therefore put in the category of 'anecdotal', but still thought of as necessary from a compliance perspective to avoid law suits and bad press. Today, more and more data is showing that workforces that have a healthy balance of mental, physical and financial well-being have a positive impact on engagement and productivity and create more profitability/efficiency. Organizations with highly effective well-being programmes designed to improve productivity report 11 per cent higher revenue per employee, 1.8 fewer days absent per employee per year, and 28 per cent greater shareholder returns among North American companies (SLF Group Benefits, 2012). Elizabeth The at HR and wellness company Rise People writes that among employers offering wellness programmes, 77 per cent saw increased employee satisfaction and 66 per cent reported increased productivity. Additionally, 63 per cent noted increased financial sustainability and growth while 50 per cent saw decreased absenteeism (The, 2017). As a result, the corporate wellness market – including health care programmes, screening, assessment, education, and apps – has reached nearly $8 billion in the United States alone, where it is expected to hit $11.3 billion by 2021 (Agarwal *et al*, 2018). Executives of some of the world's most successful companies have developed a clear understanding of the critical role these programmes play in defining an organization and making them desirable as places of employment. For example, two-thirds of organizations now state that well-being programmes are a critical part of their employment brand and culture (Agarwal *et al*, 2018). A full 89 per cent of workers at companies that support well-being efforts are more likely to recommend their company as a good place to work (APA, 2016).

So what makes up a good well-being programme? There are as many ways to address this question as there are approaches companies enlist to make it happen. However, at the highest level the best programmes focus on the following:

- **Mental well-being**: monitor the workload of employees to avoid burnout and provide regular opportunities to renew and recharge both inside and outside work, as well as providing a certain level of autonomy in tasks and work rules to give control over work.
- **Physical well-being**: beyond providing health insurance, physical wellbeing is offering employees the opportunity to improve their health through more exercise, improved nutrition, and emphasizing the importance of adequate sleep, both at night and during the day.
- **Financial well-being**: one of the biggest stressors on the workforce is money; more and more companies are investing in helping the workforce to better manage finances. A particular area of focus is helping people save for future retirement and also dealing with student debt burdens.

Significant evidence exists supporting the link between mental well-being at work and productivity – 'good work' (jobs that are skilled, autonomous, supported, secure, with good work–life balance, good income) is associated with better mental health and less absenteeism. Managing workloads across the workforce is one of the most important things companies can do to relieve mental stress. During and after the 2008 financial crisis, people saw their workloads double and even triple as workers were let go and those that were left had to pick up the slack. More recently, there is a focus on using better workforce management techniques and tools to spread the load across the employees, to smooth the pipeline of work to be done and by whom it gets done. Additionally, many organizations are relaxing work rules and work times to allow more flexibility and control over their time and place of working.

Dr Daniel Wheatley, of the University of Birmingham Business School, in his 2017 research paper, 'Autonomy in paid work and employee subjective well-being', found that:

> greater levels of control over work tasks and schedule have the potential to generate significant benefits for the employee, which was found to be evident in the levels of reported well-being. The positive effects associated with informal flexibility and working at home, offer further support to the suggestion that schedule control is highly valued and important to employees 'enjoying' work (Wheatley, 2017).

Additionally, a focus on physical health is showing evidence of the impact of tackling risk factors such as smoking, physical activity and obesity. A study of Transport for London found workers with obesity (BMI>30) take an average of three more sick days annually than those of normal weight

(BMI<25), and those with severe obesity (BMI>35) take six days more (Goettler *et al*, 2017). Helping employees change behaviours and giving them opportunities, and tools, to work on their health reaps significant benefits. In insurance giant Aflac's 2016 workforce survey, 55 per cent of employees said they would participate in an exercise programme through their workplace to help lower their health insurance cost, while 64 per cent of employees participate in their companies' well-being programme and agree that they've made healthier lifestyle choices because of these programmes (Aflac, 2016).

One area of particular focus in creating physical well-being is sleep. A flood of recent research shows that the importance of at least eight hours of sleep per day has massive personal benefits in mood and performance (Schwartz and Porath, 2014). At the same time, the lack of consistently catching eight hours of sleep a night can be catastrophic to physical well-being and productivity. Former *Huffington Post* founder and editor, Ariana Huffington, says:

> After my collapse from sleep deprivation and exhaustion in 2007 I became more and more passionate about the connection between well-being and performance. And as I went around the world speaking about my experience, I saw two things: First, that we're facing a stress and burnout epidemic. And second, that people deeply want to change the way they work and live (Mari, 2019).

Ariana used to sleep for only three to four hours a night when she was setting up and running her news media aggregation site. In 2007 she collapsed and woke in a pool of her own blood from an injury to her cheekbone. Her doctors told her she was exhausted and had to change. And once she made this change she said: 'I'm much more present in my life, much more joyful. I am, without question, a better leader, because I can look ahead with more clarity.' She went on, 'I think the biggest growth of the *Huffington Post* happened after [she slept more]. I think it's a delusion that in order to succeed as an entrepreneur you need to burn out.' Now, she's so evangelical about her bedtime routine, she sold *Huffington Post* and now proselytizes around the world on the benefits and what she calls 'the necessity of sleep' as part of her Thrive Global enterprise (Mari, 2019).

Money worries are some of the most pernicious areas of challenges for people. Having a certain amount of freedom from worry about money is something many people long for. Therefore, financial well-being has an impact on a worker emotionally, but it also impacts business productivity. Almost 25 per cent of workers report money worries have affected their ability to do their job, and one in ten say they have found it hard to concentrate/make decisions at work because of money worries. A further 19 per cent have lost sleep worrying about money, all of which impact performance (Schwartz and Porath, 2014). A 2018 study by the Centre for Economics and Business Research in the UK found that 11 per cent of workers admitted that they experienced a reduction in their work productivity due to financial distress. Nearly 25 per cent of workers surveyed stated that they were often distracted by financial worries, which ranked ahead of issues like health worries (18 per cent), family worries (16 per cent) and job security (also 16 per cent) (Cebr, 2018). As a result, financial worries have as big or bigger part in creating 'presenteeism' (people at work, but distracted) and 'absenteeism' (not showing up for work at all). In fact, it's been found that presenteeism has a greater financial cost to employers than absenteeism, as it is harder to detect productivity impacts of workers being at work physically, but mentally checked out. This makes financial well-being a particularly difficult problem to root out, as people are much less likely to discuss their financial health than they are their physical health with their employer or colleagues. To address this problem (and to measure the impact), in the United States the Consumer Financial Protection Bureau came up with a financial well-being scale:

- Control over one's finances: being able to pay bills on time and making ends meet.
- Capacity to absorb a financial shock: unexpected major outlay of cash.
- Being on track to meet financial goals: paying off debt, saving for retirement.
- Making choices that allow one to enjoy life: having freedom to do enjoyable things (Cebr, 2018).

It might be easy to put the blame mostly on workers for not watching out carefully for their own finances, but the numbers tell a different story. Consider the fact that wage growth has been stagnant across mature economies up until very recently. It takes no major leap in understanding as to why so many people are feeling the crunch; feeling out of control of their finances. It's been a vicious cycle of hanging on to one's job (or not) during the economic uncertainties following the 2008 financial crisis, then as the recovery progressed, watching the rise of house and food prices, and more recently, interest rates, all while wages have barely budged. These facts are putting more onus on companies and government policy makers to help out, if not for their people, but for themselves and society as a whole.

The good news is that more and more employers are seeing the advantages to helping their employees obtain financial well-being. As a result, one of the most active areas of programmes supporting employee well-being revolves around finances. Most employers now have robust 'financial and benefits planning' support for their employees. Many organizations have set up pension programmes that match employees' saving and educate employees on the potential of saving for the future. In some countries, like the UK, setting up pension schemes is mandatory. All workers are put into their employer scheme; if they prefer they can opt out but must do so in writing, stating that they understand the implications of not saving for a pension. A recent YouGov survey found that the most popular financial well-being support employers can offer is providing 'above minimum' matching pension contributions for employees. Over 82 per cent of employees agreed this was the most desirable form of financial support companies could give. Additionally, many employers are creating programmes that automatically enrol employees into these matching contribution plans and are providing apps and other tools for employees to engage with their financial planning (Cebr, 2018).

Lastly, advances in technology are generally seen to have more of a positive than negative impact on employee well-being, largely through facilitating flexible working and enabling more effective communication. Most organizations, however, report that advances in technology have also had adverse effects on employee well-being in their organization. An inability to switch off out of hours and the stress caused by technology failure are common hazards; however, more and more data is starting to come in that shows the 'double-edged sword' our fingertip access to technology can have on our mental well-being, both at home and at work.

Innovation: the engine driving engaged people and greater productivity

If you have an apple and I have an apple and we exchange apples, then you and I will still each have one apple. But if you have an idea and I have an idea and we exchange these ideas, then each of us will have two ideas.

CHARLES F BRANNAN, US SECRETARY OF AGRICULTURE,
FROM A BROADCAST OVER NBC, APRIL 3, 1949

Certainly, innovation is a hot topic in today's business literature. It is also over-used and not always in the right context. It is derived from the Latin word *innovare*, meaning to make something new in a complex construct. Some psychologists argue that *innovare,* or innovation, is a natural human instinct (eg van Mulukom, 2018). We are born with an innate ability to look at a thing or a situation and think through how we might improve on it. Given the right environment and circumstances, humans can innovate all the way to the moon and beyond! It has also been found that organizations, just because they are made up of humans, will not automatically be innovative. Uninspiring work and work environments actually suppress the natural human inclination towards innovation. This is why engaged people create innovation, and innovative work and work environments create engagement. The other main ingredient, once engagement is added to the recipe, is human relationships. People spark off one another. Just like musicians 'jamming' in improvisation, employees often do the same in work. In fact, many companies, such as IBM and SAP, call these internal improvisation and brainstorming sessions 'JAM'.

Productivity growth is currently a challenge in most regions of the world. However, research and development (R&D) spending was expected to rise 3.4 per cent in 2019 to approximately $514 billion. That's roughly 2.8 per cent of US GDP, the highest on record. Though the federal government and academia spend heavily on R&D, industry is the biggest contributor, representing about 70 per cent of the total. This dynamic is also playing out around the globe in countries such as China and Japan (Franz, 2017). So, with all this spend on R&D (it's a total $2.3 trillion worldwide in 2018) why are we getting such low yield on people productivity – what is going on? We have begun to outline the challenges here, but also the case for some of the ways forward. Hopefully in the previous pages, we have begun to address how we need to evolve our thinking about human capital. In my experience across many large and small organizations, we are mostly still stuck in the 20th century in how we motivate, develop, deploy and reward talent, and this is getting in the way of our ability to get a better yield. The problem is, we have not hit that critical mass of organizations that have made the changes needed that we have been discussing in the chapter. Certainly the trend is towards the positive, towards PEIP, and is accelerating, but we have not hit the tipping point – yet.

Regardless, it should not be surprising that more and more data has been pouring in for over 10 years now about how, when we engage our people effectively, it creates an engine, a virtuous cycle, a fly wheel even, of creativity:

- A report by Bailey *et al* (2015) consolidated the results of 214 academic studies, the combined findings of which revealed a significant link between engagement and innovative work behaviour.
- A MacLeod and Clarke report (2009) stated that 'engaged employees freely and willingly give discretionary effort, not as an "add on", but as an integral part of their daily activity at work'. The report then went on to reinforce that idea with case studies that highlight companies who placed an emphasis on values-driven engagement that ultimately resulted in greater innovation, among a number of other benefits.
- In 2007, Gallup found that higher levels of engagement are strongly related to higher levels of innovation. Fifty-nine per cent of engaged employees say that their job brings out their most creative ideas against only 3 per cent of disengaged employees (Krueger and Killham, 2007).

According to Gichohi (2014), employee engagement is the critical ingredient in the role of creativity and innovation at the workplace. He cites Social Exchange Theory (SET), a theoretical foundation of engagement and creative behaviour of employees. According to SET, when employees are given values by empowerment and training, they feel a sense of consideration and they repay the organization by showing engaged behaviour. This engaged behaviour of employees motivates them to perform more than their duties and results in creativity and innovation in the organization. Moreover, engaged employees are a source of creative performance – and productivity (Gichohi, 2014).

Additionally, another area that many organizations are starting to look at is one of creating more time for innovation through reducing 'organizational drag'. Essentially, organizational drag is the cumulative effect of 'unnecessary internal processes, interactions, unproductive or inconsequential meetings, and unnecessary communications' (Mankins, 2017); Michael Mankins at Bain & Co says organizational drag wastes time and saps the energy of the workforce. For example, In the 1970s, an executive received up to 5,000 communications per year. In the 2010s, executives can expect to receive 50,000 communications per year (Brantley, 2017). There is a limit to what humans can absorb, and we may be at that limit. Essentially, we are saying that unnecessary processes, interactions, meetings and communications can become a very large tax on an organization – a financial tax. A tax so expensive, according to Mankins, it makes financial capital look very cheap in comparison. Michael put it this way in a recent interview (Mankins *et al*, 2017):

Financial capital is no longer scarce. It's super abundant and, for most companies, cheap. What's scarce for most companies now is good ideas and good ideas don't just materialize, they're the product of people. People that have the time to dedicate to their work, the talent to bring creativity and ingenuity to the work they do and the willingness to dedicate at least a portion of their discretionary energy to serving customers leading into the success of the company or organization itself. The real scarce resources over the next three decades are really time, talent and energy. That's what drives the quality of ideas, the ability to execute those ideas, the number of those ideas. That's what it's really going to take to outpace the competition given that financial capital is now super abundant and relatively cheap.

He went on to say:

So there's a quote by Andy Grove from Intel that we use in the book (*Time, Talent, Energy: Overcome organizational drag and unleash your teams productive power*, Mankins *et al*, 2017), but also in an HP article a few years back, that just says you wouldn't think of letting an employee walk away with a piece of office equipment, but you let them walk away with the time of their fellow managers all the time.

Most organizations don't actually know where they invest their collective time, even though the tools are available to answer that question today, and they weren't a few years back. And as a result, that scarce resource, time, is often squandered unintentionally, or certainly not put to its highest value and best use, which is the test that you would apply for things like financial capital.

It's a bold claim, but when we step back and look at what we spend our day doing, add up the time that is not adding value but is 'required' for the day job, it really adds up. Then multiply that by all of the people in the organization and it becomes a large amount of wasted time and money, but, just as importantly, is also draining on people. This time takes away from their ability to engage with work, improve their performance and think up new products or ways of doing things (innovation). If organizations can reduce drag by even small increments, it adds up greatly over time. Recently a very astute blogger, Bill Brantley, coined a term that describes the opposite of 'organizational drag' – he came up with 'organizational thrust', which essentially is what happens when you significantly reduce organizational drag. As he put it (Brantley, 2017):

'Organizational thrust'; I coined it from the aeronautical concepts of drag and thrust. If organizations can better manage the time and talent of their workforce, then organizations will increase the energy of their workforce. A workforce of merely satisfied employees who become a workforce of 100 per cent inspired employees will produce tremendous organizational thrust. The organizational thrust that increases the number of innovative ideas and the difference makers to implement those ideas.

So what are organizations doing to reduce drag and create thrust? Mankins and his colleagues describe three areas of focus (Mankins *et al*, 2017):

- **Time:** Believe it or not, if all the normal digital communication and meetings were totalled up for a particular manager and bunched up to be completed at the beginning of the work week, the manager wouldn't be able to start more value-added work until late Thursday afternoon. This is low-hanging fruit that can be addressed with some basic discipline around meetings and communications, and also by eliminating unnecessary processes and workplace rules.

- **Talent:** Many organizations are pooling their top talent into ringfenced teams who are freed up from day-to-day meetings, communications and processes to focus on high-priority programmes. For example, they have relaxed rules around work time and place, and are even trusted to be given expense budgets that do not require detailed reports being filled out (which can take a lot of time, and add zero value).

- **Energy:** Unproductive workplaces sap employee satisfaction and engagement; we have all seen this. Productive and innovative workplaces have 'thrust' and get things done and innovate. A satisfied employee is 40 per cent more productive than an unsatisfied employee. An engaged employee is 44 per cent more productive than a satisfied employee. However, an inspired employee is 125 per cent more productive than a satisfied employee! Imagine, if you have a team of 10 satisfied employees. If you could turn each of the team members into inspired employees, you would have the productivity of a team of 25 employees without additional salary costs.

So Mankins and other experts in this space advise us to measure and get a handle on what is causing unproductive time and remove it. The tools and analytics exist today to get to the bottom of this. It is clear that by reducing email, numbers of meetings, unnecessary processes and relaxing work rules, it allows for head space to innovate and become engaged in the most interesting aspects of our work.

Additionally, if we get PEIP in balance, change our motivation and reward programmes to match 21st-century work, create a focus on improving employee well-being, be a purpose-led organization, and reduce organizational drag, it's not surprising that people will find the 'head space' to think up new things. Engaged people do more stuff, better – new products, new ways of doing things, time to provide better customer service. It becomes a virtuous feedback loop of effectiveness: engagement creates innovation – innovation creates engagement. It's also a good deal of fun working in this kind of environment: more collaborative, buzzy and fulfilling. Employees in these organizations are not only trusted to come up with new ideas but are positively reinforced and supported for doing so, even when it does not always pan out. These days almost everyone is in agreement that for organizations to grow, be more productive and remain competitive, a sustainable pipeline of new thinking, new ideas – innovation – is critical. Clearly, another area of emerging understanding is around the link of engaged employees to innovation, and vice versa. Let's take a deeper look at this in Chapter 3.

References

Aflac Workforces Report (2016) Large company business trends: 2016 Aflac WorkForces Report results for businesses with more than 5,000 employees. Available from: https://www.aflac.com/docs/awr/pdf/2016-detailed-findings/awr.2016-fact-sheet_large-business-trends-5000.pdf (archived at https://perma.cc/L7NU-VM89)

Agarwal, D, Bersin, J, Lahiri, G, Schwartz, J and Volini, E (2018) Well-being: A strategy and a responsibility [blog] *Deloitte Insights*. Available from: https://www2.deloitte.com/insights/us/en/focus/human-capital-trends/2018/employee-well-being-programs.html#endnote-sup-8 (archived at https://perma.cc/P526-D7PY)

APA (2016) Workplace well-being linked to senior leadership support, new survey finds [blog] *American Psychology Association*, 1 June. Available from: https://www.apa.org/news/press/releases/2016/06/workplace-well-being (archived at https://perma.cc/R5XA-4H77)

Bailey, C, Madden, A, Alfes, K and Fletcher, L (2015) The meaning, antecedents and outcomes of employee engagement: A narrative evidence synthesis, *International Journal of Management Reviews*, 19 (1), pp 31–53. Available from: http://sro.sussex.ac.uk/id/eprint/54474/ (archived at https://perma.cc/3T96-N5RA)

Braconier, H (2015) Determinants of tertiary graduations, OECD Economics Department Working Papers No. 1138, OECD Publishing. Available from: http://dx.doi.org/10.1787/5js4hmvns9hh-en (archived at https://perma.cc/5H39-CJRY)

Braconier, H, Nicoletti, G and Westmore, B (2014) Policy challenges for the next 50 years, OECD Economic Policy Papers series, OECD iLibrary, 2 July. Available from: https://doi.org/10.1787/5jz18gs5fckf-en (archived at https://perma.cc/6JFG-R65W)

Brantley, B (2017) How organizational drag is wasting the time, talent, and energy of your agency's workforce [blog] *GovLoop*, March. Available from: https://www.govloop.com/community/blog/organizational-drag-wasting-time-talent-energy-agencys-workforce/ (archived at https://perma.cc/ZQW7-T9YF)

Brynjolfsson, E and Hitt, L (2000) Beyond computation: Information technology, organizational transformation and business performance, *Journal of Economic Perspectives*, 14 (4), pp 23–48

Brynjolfsson, E and McAfee, A (2011) *Race Against the Machine: How the Digital Revolution is accelerating innovation, driving productivity, and irreversibly transforming employment and the economy*, Digital Frontier Press, Lexington, MA

Cebr (2018) Financial wellbeing in the workplace [blog] *Centre for Economics and Business Research*, October. Available from: https://cebr.com/reports/financial-wellbeing-in-the-workplace/ (archived at https://perma.cc/NZK4-VKNQ)

Crunden N (2016) Help mobile workers feel less remote, *Occupational Health & Wellbeing*, 68, p 11

Demerouti, E, Bakker, A B and Halbesleben, J R B (2015) Productive and counterproductive job crafting: A daily diary study, *Journal of Occupational Health Psychology*, 20, pp 457–69

Dweck, C (2014) Self-theories: The mindset of a champion [blog] *Gostanford*. Available from: https://gostanford.com/sports/2014/5/2/209487946.aspx (archived at https://perma.cc/53RQ-5B9L)

Edelman (2012) Goodpurpose: Global consumer survey. Available from: http://www.fairtrade.travel/source/websites/fairtrade/documents/Edelman_Goodpurpose_-_Global_Consumer_Survey.pdf (archived at https://perma.cc/BQW8-APJZ)

Enehaug H (2017) Ten successful years: A longitudinal case study of autonomy, control and learning, *Nordic Journal of Working Life Studies*, 7, pp 67–89

EYGM Ltd (2016) Winning with purpose: EY entrepreneurial winning women conference, May 2016. Available at: https://www.ey.com/cn/en/services/strategic-growth-markets/ey-asia-pacific-entrepreneurial-winning-women-2016-program-major-events (archived at https://perma.cc/4NWB-LWBA)

Franz, J (2017) Innovation is driving economic growth and sparking productivity gains [blog] *Capital Group*. Available from: https://www.capitalgroup.com/pcs/latest-perspectives/innovation-driving-growth.html (archived at https://perma.cc/Q89T-G9PC)

Gichohi, P M (2014) The role of employee engagement in revitalizing creativity and innovation at the workplace: A survey of selected libraries in Meru County – Kenya, *Library Philosophy and Practice*, 1, pp 1–33

Goettler, A, Grosse, A and Sonntag, D (2017) Productivity loss due to overweight and obesity: A systematic review of indirect costs, *BMJ Open*, 7 (10), e014632. Available from: http://dx.doi.org/10.1136/bmjopen-2016-014632 (archived at https://perma.cc/CMF8-9HN6)

Guillemette, Y and Turner, D (2018) The long view: Scenarios for the world economy to 2060, OECD Economic Policy Papers, 22. OECD Publishing, Paris. Available from: https://doi.org/10.1787/b4f4e03e-en (archived at https://perma.cc/8SML-JFZ7)

Jorgenson, D W (2001) Information Technology and the US Economy, *American Economic Review*, March

Krueger, J and Killham, E (2007) The innovation equation: Strengths development + engagement = innovation, according to a Gallup study, *Business Journal*, 12 April. Available from: https://news.gallup.com/businessjournal/27145/innovation-equation.aspx (archived at https://perma.cc/5GGV-85SZ)

Lee, A, Willis, S and Wei Tian, A (2018a) Empowering leadership: A meta-analytic examination of incremental contribution, mediation, and moderation, *Journal of Organizational Behavior*, 39 (3), pp 306–325, http://dx.doi.org/10.1002/job.2220 (archived at https://perma.cc/U9ZM-HGW2)

Lee, A, Willis, S and Wei Tian, A (2018b) Empowering employees works, and when it doesn't, *Harvard Business Review*, 2 March. Available from: https://hbr.org/2018/03/when-empowering-employees-works-and-when-it-doesnt (archived at https://perma.cc/YL9J-8K3Y)

Leppänen, A (2002) Improving the mastery of work and the development of the work process in paper production, *Relations Industrielles*, 56 (3), pp 579–609, https://www.erudit.org/en/journals/ri/2001-v56-n3-ri366/000083ar/ (archived at https://perma.cc/C9B4-7XXB)

Liao, H et al (2016) ICT as a general-purpose technology: The productivity of ICT in the United States revisited, *Information Economics and Policy*, 36, pp 10–25, https://dspace.lboro.ac.uk/dspace-jspui/bitstream/2134/21850/3/LI_ICT%20paper%20IEP.pdf (archived at https://perma.cc/RAY3-NQLT)

MacLeod, D and Clarke, N (2009) *Engaging for Success: Enhancing performance through employee engagement*, Office of Public Sector Information, London https://dera.ioe.ac.uk/1810/1/file52215.pdf (archived at https://perma.cc/JV58-RAXG)

Mankins, M (2017) *Time, Talent, Energy: Overcome organizational drag and unleash your team's productive power*, Harvard Business Review Press, Boston, MA

Mankins, M, Harris, K and Harding, D (2017) Strategy in the age of superabundant capital, *Harvard Business Review*, March–April. Available from: https://hbr.org/2017/03/strategy-in-the-age-of-superabundant-capital (archived at https://perma.cc/28WN-T9MG)

Mari, K (2019) The joy of sleep: An interview with Arianna Huffington [blog] *Thriveglobal*, 2 January. Available from: https://thriveglobal.com/stories/benefits-sleep-interview-arianna-huffington/ (archived at https://perma.cc/R2V5-SSYT)

O'Boyle, E Jr and Aguinis, H (2012) The best and the rest: Revisiting the norm of normality of individual performance, *Personnel Psychology*, 65, pp 79–119

OECD (2004) *The Economic Impact of ICT: Measurement, evidence and implications*, OECD, Paris

Pauling, L et al (1964) *The Triple Revolution*, The Ad Hoc Committee on the Triple Revolution, Santa Barbara, California. Available from: http://scarc.library.oregonstate.edu/coll/pauling/peace/papers/1964p.7-01.html (archived at https://perma.cc/7699-G9FY)

Pink, D H (2011) *Drive: The surprising truth about what motivates us*, Canongate Books, Edinburgh

Reilly, R (2016) Five ways to improve employee engagement now [blog] *Gallup*. Available from: https://www.gallup.com/workplace/231581/five-ways-improve-employee-engagement.aspx (archived at https://perma.cc/NR8B-EZNW)

Schwartz, T (2013) The energy project: What is your quality of life at work? [blog] *Harvard Business Review*. Available from: https://hbr.org/web/assessment/2013/11/what-is-your-quality-of-life-at-work (archived at https://perma.cc/8SFQ-RRHB)

Schwartz, T and Porath, C (2014) Why you hate work, *New York Times Sunday Review*, 30 May. Available from: https://www.nytimes.com/2014/06/01/opinion/sunday/why-you-hate-work.html?_r=1 (archived at https://perma.cc/H6KU-P9CX)

Sickles, R C and Zelenyuk, V (2019) *Measurement of Productivity and Efficiency: Theory and practice*, Cambridge University Press, Cambridge and New York

Silver, C (2019) Top 20 economies in the world ranking the 'richest' countries in the world [blog] *Investopedia*, 7 June. Available from: https://www.investopedia.com/insights/worlds-top-economies/ (archived at https://perma.cc/W3EN-4UN2)

Sisodia, R, Sheth, J N and Wolfe, D (2014) *Firms of Endearment: How world-class companies profit from passion and purpose*, Pearson Education, Upper Saddle River, NJ

SLF Group Benefits (2012) A Strategic Dose of Wellness: Your prescription to a healthier organization, research based on the 2011 Buffett National Wellness Survey, Sun Life Financial, Canada. Available from: https://www.sunlife.ca/static/canada/Sponsor/About%20Group%20Benefits/Group%20benefits%20products%20and%20services/The%20Conversation/Bright%20Papers/files/1748-03-12-e.pdf (archived at https://perma.cc/6DC8-SV7V)

Taylor, T (2019) The puzzle of the US productivity slowdown [blog] *BBN Times*, 5 February. Available from: https://www.bbntimes.com/en/global-economy/the-puzzle-of-the-us-productivity-slowdown (archived at https://perma.cc/KAC8-GZAT)

The, E (2017) 25 fascinating workplace wellness statistics, Rise. Available from: https://risepeople.com/blog/fascinating-workplace-wellness-statistics/ (archived at https://perma.cc/3MC8-DC6P)

van Mulukom, V (2018) The science behind going with your instincts [blog] *WeForum*, May. Available from: https://www.weforum.org/agenda/2018/05/is-it-rational-to-trust-your-gut-feelings-a-neuroscientist-explains (archived at https://perma.cc/NMR3-TX2K)

Wheatley, D (2017) Autonomy in paid work and employee subjective well-being, *Work and Occupations*, **44** (3), pp 296–328. Available from: https://doi.org/10.1177/0730888417697232 (archived at https://perma.cc/SD5K-GPGB)

03

People engagement, innovation and performance – PEIP

The impact of diminishing people productivity presents a formidable challenge for all of us. It's a serious problem, and the trends that are breaking over us today only make the challenge greater (these trends also represent an opportunity – more on this in the next chapter). However, the good news is that the fixes that are required to turn the situation around are all available to us today – proven solutions. In a way, we can actually look to the recent past for the solutions; they worked then and can work now. Dust them off and put them back to good use. Therefore, there is a great deal of reason to be optimistic about the future, for two reasons: *The Present*, and *The Past*.

The Present: in my recent travels and time spent with companies both big and small, it's clear there is a growing focus and a tremendous amount of energy and desire to address people engagement and productivity. This wave has been building for a long time and is now cresting as leaders understand that there are not a lot of areas left in organizations to cut costs or financially engineer more profit. Most companies have undergone some kind of 'transformation' programme, but the results are sketchy as best. Achieving a successful organizational transformation is far from an easy feat. According to the McKinsey Transformation Change survey, just 26 per cent of companies accomplish their performance objectives and even fewer lay the groundwork for sustained change and positive results (Bucy *et al*, 2016). Implementing new technology and/or new organization structures has had a limited impact on the cost structure and on the value of many companies.

However, improve the engagement of your workforce and drive improved performance and this goes straight to the top and bottom line – and, for publicly held companies, a bump in the share price, for government organizations, improved taxpayer services and tax revenue savings. This idea is gaining more of top management's attention and is why we see management boards and CEOs pushing their organizations to think and do differently in the workplace today. Many senior executives are now measured by the board on their employee engagement and people performance metrics. It's why there is a booming business for 'engagement solutions' and 'people surveys' and for emerging cloud HR IT solutions like SAP SuccessFactors and Workday, which are being tapped by organizations to help them improve employee experience, engagement and productivity. HR is restructuring how they provide services by taking advantage of the automation these cloud HR systems provide, freeing them up to support managers who are now doing most of the talent management activities that HR used to do. These cloud HR systems allow the organization to push the centre of gravity for people management down to the line management. They are relatively simple to use and make line managers look like HR experts, if implemented correctly. The organization is now freed up to focus on the things that matter: the performance of the organization. A win-win for all involved. It's a quiet revolution underway that is changing work and long-held business management principles.

The Past: in the 1990s, as the internet was starting to become a tool for making businesses more effective and reach more customers, there was a great deal of energy and investment put into aligning people to the new technology. The new technology was such a massive step change from what went before, and the amount of money that was being invested so completely unprecedented, that organizations were careful to focus on the human element of the change. Entire new disciplines were founded – for example, change management (aligning people to the changes ICT was bringing to the workplace) – and small consulting companies like Andersen Consulting became multi-billion-dollar businesses. The changes that technology was bringing were understood, and there was much focus put on making sure people were able to effectively harness these new tools to drive performance. In the United States during this time a focus on both sides of the equation – technology/people – produced astonishing results, with US people productivity, company profits, share price and national GDP approaching record highs. There is an excellent *Harvard Business Review* study on this period that documents the 'perfect storm' of investment in IT and people, finding this as the main reason for a 10-year-long 'blip' of productivity, growth in wages and company value creation that has not been repeated since. Around 1989 to 1990 there were predictions by award-winning economists such as Paul Krugman that the stagnation in human productivity that started in the 1970s would continue, and most likely get worse. In fact, productivity growth increased only modestly in the early nineties but then surged after 1995, averaging 2.8 per cent from 1996 to 2000, and the pessimism of the 'computer productivity paradox' gave way to near-universal belief in a 'productivity resurgence' led by information technology. Official estimates of potential growth had to be raised repeatedly during this period. From 1997 to 2001, the US Congressional Budget Office more than doubled its 10-year projection of non-farm business productivity growth from 1.2 to 2.7 per cent (Jorgenson *et al*, 2008). The combination of investment in technology and people, together with a cycle of deregulation in the United States and the subsequent fiscal policies of the US Treasury, created the perfect conditions for this surge in productivity and GDP. It was a golden age of economic good news stories and real value creation which had not been seen before, with people and technology being the main drivers. There was talk of the US Dow Jones hitting 'the 20,000' mark back in the late 1990s (it was in the 11,000-point range in the early 1990s). There was a major focus on getting the right people, in the right place at the right time, with the right skills and motivation, to get the most out of the investment in technology: the first version of PEIP was born.

By contrast, in Europe there was a different story emerging during this period. Europe was less inclined to take the headlong plunge into the internet age than the United States. Less investment was being made into these new technologies and even less into people. Add to this a far more restrictive regulatory environment, and the story emerges as the opposite image of what took place in the United States during this period. In retrospect the situation provided an unintentional 'test vs control group' for the power of aligning people to new technology. Average annual labour productivity growth (measured as GDP per hour of work) in the United States accelerated from 1.2 per cent in the 1973–1995 period to 2.3 per cent, reaching a peak of over 5 per cent from 1995 to 2006. Conversely, the 15 European Union countries that constituted the union up to 2004 experienced a productivity growth slowdown between these two time periods. For these 15 countries as a group, labour productivity growth declined from an annual rate of 2.4 per cent during the period 1973–1995 to 1.5 per cent during the period 1995– 2006 (van Ark *et al*, 2008). In fact, the latter period was the first measured case of divergence in productivity growth after Europe had caught up with the United States in the post-war period. For about 10 years, the two regions moved in lock-step on the subject of productivity. This caused a flurry of studies trying to understand what was going on, with most economists coming to the same conclusions on the data: in the late

1990s Europe was lagging behind in moving to a technology-driven knowledge economy relative to the United States. Europe was not following the US in getting the right people in the right place at the right time, with the right skills and motivation, to take advantage of the emerging technologies.

I was fortunate enough to be able to directly observe the phenomena described above across both regions as I was working in the United States up until 1997 and then in Europe from that point on. When I arrived in Britain in 1997, I noticed a very different level of maturity around embracing ICT in the businesses I was working with as a management consultant. In the US, adopting new technologies and aligning people to these technologies was happening across most industries by 1997. In Europe, by contrast, I found that the big ICT projects were mainly restricted to the big telecommunication companies (telecoms) such as British Telecom. The rest of industry seemed, in my experience, to be almost proud 'Luddites' who were resisting the new technology and new ways of working. There was significant reluctance to follow the Americans down the path of using the internet and ICT. It was seen as a massive investment with very uncertain outcomes, so best let the 'Yanks' go first! Luckily for Europe, most of the European Telecoms bucked this trend and invested heavily from the beginning, laying the groundwork and the infrastructure that was going to allow Europe to catch up, eventually.

However, fast-forward to 11 September 2001, and the geopolitical and national security shockwave that was unleashed globally by the attacks executed by Al Qaeda on the World Trade Center and the US Pentagon, causing the deaths of over 2,000 civilians, and a subsequent recession. This, combined with the bursting of the dot-com bubble in 2000, led to a perfect storm of uncertainty. Although the economic impact of these two events proved to be short-lived, with the recession of 2001 turning out to be one of the briefest and shallowest in history, the uncertainty that this unprecedented attack created for the psyche of global political and business leaders significantly disrupted the accelerating investment in people and technology that had preceded the terror attacks. Post 9/11 up until the Great Recession beginning in 2007, the investments being made were smaller scale and emphasized the technology over the human element. What I observed over and over again during this period was companies trying to cut costs (and reduce risks) of IT implementations by reducing or completely removing any investment in the people element of these programmes. In Accenture (which had rebranded from Andersen Consulting during this period) we found the demand for our change management services greatly reduced, which required a reorganization of our practice in this area. This type of change management business focused on aligning people to technology, and it never really recovered post 9/11. To my mind, and in my experience, this has been one of the most glaring causes for ending the period of growth in people productivity that is still impacting us today. This de-coupling of IT and people has had a tremendous drain on the world economy, which we are only recently beginning to address.

Nonetheless, there are some great lessons to be gleaned from the recent past and embedded within are the solutions that we can leverage to fix the present and future. The remainder of this chapter is going to leverage what we can glean from the past 15 or so years and focus on three key areas to get us back to where we need to be:

1 Working smarter, not harder.
2 The integrated human capital lifecycle: lays the foundation for PEIP.
3 Solving the productivity paradox: unpacking PEIP for driving peak people performance.

Work smarter, not harder – it's OK, really

It's not the load that breaks you down, it's the way you carry it.
       LENA HORNE, AMERICAN PERFORMER AND CIVIL RIGHTS ACTIVIST

I moved to London in June 1997 when I transferred from the Columbus, Ohio, office of Andersen Consulting to the London office. I took up my role as a manager and, just as I was settling into my new work location, August rolled around. I noticed how suddenly almost everyone seemed to disappear, both in our offices and at the clients' offices. The normally gridlocked London streets seem to miraculously free up and traffic flowed noticeably better than just days before. This felt a bit strange, and I started to wonder if I was missing something. My British wife, also a former Android (as we Andersen consultants were known), was pregnant with our first child. As a result, we were not very mobile and staying close to the local hospital preparing for imminent birth seemed sensible. Over dinner one evening I remarked on how quiet it was in the office and around the city. She said, 'Oh yes, if it wasn't for the baby, we would be taking off for holiday too.' So, I wondered to her, when would everyone be coming back from holiday? She said 'end of August', which floored me as I could not imagine even a one-week 'holiday' in August, let alone two or three weeks. It's just not something that Americans would normally do. Seemed crazy to me, as not a lot of work was getting done for an entire month – 1/12th of the year, gone! But this was not the end of the 'holidays' over the coming months heading into autumn.

No sooner, it seemed, had everyone arrived back from summer holidays, when, what seemed only weeks later, the 'school holidays' (or 'half-term' holiday as it is known) appeared. Again, large numbers of people – particularly with children – packed up and went on another break. It was astonishing to me coming from mid-west Ohio, where the work ethic was 'work all hours God gives you'. By the time Christmas rolled around, it seemed to me a lot of time off had been taken, and we were on the verge of the end-of-year holiday – which I was a bit more comfortable with, as even in Ohio we would typically take a week off over Christmas. Come January, when everyone was back to work, I started to notice something different about my teams of people in the UK, relative to my American teams. After each one of these regular holidays over the previous four months, the team came back very energized, focused and productive. Engagement with work was strong and people got a great deal of work done, and at a pace. They were fresh with ideas and ready to go for the new year. Then, sure enough, another school half-term holiday rolled around and the whole cycle started again. Throughout 1998, my first year in London, these regular breaks came up, and each time the teams came back, they were highly productive and engaged. They did not have the persistent weariness that I often found in my American teams after long months of no major breaks in the schedule. I quickly realized that, contrary to what I was told about 'lazy Europeans' who were on vacation all the time and produced less than Americans, it was my UK teams that were getting more done, and with better quality, while taking *more* (much more in some cases) time off on a regular basis. Working *less* actually produced *more*. It was a revelation, and slowly over the years I have tried to accustom myself to taking regular holidays, though I have to admit it took some practice and a lot of getting used to – I had to change the way I was thinking: work smarter, not harder, and get some rest on a regular basis. Yes, I could live with that.

Working smarter is doing more

It's very tempting to just throw more hours and more people at the productivity challenge and hope to correct it (van Ark *et al*, 2008). In fact, working more hours with more people is one of the key reasons why productivity is declining. The data shows that the more people we throw at the requirement to increase productivity, the more we inhibit it. We have to think and work smarter – not harder. In recent years our knowledge of how the brain works, how the brain is wired, has increased substantially. One of the more interesting and startling conclusions is that the human brain can only sustain maximum concentration for, at best, four hours a day. The brain is like a bank account, where the more concentration energy you spend, the more you deplete the savings. The only way to top up the concentration savings is with more rest – not with more work. Yet since the Great Recession, we have seen the average hours that people work going up steadily. In the United States, for example, the average American works 47 hours a week, with four in 10 working at least 50 hours, according to Gallup; this is up from 45 hours, pre-recession (Saad, 2014). Former Silicon Valley strategy consultant Alex Soojung-Kim Pang reached his four-hours-a-day conclusion while researching his book on how famous intellectuals have worked across history, *Rest* (Pang, 2017). Pang found that many historical figures all had similar lengths of concentration periods, most notably Charles Darwin, who worked for two 90-minute periods in the morning, then an hour later on, while mathematician Henri Poincaré worked from 10 am until noon then 5 pm until 7 pm.

While no one is going to pretend, just yet, that we are all going to suddenly take up artistes' hours, it's worth noting that some companies are successfully experimenting with shorter work days and work weeks. Take the example of Perpetual Guardian in New Zealand; their employees worked 32-hour weeks in March and April of 2018 and now the company wants to make the policy change permanent, according to the *New York Times* (Graham-McLay, 2018). The firm, which manages estates, trusts, and wills, says employee productivity increased and Perpetual Guardian supervisors saw improvements in employee attendance and creativity during the experiment. Company founder, Andrew Barnes, told the *Times* that a permanent policy change would benefit mothers the most, allowing them to complete a full-time amount of work in fewer hours, and the policy could also lead to lower electricity bills and fewer cars on the road during rush hour.

Another example, a few years back, did not work out so well for the State of Utah. In 2008, Utah became the first state to require state employees to work four days a week. Former Utah Governor Jon Huntsman's decision to mandate four 10-hour days was meant to increase efficiency, conserve energy, and help retain employees, but a 2010 legislative audit showed that the state did not save money this way, and the employees went back to working five days a week the following year (Dembe, 2016). While the four-day workweek did not benefit the state as a whole, it was found to work better at municipal level. The city of Provo functioned on a four-day week for years before the governor's decision. These days, the Provo mayor's office and other departments are open 7 am to 6 pm Monday through Thursday. John Curtis, the city's mayor, said the system led to improvements in workers' morale and seemed to bring in savings as well (Loftin, 2011). Curtis added that four-day work weeks could be better suited for local governments than state governments (Kotecki, 2018).

A two-year trial of a six-hour working day at a care home for elderly people in the Swedish city of Gothenburg proved that a shorter working day lowered sick leave by 10 per cent (Bernmar, 2017). Other perceived health benefits of the care workers were reductions in stress and increased alertness. The residents at the care home also reported that they felt they were getting better care and more time with the nurses. Healthier employees will have more energy and be more motivated to do their job versus overworked, stressed, exhausted employees, who will have less energy and motivation and ultimately take longer to do a task because they lack the same level of alertness of someone working shorter days. Overworked people tend to eat more, stress more, and exercise less; if this becomes a continuous cycle it can create myriad underlying health issues (Bernmar, 2017).

Working smarter is not working to the deadline

Parkinson's Law states that 'work expands to fill the time available for its completion'. The way our brains are wired means that the more time we have to complete a task, the more time we have to procrastinate and overthink/overdo a task, often filling that time with stress about getting it done. When I look back at the various projects I have been a part of, I have certainly seen this to be the case. I can remember numerous HR transformation projects where we were implementing new HR strategy, technology and processes, feeling keenly the importance of getting these projects done on time. As anyone who has been close to one knows, when an HR project goes awry, this often means people don't get paid – no one wants to be the cause of that! Nothing like a deadline to focus the mind, we say. As a manager I used to ask myself how we would get into these situations so often. What was I doing wrong that allowed this to happen again? As a team we would joke during those midnight pizza runs, about the 'all-nighter' we were pulling; it was like being back in college. When I reflected on the crazy things we were doing I was grateful the task always got completed because we always powered through to meet that 'now urgent' deadline. However, in retrospect maybe it was not something to be proud of.

A few years back, having read about Parkinson's Law, it dawned on me what was going on and some ideas emerged how to do things differently. On the next project, we reorganized the plan and the teams in a way that focused minds sooner rather than later. We looked to assign *less* time to key project workstreams rather than more. We challenged each workstream leader to a 'bare minimum' amount of time to be assigned. Additionally, rather than have big chunks of work with many tasks and dates for completion way out into the future, we reconfigured to a number of much smaller chunks of work with dates for completion no more than two weeks out. The idea was to demonstrate to our procrastinating brains that there were no huge pieces of work with dates out over the horizon, requiring us to focus more quickly and hunker down to the task in hand. The other principle we put in place was to know what 'done' means. In other words, we employed a 90/10 rule where we avoided pushing for perfection all the time, and agreed that '90 per cent is good enough'. There was to be no 'navel gazing' over tasks, and more of a 'get it done and move on' attitude. The results were pretty amazing. No deadlines missed, quality of work excellent and, most importantly, the team were happy and unstressed, pleased with the outcomes. People felt super productive yet without the weariness of the late nights and rush to completion.

Working harder can make you sick

We all know that when we're tired we are most prone to mistakes. People that are close to burnout can make serious, sometimes fatal, errors. Most snow skiing injuries come in the last hour of the slopes being open, after people have been exerting all day and are having the last downhill for the afternoon. That is when the accidents strike, and the snow patrols get most busy. The science is coming in fast and furious these days that shows the huge importance of getting seven to eight hours of sleep per night. Studies show that without it, we do not have the same control over our emotional health and our judgement becomes impaired. Henry Ford spotted this over 100 years ago and took a radical step to address it when he saw the carnage that was taking place on his factory floor. He doubled his workers' pay but cut their working hours from nine hours to eight hours a day. He took a lot of heat for this from his competitors, but in the end they followed his lead and did the same. But he saw production rise and profits boosted at Ford, along with fewer employee incidents on the shop floor. His competitors soon followed suit.

Here in the 21st century we are starting to see a similar trend towards focusing on employee well-being, and seeing similar results as Henry Ford saw. Take, for example, the US insurance giant Aetna. Their CEO Mark Bertolini introduced a number of wellness programmes to help his workforce become more productive. Bertolini went even further than just your typical wellness programme, putting in place an opt-in cash incentive programme where his firm would pay $300 to workers who attested that they got seven or more hours of sleep for 20 nights a month (Osborne, 2016).

Duke University measured the impact and first year of the programme; they found a 7 per cent reduction in health care costs and a 62-minute-per-person improvement in productive time (Snyder, 2016). Sleep guru Arianna Huffington said of Bertolini's programme: 'What I've heard more about when we talk to the [Aetna] employees is not the $300… It was the fact that the CEO of the company was telling them that getting enough sleep was good for the bottom line of Aetna, that there was no trade-off between the two' (Snyder, 2016).

Smarter data can be more insights

Big data is not a good thing when it comes to people data. The key to success is not *quantity*, but *quality* (and focus). The challenge is to resist the temptation to create and process large volumes of data and embrace a more targeted approach. In fact, some argue that HR data is *never* big data. Consider this: most companies have either hundreds or, at most, thousands of workers – not millions. On the other hand, these companies are running customer analysis data models on a regular basis on millions of potential customers; for example, your typical cellular phone provider has anywhere from 2 million to over 20 million customers. It's safe to argue that virtually no organizations have this many employees to run data on. So, the challenge comes for HR to ignore the broader big data noise and focus on smaller and more manageable sets of data. To focus on what I call the 4 Cs, workforce data must be properly consolidated, cleansed, consistent, and current to make the right decisions. Big data is not helpful when it comes to people data.

FIGURE 3.1 Workforce analytics: predicting the future (not the past)

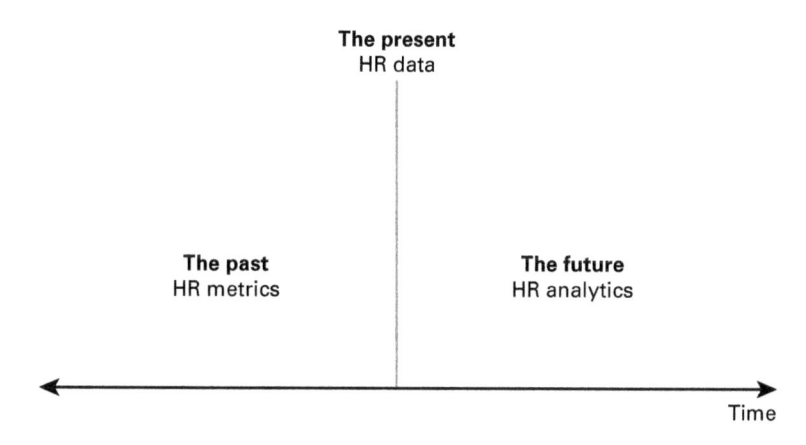

```
                    The present
                      HR data
                         |
                         |
                         |
                         |
        The past         |        The future
        HR metrics       |        HR analytics
                         |
   <---------------------+--------------------->
                                           Time
```

The other key thing to understand about people data is the difference between HR metrics and HR analytics. Understanding the difference helps to skinny down the amount of data that is being collected and processed. A helpful way to illustrate this is in the graph at Figure 3.1. If we focus on the timeline, divided into past, present (0) and future, we can divide analytics and metrics into two buckets. Everything from present and looking backwards is a 'metric'. It's about collecting data and measuring something that has happened in the past. An 'analytic' is everything from the present looking forward into time. An analytic takes metrics, applies predictive models to this data and makes a forecast about the future – HR metrics converted into HR analytics. HR metrics are not second to HR analytics. In fact, you cannot have analytics without metrics and vice versa. The key is to understand the difference to make best use of the information and not get lost in the noise, hurting our productivity and effectiveness.

The things we thought made us more productive and that we thought allowed us to get more done actually have the opposite effect. The data and recent experience show us that there are a lot of reasons to challenge our long-held beliefs about work and how we do it. I must admit, as a midwestern American baby boomer who was brought up on a Protestant work ethic, my immediate go-to reaction to some of these ideas is 'why change?' These ways of working have been around for decades, and we seemed to get on fine. However, it's becoming harder to argue with what I see with my own eyes and experience in my day-to-day work.

These new ways of thinking about how we work smarter lead to the next, and core, point, which is to change how we *organize* ourselves to do more productive work. As the ancient Persian poet philosopher Rumi said: 'Everyone has been made for some particular work and the desire for that work has been put in every heart.' The trick is to get the right people, in the right place, at the right time, with the right skills and the right motivation. Match people to 'particular work', together with the 'desire for that work'. This is people engagement, innovation and performance (PEIP).

The integrated human capital lifecycle is working uber-smart

The first step in creating people engagement, innovation and performance in an organization is to understand the power of putting in place an integrated human capital lifecycle – the power to put your workforce in the best position to succeed and, more importantly, to help your organization execute on organizational imperatives through a seamless employee experience (see Figure 3.2). The power comes in developing the ability to attract and retain, motivate and develop, connect and enable, and deploy and manage the workforce in an integrated fashion with real-time data and analytics. Having this ability creates organizational agility and allows top management to drive enterprise strategy into the organization rapidly and on a consistent basis; a sustained capability to drive change and transformation.

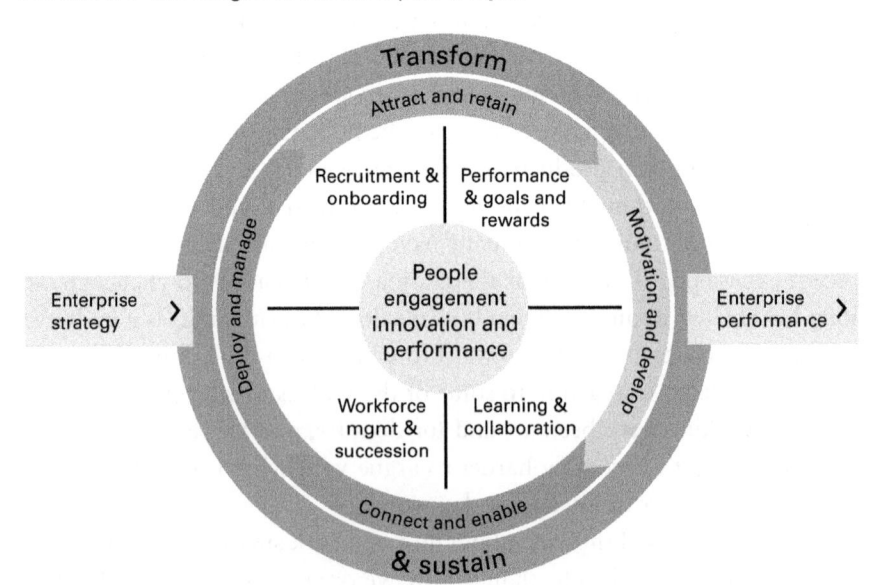

FIGURE 3.2 The integrated human capital lifecycle

Let's look at this model, first, from the point of view of the CEO. Her job is actually pretty straightforward: she is in charge of developing the enterprise strategy. She looks across the landscape of the environment the organization operates in, considers the impact of external factors, gauges the economic situation, assesses the market for customer requirements (or taxpayer requirements) and formulates the 'go-to-market' plan for the year, or next few years. From this information she develops an organization strategy and direction with the board and top management and prepares it for communication to internal and external stakeholders.

Once ready and agreed to, the difficult and most risky part starts: handing over the strategy to the organization to execute. Any CEO will tell you that this is the part that they dread. They hand off their baby to the real world and hope for the best for their 'offspring'. As most senior executives will tell you, no enterprise strategy fully survives its first contact with the organization. In fact, if 50 per cent of it survives intact, most CEOs will chalk that up as a victory. Many accept this is the nature of organizations and try to account for it with 'contingency planning'. The plan is handed off to senior executives and middle management, who all have their own take on what it means. Even with 'cascaded' management objectives, which are supposed to align to achievement of the plan, there remains significant 'leakage' of intent. The plans and objectives are open to interpretation by the management layer. But this is only the first challenge. The next comes when middle managers each take their part of the plan and organize their workforces to execute it. The strategy hits another level of interpretation. Worse, it's often not clear how to get the right people in the right place at the right time with the right skills to do the job required. Very few organizations have a sophisticated strategic workforce planning capability to organize teams effectively. Most workforce planning consists of seeing who is around and who is available in each team. Immediately execution becomes sub-optimal.

Most organizations these days are pretty good at developing team and individual annual performance objectives; however, after that it's a bit of a free-for-all. Performance objectives should stretch people to motivate them and help them grow. However, to work effectively, this requires individual learning plans that provide development in a 'just-in-time' model to fill skill gaps as the year (and the plan) progresses. Additionally, connecting people and enabling them with technology tools to make them more productive allows teams to learn from each other and spread that knowledge rapidly across the organization, enabling effective execution. Next, if we deploy and manage the right people to the right jobs, rather than staffing whoever might be available, performance can be further refined to execute on the plan. Having these steps in place not only improves execution on the organization strategy, it goes a long way to engaging and retaining top talent, who then tell their friends, allowing the organization to attract top talent – a virtuous cycle, and one that creates much-improved execution on organization strategy. Once in place, this virtuous cycle allows the organization to more rapidly drive change into the workforce. New strategy can be developed on a regular basis and handed off to the other organization to execute, creating a constant ability to transform and sustain change, which is the nexus of today's 'agile' organization.

Now, let's look at the model from the employee perspective. Imagine you have just been hired into a new organization. On day one, you are given your laptop or tablet and when you turn it on up pops the employee portal. It's simple and intuitive, and also has a chat bot available for you to ask questions and help you find things – either voice activated or typing into the keyboard. The chat bot points you to the main tile for your onboarding. When you click on the Onboarding tile, it has a schedule of meetings for you to meet your new manager and your colleagues. Additionally, a draft of your performance goals and objectives is in your in-box from your manager. When you go into your goals, you find five simple objectives for the year with clear measurements for achievement. Once you have finished reading them, you can ask the chat bot to set up a meeting for you with your manager to review and finalize your performance and goals.

The Onboarding chat bot also shows you your draft development plan, which is linked to your five objectives, suggesting courses that you should schedule in your first year to increase the likelihood of being successful. It has already scheduled your first orientation and placed it into your diary. Once you have accepted the invite for the orientation course, the chat bot asks you if you would like to be taken to the organization's internal collaboration tool. In there you can see your employee profile is already set up listing out your role and manager, as well as some background about you including skills and competencies. You push the 'publish' button after making a few edits and you are now 'live' in the 'JAM' collaboration system. It's very similar to LinkedIn and Facebook, but for internal use – lots of lively chat threads to choose from where you can start to join the conversation. From here the chat bot asks you if you would like to see what projects and roles are available for you within your team.

Next, you go into the organization's strategic workforce planning tool, called the Job Marketplace, where you can start to peruse current roles that match your skills and experience from your employee profile. You place-mark a few that look interesting and have a '90 per cent or greater fit' indicated, which you can discuss with your manager in your first meetings. Lastly, the chat bot takes you into the career planning tool, where you can see the different career paths and example roles that you could grow into. These are part of the organization's succession planning process. Like the Job Marketplace, you can project yourself into roles, but these are all in the future and about your growth in the organization, based on your background and skills and, more importantly, on your ambitions for your career in the future, two years and five years out. Underpinning all of what you experience in this first interaction with the organization is one source of data provided for all the actions you take, and all of it sits within one system. No going in and out, logging in and out and finding information in spreadsheets or different systems. It is up to date and available 24/7 on any device you use, giving you the flexibility to manage your own career and day-to-day job anytime, anywhere.

The power of an integrated human capital lifecycle cannot be underestimated. The ability for an organization as a whole, and for an employee as an individual, to be plugged directly into this virtuous cycle allows a CEO and executive team to regularly change direction, as needed, and for the employee to have what they need to execute as strategy evolves. Not surprisingly, execution is enhanced, while engagement and productivity see measurable improvement. This approach is not theoretical; it's in use in many of the world's best-run companies and it should not be a surprise that they outperform in their industries. Organizations that I have seen who have implemented an integrated lifecycle as described here have a distinct competitive advantage in terms of business and shareholder value, but also in terms of the talent that they attract. The best people gravitate to organizations that can show candidates a concrete and proven approach to bringing them into the organization, giving them clear objectives and development plans, and deploying them to interesting work that can help them grow their career.

Take insurance company PEMCO, for example, an organization that has had a plan for tackling integrated talent management head on since 2009. Headquartered in Seattle, PEMCO is a mid-sized company of about 620 employees serving the north-western United States (Downs, 2012). It has a rich 63-year history with roots in the public educator market, which is still one of its largest segments of policyholders today. Like most insurance organizations in recent years, PEMCO has experienced a tremendous amount of change, leading to significant organizational, cultural, and strategic shifts in how it does business and what it offers to consumers. The channels through which consumers access insurance products has changed dramatically, with most business done online these days. Through it all, the company's leaders know that competition for great talent is tough and the climate for existing employees can be even more challenging, so 're-recruitment' is top of mind. What started as putting together some tools for talent management five years ago resulted in the launch of a new talent development programme that promised to reframe how employees think about their careers at PEMCO and alter the company's mindset of what talent strategy is all about.

At PEMCO, the talent management approach is defined as the activities and processes throughout the employee lifecycle: recruiting and hiring, onboarding, training, professional development, performance management, workforce planning, leadership development, career development, cross-functional work assignments, succession planning, and the employee exit process. It has had several building blocks in place for several years, including competency-based position profiles and performance appraisals, an effective recruiting process with use of behavioural interviewing, and a professional development plan (PDP) process. They now have a completely integrated human capital lifecycle which has allowed them to create 'talent pools', from which employees' careers are managed and grown. People in the talent pools use their PDP to: 1) put in place learning plans to help them build their skills and personal growth; 2) identify current roles that they could move into that match to their new skills; and 3) map out future roles that they could grow into, as part of the company's succession planning.

When piloting the programme, PEMCO decided to start with manager through executive roles with the intent to expand it to other key roles in the future. This approach allowed time for everyone to get used to the process and tools available to help identify and document succession candidates. This also created top-down transparency and senior-level buy-in. According to Patricia Hitch, senior organizational development consultant at PEMCO, the key is to make as much of the process as visible as possible to the degree that it makes sense (Downs, 2012). 'Transparency has helped because then there are no questions left – there's nothing hidden about the process,' she says. 'Employees have started to trust the management' as they see them walking the walk, talking the talk.

Although the effect of the programme on employees' careers and employee engagement has taken time to assess, more than 85 per cent of employees participated in talent pools; of those, 88 per cent completed the assessment for the pool they chose. Employee interest in succession roles was strong, with 72 participants for 59 roles. An impressive 98 per cent of employees turned in their PDPs by a May 31 deadline, exceeding a goal of 90 per cent. Executives led by example, all submitting their updated PDPs before the deadline, including CEO Stan McNaughton, who also publicly shared some of his development goals. Business agility and business performance all improved, as did engagement scores of the workforce (Downs, 2012).

The power of the integrated human capital lifecycle to put the workforce in the best position to succeed is proving to be the critical foundation to implementing PEIP. In fact, it is a pre-requisite to getting it right.

PEIP: solving the productivity paradox for driving peak people performance

It's not surprising to find that 77 per cent of CEOs see availability (or non-availability!) of key skills at the right time, in the right place, as the biggest threat to their business performance (PwC, 2017). Show the PEIP model (see Figure 0.2) to any CEO or management board member, and it is a safe bet that they will say this is a capability they want in their own organization. (Show the same model to employees and you get an even more enthusiastic response – we'll come back to this later in this chapter.) The question is: how? There are three main capabilities that need to be in place:

1 HR operating model and processes that support an integrated human capital lifecycle.
2 Tools and technology that make it simple for managers and people to operate effectively.
3 Behaviours and mindset that prioritize putting people in the best position to be successful.

Let's take a look at these capabilities in some more depth.

HR operating model

The key step in moving forward to create an integrated human capital lifecycle and to head towards PEIP is to create a shift in the HR operating model. We touched on the model briefly in Chapter 1 (see Figure 1.1). HR organizations are continually balancing two 'value agendas': first of all, running an effective and efficient HR back office – saving money (bottom of the model); second, enabling people productivity and engagement – creating value (top of the model). The challenge, as almost any HR professional will tell you, is that they spend the majority of their time focused on the bottom half of the model because, first, it is what the organization expects (and is used to) and, second, it is required because much of the HR back office is still manual or done with antiquated systems and processes. The opportunity here is to use the goal of PEIP to drive change, as improved people performance can only be achieved by skewing the balance of what HR does to the strategic part in the top of the model.

In order to do this, investment is required in terms of money and time. Fact is, if the bottom half of the model is not working effectively and efficiently it is difficult to make the case for investment in the top half. The price of admission to PEIP is getting the basics, the foundations of HR operations, right. In Chapter 5 we are going to look in detail at making the case for change, so, for the moment, let's assume the case has been made for the time and the money to make the shift in focus. The organization needs to be prepared by HR for a shift in mindset about what HR does and how it is done. For example, when the back-office operations are automated, and self-service is made available to employees, it inevitably causes some questions (and, often, some consternation) as people are used to having HR do many of the tasks in the lower part of the model. However, if self-service has been implemented effectively, and the technology is intuitive and easy to use, people quickly find it is a much better arrangement – they have more control. It's a great way to sell the idea, but if the organization is not sold on the new model, it can often lead to failure, so this part cannot be underestimated.

If the organization has been successful in making the transition to automate HR back office and self-service, the next job is to retool and redeploy HR teams to focus on the more valued-added, more exciting aspects of helping people be more productive and engaged. The move to changing the balance towards the top half of the model needs to be planned and carefully managed. Often, organizations take this opportunity to cut HR headcount. In my experience this is almost always a mistake. Any moving of people out of the HR function should not be done based on fewer people needed due to automation. The focus should be on first, understanding the skills and capabilities of HR teams and second, understanding clearly what the new roles required are. From there the gaps can be understood, and a plan put in place to address with current HR teams, or sourced externally. Only then, once this analysis has been done, should there be headcount reductions. In my experience, most HR organizations have the skills and capabilities to perform the roles required in driving PEIP, but have typically not been put to best use given the usual focus on more transactional types of tasks. For example, very often HR teams have many people with diverse backgrounds who either have an education background, prior work experience or both in roles like:

- HR Strategic Advisory
- Strategic Workforce Planning
- HR Analytics and Statistics
- Finance
- Organization Behaviour

All of which could be put to much more valuable use if focused on people performance. Before PEIP is implemented in the organization, this should be done for HR first. This is a good place to run pilot programmes and is what most of the successful HR transformation programmes do. Let's take a look at a real example.

CASE STUDY
IBM Part I

IBM is a very good example of one of the first companies, in my experience, to seek out PEIP as corporate strategy. The company has a long tradition of excellent people management and development practices and is a good example of utilizing the principles inherent in creating PEIP. In 2005, the organization embarked on an HR transformation, led by the senior vice president (SVP) of HR, Randy MacDonald. Randy was a very forward-thinking HR professional who came, originally, from sales, so had a solid business background and understood the power of effective HR. Additionally, CEO Sam Palmisano was the successor to Lou Gerstner, who was famous for people-led transformation and innovative leadership approach. In his memoir *Who Says Elephants Can't Dance?* (2003), Gerstner said, 'You don't "win" with strategy, you win with people… In the end, an organization is nothing more than the collective capacity of its people to create value.'

When I joined IBM in 2006 as an executive to lead their global human capital consulting practice, it was clear the company's strategy was to take what Gerstner had accomplished to the next level. In my first meeting with Randy after joining, he outlined to me Palmisano's desire to get the right people in the right place at the right time, as a critical strategic imperative, particularly since IBM had recently acquired PWC Consulting. A new unit was created, IBM Global Business Services (GBS), comprising more than 60,000 IBM and 30,000 transferring PWC Consulting professionals, led by Ginny Rometty (who eventually succeeded Sam as CEO).

As a result, IBM created the world's largest consulting services organization, with operations in more than 160 countries. The assimilation of 60,000 professional services consultants from PWC into what was a hardware-and-software sales culture was a significant change of strategy for IBM and was critical to the next phase of transformation for the company. It was an enormous undertaking, one of the biggest human capital projects in the world, and required a new way of thinking and doing inside IBM.

To make this new organization most effective, to drive the value from the acquisition, there was a need to drive change in the HR operating model and capabilities. Getting 60,000 consultants busy and generating revenue was a different model than the nearly 100-year-old tradition of IBM being a hardware and software business. The company understood that new HR technology was going to be required as the current HRIT landscape was fragmented and non-integrated into all the financial systems. There was a need for one single 'source of the truth' for HR data.

On the HR operating model, key questions needed to be answered: How and where would HR operations be conducted – centralized, or regionally? Who would mainly be responsible for managing talent – managers and/or HR? And, lastly, how would shared services be used to support the model? These are questions every company faces these days, but IBM saw the opportunity back in 2005 and wanted to grasp the nettle now to facilitate changes to the business model.

In my first few months in IBM a new HR operating model began to emerge as a result of a number of regional strategy sessions to understand the lie of the land and discussions on potential changes. The main questions under consideration:

- Should HR operations be decentralized into the regions and lines of businesses?
- Should shared service centres be expanded into local regions; HR administration automated where possible?
- Should managers take more responsibility for talent management (with HR business partner support)?

On the surface, these questions may seem fairly uncontroversial and make sense generally, especially today; however, back then, for large, complex, international organizations these were profoundly impactful changes requiring new ways of thinking and doing and also new skills and capabilities for management. Like most companies, the organization was used to HR as it was: semi-centralized and responsible for many of the talent management processes. After all, 'this is what HR does' and 'why change if it isn't broken?' are things that most organizations ask themselves when on a journey of change to the HR operating model. Both are understandable points and important for any change programme to take under consideration; the impact of a change to HR processes and technology cannot be underestimated. The changes can require a great deal of energy and time of the leadership who are trying to meet quarterly and annual goals at the same time. For the line managers, they are not all equipped with the skills or tools to do performance management, learning, succession, recruitment, compensation, staffing; this also needs to be taken into account by HR. Push back from line managers was anticipated and planned for as well as an explanation of the tools that were going to be put in place to allow the business to operate in the new model. Like most companies at that time, the tools that IBM had in place were clunky, inflexible and anything but intuitive. This was all that was available at that point in time. SAP HR, Peoplesoft or other similar on-premise, highly customized systems were the platforms of the day. Using them required extensive support from HR and IT as well as HR Business Partners. Any new HR operating model was going to put extra requirements on the leadership and line managers and having easy-to-use technology to facilitate change was seen as critical. So, this is where IBM found themselves; with a great opportunity, as well as a set of challenges – however, the timing was perfect given the changes in the business. The HR team set to work on a programme and to gain buy-in. The first step towards PEIP was now underway, and the future of IBM as a software *and* services company was in their hands.

Tools and technology

On paper, it may seem straightforward to change the HR operating model; however, if the tools and technology are not available to allow managers to get the right people in the right place at the right time, to help them take up the task of managing talent, it will be difficult to get them on side. The first question is usually 'what's in it for me?' and, without effective and efficient tools and technology in place, the answer is going be 'more work for you'. Not what anyone wants to hear in the midst of a major change in ways of working. If the solution is to push the centre of gravity of HR operations down into the business, it's not really fair, or very inspiring, to have to use spreadsheets or clunky talent systems that require weeks of training to learn how to use.

This is where the next step in the transformation of the HR operating model comes in. It should be implemented in sequential order – 1) operating model; 2) tools and technology – and it is here that most organizations make a key mistake. Often, when undertaking an HR transformation programme, it starts with a new HR system; particularly these days when there is significant focus on moving to cloud IT systems as they are less expensive to acquire, implement and run. Typically, this puts HR in the situation of reacting to and having IT drive the HR transformation programme, making it all about new technology. Often this takes place before changing the HR operating model, which is not only the backwards way around, it is often the reason HR transformations fail. A point of warning: don't fall into this trap. It is in everyone's interest that HR change the way it operates according to what the business requires in order to take the most advantage of these powerful new technologies. Let's take a look at what IBM did.

CASE STUDY
IBM Part II

The start of the HR change programme had begun some months before the operating model discussions, focusing on implementing an SAP HR on-premise HR system globally (in 2005–06, cloud HR systems had yet to become scalable and robust enough to serve as the central HR system for a company the size of IBM). It is understandable how this happens, as the main attraction of systems like SAP HR and Peoplesoft was that, when implemented across an entire business, they gave HR 'one version of the truth' for HR data. Additionally, these systems were critical to setting up efficient and effective HR shared services and employee self-service, so it was quite common that these programmes kicked off with an implementation of one of these on-premise HR systems. The main downside of these was that they required a significant amount of customizing to fit an organization and its HR processes, so once programmed against one type of HR operating model, it was extraordinarily difficult to make changes. Therefore, if the system was customized to suit the existing model, it would be very difficult to transform the HR operating model henceforth. Additionally, for the users, these systems were not designed to make people more productive, they were designed to create compliance to the organization's policies and processes and were anything but intuitive and easy to understand.

If the SAP HR system implementation project carried on as it was designed, it was going to set in stone the *old* HR operating model, making it difficult to migrate to the new model. Also, since managers were going to be picking up a significant part of the talent management activities, the unintuitive SAP HR system was going to require a significant amount of training and HR support.

At about this time, I had joined IBM and met with Randy about the project to give him some of my observations of how it was going. Having done a number of these projects for clients while at Accenture, I could see some familiar trends emerging in the IT implementation. We had a two-hour meeting and at the end, the following was agreed:

1 Briefly postpone the rollout of SAP HR in order to finish the HR operating model work and to re-baseline the system configuration, timelines and roll-out plans.

2 Design and develop a front-end portal to put on top of SAP HR for the managers so that the system would be easier to understand and use.

3 Reconfigure the project team (a cross-discipline team of GBS SAP HR consultants, HR team and IBM IT teams) by putting in place experienced people from my GBS HR consulting team to help with the implementation; this would reduce risk, time wastage and improve execution.

The most interesting part of the re-tooling of the project ended up being the designing and mocking up of an employee and manager portal to sit on top of SAP HR to improve the user experience. From my perspective, I thought the HR team's new HR operating model was exactly what was needed; however, I was worried about answering the 'what's in it for me?' question, given we were going to be asking line managers to pick up a significant amount of talent management activities with clunky tools and technology. There was already significant resistance to this idea in senior management as the focus needed to be on executing in the day-to-day business. We needed to get them onside by showing them what the future would look like for managers and how it would make them better managers.

The HR team, together with a few top designers from internal IT, began mocking up what the portal would look like, using the future operating model motto of 'right people, right place, right time' (which would become the Workforce Management Initiative – more on this later in the chapter) as the guiding principle. The idea was to bring together onto one internal site, performance and goals management, learning, succession, staffing and employee collaboration. This portal could be used by managers to manage talent, and by employees to have access to a personal development platform. Oh, and the other thing thrown in at the last moment, and which proved to be genius, was an employee contacts database. This turned out to be the most popular part of the portal! Really what IBM was doing was creating an early version of what the SuccessFactors and Workday platforms would become five years later.

To address the concerns about the new HR operating model at senior levels, we set up a meeting with senior line managers in the company, to demonstrate to them what the future would look like. We let them try out a mock-up of this new portal, so they could see how managers would manage talent and get the right people in the right place at the right time, and do so with not too much extra work. The session was a success. By being able to see the future, and 'see what's in it' for them, changed the mood about the proposed changes in the HR operating model and technology. They could see that we were providing the tools to make it as painless as possible and that it would not require much training or time out of the business to do talent management.

True, this project was over 10 years ago, but I think the IBM story is still very relevant, as IBM back then was where most organizations are today. Most organizations today are looking at their HR operating model and their IT landscape and coming to similar conclusions as Randy MacDonald and Sam Palmisano. They want to get right people, right place, right time, and see the advantages this can create. Additionally, many organizations have outdated SAP HR, Peoplesoft or Oracle Fusion (or other) systems, see the bright shiny new cloud HRISs like Workday and SuccessFactors, and see the need for change. Others have no legacy HR system, yet still see the need for change and acquisition of a central HRIS. IBM just had the foresight to move first and move decisively. Having acquired 30,000 new consultants, all of whom needed to be put to work (generating revenue), focused the mind and investment.

The good news is, compared to 10 years ago, the power and the usability of this new generation of HR systems is astounding. They are much more akin to Facebook and LinkedIn, requiring very little training to use them. In fact, the learning required is more focused on teaching the line manager how to have performance conversations, how to make rewards and compensation decisions, succession plan, and other more strategic activities. So, rather than an HR business partner and the line manager focusing on transactional types of activities, they can focus on things that make people better, make people more productive.

Also, implementation is significantly simpler as these systems do not require customization and therefore the services of costly systems implementation consultants. These systems come complete with a set of 'best practice' processes already built in. The work involved in implementation is more focused on changing the HR operating model and processes to fit to the best practice processes that are already configured in the tool. As we have seen, this is the right way round when making the changes to HR that improve effectiveness of HR and, more importantly, the workforce. It's a good time to be making operating model and technology changes in HR.

Mindset, behaviours and skills

While the new HR operating model and technology is being put in place, another key aspect of successfully implementing PEIP is understanding the substantial shift in mindset that is required to make the change successful. The vast majority of organizations are set up along very traditional lines of thinking and doing that have been around for more than 150 years. Business schools still teach very traditional models of management science that really have not changed much since the 1950s, which means there is no collective memory of doing anything any differently. Whether we admit it or not, people are still seen as 'widgets' to be hired, fired or retired, based on current business and economic conditions. Widgets are typically seen in terms of what value they produce, and how much they cost to produce that value. True, there are new people management ideas and thinking finally emerging, but for the most part what is described here is the default.

This kind of thinking leads to what is, in my experience, the biggest mistake organizations make over and over again. One of the biggest destroyers of value in an organization is what I call the 'hire and fire binge' school of management thinking. When times are good and business is robust, organizations will bring in large numbers of new people and skills. When those good times inevitably turn, the hiring binge turns into a firing binge; people are let go in significant numbers, to get the cost base aligned to the economic conditions. The disruption to business activities and focus, alone, should make a manager or CEO take a moment of pause. We have all experienced it: the dreaded 'restructuring' phase of the business cycle.

The binge, on either side of the equation (hire or fire), causes a rush in business decision making that often leads to the wrong person in the wrong place at the wrong time; the complete opposite of PEIP. The rush to get people in when business is good often sees managers taking advantage of the spigot being opened and a move to get people – sometimes any people – in before the spigot gets turned off again. Not the ideal situation in which to make the best business decisions. Then, on the opposite side, when business conditions turn, the rush to get people out of the business leads to decisions that end up taking the right people in the right place at the right time, out of the business. The rush typically causes a focus on the cost of an individual, or team, rather than a focus on whether they are the right person with the right skills. Again, we have all seen this, when suddenly good old Steve in the R&D department, who everyone agreed is one of the top performers in the team, suddenly disappears when the 'restructuring' takes place. Everyone is, rightly, perplexed as to how this happened.

The late 1990s and early 2000s show us an excellent example of this hire-and-fire binge – a rather extreme example, but it makes the point. The excitement created around the emergence of the internet as a new business model caused what became known as the dot-com bubble. Between 1990 and 1997 the number of households in the United States owning computers increased from 15 per cent to 35 per cent as computer ownership progressed from a luxury to a necessity. This marked the shift to what became known as the Information Age, when a section of the economy became strongly based on ICT, many new companies were founded, and inside existing businesses whole new divisions were created to take advantage of this rapid shift. It was an exciting time when the possibilities seemed endless. If someone had any ICT engineering/design or sales background, they were in hot demand from startups, but, even more so, in existing and established organizations that were looking for a new route to market for new revenue streams.

At the same time, on the other side of the coin, relatively lower interest rates increased the availability of capital when the US government lowered the top marginal capital gains tax to stimulate business activity, but also made people more willing to make more speculative investments. Netscape Communications Corporation made an initial public offering (IPO) on Nasdaq on 9 August 1995 and was extremely successful – the stock closed at $58.25, giving the company a value of $2.9 billion (Shinal, 2005). Several months later in 1996, Yahoo! made one of Nasdaq's most successful ever IPOs. That same month, internet companies Lycos and Excite also went public. All this generated high interest in investing in internet companies.

Certainly the new ICT startup businesses were doing significant amounts of hiring; however, they were relatively small organizations that had not existed previously and only made a dent in the potential these technologies could present. The more interesting industry where massive hiring was taking place globally was the major telecoms businesses, who were at 'ground zero' of this new economy, providing both infrastructure and new services/products for the Information Age. At the time, I was working in Andersen Consulting in London and my main client was British Telecom, now BT. It was like having a front-row seat at the biggest economic event to take place since the advent of the cotton gin. I was impressed by the speed with which the senior management at BT moved to take advantage of the business potential for this 'new economy'. The business units were not only gearing up for the development of new 'IP-based products' but also focused on changing the configuration of their workforce to support it. The BT of the late 1990s was still heavily unionized and was therefore limited in what it could do with its existing old-school telecommunications engineering workforce; therefore, they had to hire significantly to get the new skills required. Additionally, there was a major focus on reskilling the retail and wholesale customer sales and service workforce to prepare them to sell these new products and services. BT's HR organization was at the centre of this transformation of the workforce – a workforce that had looked the same since the 1920s. They invested heavily in the skills needed to embrace the new economy, and they were careful about changing the composition of the workforce away from traditional telecoms engineering skills and towards the more ICT engineering skills. BT was heavily regulated in terms of what they could do with the existing workforce, so this forced a careful consideration and plan to make the changes required to change the balance of the workforce – they could not embark on a 'hire and fire binge'. This turned out to be a blessing in disguise.

As for other telecoms who had been private companies for many more years than BT and had far fewer restrictions on what they could do, they went on an unprecedented binge of hiring and firing. They wholesale moved out large numbers of 'old school' engineers and wholesale hired almost anyone who had some kind of 'internet' skills in their resumé. These companies were very concerned about potentially being disaggregated by the startups, and moved fast to look more like them and less like the old telecom dinosaurs they were. Scant attention was given to the details of who was being hired and fired, as the data did not exist on who were the top performers in the organization and where people were best deployed to fit the new economic realities. The very opposite of PEIP was happening. It was a 'numbers game' of widgets acquisition and de-acquisition.

In and around early 2000 and late 2001, two events happened in quick succession that would reverse all that had been taking place the previous five years. The dot-com bubble had reached unsustainable proportions. Telecoms in Europe overspent on purchasing 3G licenses from governments and went heavily into debt. Investors began to question the business models and lack of profit being created in these new businesses. On 3 April 2000, Bloomberg published an article that stated: 'It's time, at last, to pay attention to the numbers' (Yang, 2000). Later that day a one-day 15 per cent decline in the value of shares in Microsoft and a 350-point, or 8 per cent, drop in the value of the Nasdaq proved to be the first sign of trouble (Yang, 2000). On 9 November 2000, Pets.com, a much-hyped company that had backing from Amazon.com, went out of business only nine months after completing its IPO (Richtmyer, 2000; MSNBC, 2016). By that time, most internet stocks had declined in value by 75 per cent from their highs, wiping out $1.755 trillion in value (Kleinbard, 2000).

Then the unthinkable happened. At 8:46 am on 11 September 2001, hijackers aboard American Airlines flight 11 crashed the commercial airliner into floors 93–99 of the North Tower of the World Trade Center, killing everyone on board and hundreds inside the building. The spasm of shock and uncertainty was greater than that after the Japanese had bombed Pearl

Harbor, nearly 60 years before. Immediately organizations hunkered down as the economic gloom that had precipitated the Dot-com crash was now dramatically accelerated.

This began yet another epic firing binge. Organizations took the axe to large swathes of their workforce without much thought about who exactly they were getting rid of. No matter what, costs had to be taken out immediately to preserve profits during this unforeseen shock. The major consulting firms, including Accenture, began to warn their clients that by cutting so deeply and with such abandon, they were likely losing a significant amount of the new skills they had developed and hired during the previous hiring binge; that much of that talent would be lost, with little understanding of the future impact. I recall conversations with senior executives at a number of organizations that I was working with at the time, in both telecom and financial services, that they did not have the data – or the time – to do any deep analysis of who they were letting go and the future impact. Many of these organizations did not even have an accurate view on who were their top performers. I recall one senior executive telling me she felt like she was 'flying blind in a fog without proper instruments' to guide her; how uncomfortable this was and, knowing the risk that was being taken, it was still going forward.

Then, almost as equally unexpected, the economy began to snap back to life in early 2003. The recession caused by the earlier shocks ended up being one of the 'shallowest' on record. The workforce supply pendulum was beginning to swing back the other way and companies were starting to realize their mistake. They had lost some of their best talent because they first overreacted and second, did not carefully plan who went and who stayed. The spigot was back on and organizations were back to a hiring binge, yet again without a plan or the data required to make sure they were getting the right people in the right place at the right time. An enormous amount of time and resource had been wasted and had to be corrected. There were vows of 'never letting this happen again' and 'we learned our lesson'. The reality, however, in my experience, was very different. Organizations were right back to the old habits; the mindset had not changed.

Mindset drives behaviour. In this case, mindset did not change and therefore behaviour remained the same. Once again, organizations went headlong into the market for skills, scooping up as much as they could lest the competition do the same. And this continued until the next shock, The Great Recession, that began in late 2007. However, not all organizations followed the old playbook. A number of them realized their mistake and resolved to do things differently this time.

CASE STUDY
IBM Part III

One of the organizations that saw an early opportunity around the idea of PEIP was IBM. A key aspect of the HR transformation was putting in place a solution for solving the equation of workforce supply and demand across the company. As the new HR operating model was being rolled out with the SAP HR system, the pieces were falling into place to have the data and processes to allow putting in an approach to get right people, right place, right time.

> *One of the reasons people come to work for IBM is because we take workplace flexibility seriously. On any given day, worldwide, one-third of our people are not in an IBM location – they are working onsite with customers, telecommuting, or are mobile. Today, we must reconsider our traditional concept of work and how it gets done, because our Workforce Management Initiative allows our workforce to serve customers as never before.*
> SAMUEL J. PALMISANO, IBM CHAIRMAN AND CHIEF EXECUTIVE OFFICER

The HR organization started a project called WMI, the Workforce Management Initiative, the goal of which was to create a two-way dialogue between the workforce and management about available roles and how best to resource them. Managers could post roles that needed staffing in the WMI portal and staff could log on to see what roles were available and reach out to find out more. It was a 'free market' for matching supply and demand, internally creating efficiencies around getting right people, right place, right time but also putting some control in the hands of employees. This project gave HR a new, more strategic role in the new HR operating model: strategic workforce planning broker. HR acted as the guide, adviser and sometimes referee to make sure WMI ran efficiently. This made the overall company strategic workforce planning efforts more effective, while at the same time improving workforce engagement by involving and providing them some control over their current and future roles; very good use of time and skills all around. Not surprisingly, this programme proved to be very popular, and as more and more managers and staff got comfortable with it, it began to drive a change in the way people thought and behaved. No more reactive and one-dimensional matching of people to roles; people's mindset and behaviours changed to be more forward thinking, looking ahead as well as becoming open to new types of work inside the organization, instead of having to look externally. IBM was able to get the right people with the right skills in the right place at the right time with the right motivation. A competitive advantage was born.

It turned out that this WMI capability was very timely for IBM. Come end of 2008, and the collapse of Lehman Brothers, the next major recession began, which proved to be both global and historically severe. The shock sent the United States into an almost immediate shedding of jobs with monthly job losses averaging over 700,000 from October 2008 through March 2009 – the most severe six-month period of job losses since 1945 (Goodman and Mance, 2011). Business activity slowed dramatically in the US and GDP went into reverse. IBM and other high-tech companies saw business slow markedly, particularly in the US. Usually in this case companies will immediately draw up plans to lay people off to reduce costs. However, IBM used its new HR operating model and technology, together with WMI, to rebalance the workforce towards markets that were still robust. In 2008, China was booming and was largely unaffected by the Great Recession, and IBM was able to shift key staff to Asia from the US and Europe to fulfil demand there. IBM was able to react rapidly to the challenging market conditions and get the right people in the right place at the right time and retain top talent, rather than lose it and have to re-hire later. This was a watershed moment in the IBM HR organization. During the Great Recession, IBM hit near-record profits and near-record share price performance, and many in the organization commented that the new approach was allowing IBM to maintain peak performance and to retain top talent. A new set of tools and new management behaviours won the day. What emerged was a steadier approach to workforce supply and demand and the workforce had more say in where and how they worked. The ideal situation for any employee or employer. PEIP had arrived.

PEIP unpacked

As we have seen, once there is an efficient HR operating model in place, supported by modern tools and technology and a change in mindset and management behaviours, we can transform work for both the organization and, more importantly, the individual. As we have seen there are five critical dimensions for PEIP: right people, right place, right skills, right time, with the right motivation. All of which are meant to be seamlessly integrated from a process, technology and mindset perspective, each piece building on the other, creating ever-increasing value as each of the dimensions comes online. Let's unpack PEIP in the context of what we learned above.

Right people

Ultimately the definition of 'right people' is completely up to the organization. I have yet to run into an organization that did not have a pretty good grip on the type of people they want working for them. It's fundamental, and therefore the vast majority of organizations have a clear model for who they are and what the workforce makeup should be. There are two sides to the 'right people' equation: those externally that you want to attract, hire and deploy, and those already in the organization that you want to engage, retain and deploy.

This is where the employer brand becomes crucial. In both cases, the *right people* will identify with and buy into who you are and what you do and either choose to join you or choose to stay. Having this clear is the first step in unpacking what PEIP means for your organization. The following list from SHRM is a great summary of the most effective steps to creating an attractive employer brand:

- **Know the organization's business, vision, mission, values and culture** to understand the organization's business objectives and what talent is needed to accomplish those objectives. Define the company's unique attributes.
- **Conduct internal research** to understand how the organization is perceived by its current employees, as well as by its target candidate group, and what these employees or potential employees want from the organization. Identify top talent, and ask what those employees like about working for the company. Determine the attributes of these star employees that the organization would want to attract.
- **Conduct external research** to learn how the organization is positioned in relation to the competition. Research may be conducted through applicant surveys, as well as via internet searches, social media or firms that conduct reputation monitoring.
- **Define an employee value proposition** that clearly communicates the value of the brand the organization is developing. The employee brand should truly reflect what is special about the organization and must be aligned with its customer brand.
- **Develop an employee marketing strategy**, which should have a two-pronged approach. First, the recruitment strategy should focus on reaching the targeted applicant base. Attention should be directed to the career page, recruiting sites, social media and other external recruitment sources. The second prong centres on consistently communicating the employee value proposition to current employees to retain and engage them. Use employee testimonials to affirm the brand.
- **Align the employer brand with the overall company brand** – work with the marketing and communications groups to ensure a holistic branding approach.

- **Ensure that the people and management practices support the organization's employer brand** – training, coaching, compensation and other HR-related practices can be used to support the brand.
- **Develop and use metrics** to assess and track the success of the employer brand. Metrics may include quality of hire, brand awareness, employee satisfaction, employee referrals or other metrics.

This approach from SHRM is ideal as it is all about knowing your employees thoroughly, creating an attractive vision/purpose, then executing on the plan while measuring the results, so that changes can be made as needed. Take NPR (National Public Radio) in the United States, which is a partially government-funded company that used to have a somewhat stodgy brand. They undertook an employer branding exercise that was, as SHRM recommends, heavy on people data and measurement to guide the development of the brand. NPR saw the following results (Schmidt, 2013):

- Saved over $100k/year in job postings and recruitment marketing.
- LinkedIn, Facebook and Twitter are all in their top 10 sources of applicants and hires.
- Twitter has become a top source of hire, helping to find a variety of passive candidates including key senior-level hires.
- A multi-channel employment branding campaign, #NPRlife, generated over 1,400 Instagrams and 6,000 tweets shared by many of our 800 colleagues.
- LinkedIn Talent Brand Index (TBI) is higher than most organizations in media including the *New York Times*, CNN, ABC, *Washington Post* and more.
- Our social media recruiting efforts have been featured in the *Wall Street Journal*, *Mashable*, the *Washington Post*, *Social Media Examiner*, *Non-Profit Quarterly*, *MediaBistro*, *Twitter Stories*, *PBS MediaShift*, *SmartBlog on Social Media*, *Integrated Media Association*, the *Daily Muse*.

The external employer brand should be designed to be used and have a similar effect on existing employees, where the focus is more on retention rather than recruiting. However, some argue that the best employee retention programmes treat retention as a constant internal recruiting process. Where every day you are re-recruiting your top people in order to keep them. Unfortunately, many organizations focus too much on the external use of their employer brand and forget to involve the internal marketplace of their own employees in this process. The unforeseen consequences of this are new employees coming in with a particular message in mind of what the organization's vision and purpose are, which does not align to the existing employees' thinking and messaging, creating disappointment and confusion for both. Creating a disconnect like this with an employer brand can actually be damaging to the organizations.

The most successful employer brands address this by being clear about who is responsible for developing and implementing the internal (and external) brand. In its 2020 Outlook, The Future of Employer Branding report, Universum surveyed more than 2,000 senior executives on their perception of who has accountability for employer branding activities (Universum, no date). The results paint a confused picture: 60 per cent felt that responsibility for the organization's employer brand lies with the CEO, which while commendable is also somewhat unrealistic (the average CEO already has more work on their plate than can be accomplished in a day and adding more isn't the answer); 37 per cent of respondents felt that the board of directors should be responsible for employer branding; 32 per cent felt that it's the realm of HR; 29 per cent passed the baton to group heads; and 28 per cent deferred to marketing (Beyer, 2019).

Fact is, it's a team effort, but with the ultimate messaging defined by the CEO and board. The CEO is usually in constant communication both internally and externally about the organization, and his/her message needs to be consistent and reinforce all other communications. This is where the 'Employer Brand Team' comes in – the team responsible for delivering on the board and CEO's vision for the internal brand of the company:

- **HR/Recruiting:** your recruiters and HR team are on the frontlines of your recruiting efforts, tasked with selling your company to applicants as well as to existing employees. They're answering the tough questions and gaining insight from everyday activities.
- **The CEO's direct reports:** the senior leadership of the organization. It all starts from the top with leadership direction and focus. To succeed, the employer brand needs visibility into the organization's goals and expectations. Before any work begins, senior leadership should provide guidance in the form of short- and long-term growth plans for the company and its current employees and any associated staffing needs for external.
- **Marketing:** tasked with developing the strategies and creative materials that help sell products and services. Getting the right message in front of the right audience at the right time is what they do, and their expertise

leads to employer branding materials that create the experience the organization is creating. They can utilize the feedback gathered by the recruiting team to develop targeted candidate personas and craft compelling marketing materials internally and externally.

- **IT:** 79 per cent of recent job seekers used online resources and information in their latest employment search, and 34 per cent reported it was the most important resource they utilized (Smith, 2015). Over 85 per cent of employees say they get their main internal messaging from the company portal or email/collaborations system (Smith, 2015). The employer brand needs to be online and attractive. The IT team should have a say at every step of the process, ensuring the efforts are developed in a digital-friendly manner.

Imagine the power for both the individual (external or internal) and the organization, if your workforce is made up of people who belong there and enjoy working with each other. A sense of team and camaraderie can be created quickly and effectively when the right people come together and 'spark' off each other. Magic can happen.

A key part of *right people* is understanding what skills you need in the organization, and what skills you need to attract externally. Additionally, the most effective organizations know what skills they are going to need in the near future. So let's take a look at the next part of PEIP: *Right skills*.

Right skills

One area of significant concern in recent years for most senior executives is ensuring that the organization has the right skills and capabilities for the immediate term, but even more importantly, the future. Having the right skills in an organization has the potential to transform work and drive growth and prosperity in the global economy. However, in many countries, imbalances between the supply and demand for skills lead to significant skill mismatches and shortages, with as many as three in five workers in OECD countries employed in jobs that do not make the best use of their skills. At the same time, a large number of employers report hiring problems due to skill shortages (OECD, 2017a).

In the EU, the number of open positions that cannot be filled with the right skills has hit a record number. In September 2018, there were almost 3 million vacant posts advertised in the European Job Mobility Portal, EURES, most of which were open due to lack of applicable skills (Eurostat, 2019). The number of job openings in the United States rose to a record 7.14 million in August

2018, reflecting strong growth in the economy and the best labour market in decades; again, most of these could not be filled due to skill shortages in areas like IT, finance and construction (Bartash, 2018). Add to this that, on average, over a third (36 per cent) of workers in OECD countries are either over- or under-qualified for their jobs (17 per cent and 19 per cent respectively (EURES, 2019)), reflecting both weak skills demand and an insufficient supply of skilled workers, and the challenge comes into stark contrast. While some degree of mismatch between the supply and demand for skills is inevitable, the cost of persistent skill imbalances for individuals, employers and society is substantial. Skill imbalances can lead to lower earnings and job satisfaction for workers, stunted productivity, and reduced economic growth (OECD, 2017b).

The skills gap is not new; however, it has been widening for over 10 years now. Though a robust world economy has certainly contributed to exacerbating the situation, the underlying challenges for the skills gap are more fundamental than an upturn in the economy. The acceleration of globalization and the rapid pace of technological advancement have not only created new positions (net of those lost due to automation) to be filled, but have created completely new jobs that did not even exist five years ago. A handful of US colleges now offer majors in programmes that didn't exist a few years ago, such as robotics engineering, game design, cybersecurity, and workforce data science, but this is nowhere near enough to meet demand. Most educational institutions, never ones to move quickly in the face of change, struggle to keep up in this rapidly changing world. As a result, skilling and re-skilling to fill roles is more and more falling to organizations and even increasingly to the individuals themselves to address.

Starting with individuals and organizations working together to address the skills gap is probably the right place to begin to address the challenge. It's at the 'coal face' that the urgency is felt and the detailed understanding of what is required is found. Government and the education sector should focus their efforts on supporting employers and employees in developing the right skills for the front line of the business need. And indeed, this is what is happening. Driven from the top at CEO and board level, there is a significant amount of effort, investment and time being given to the subject of fulfilling current skills gaps and looking out into the near future to forecast what will be required. Sharing this information with government and education institutions helps put in place plans to change curricula to adapt to the change.

For example, many companies are developing what they need from among the existing workforce, including from many of the employees potentially displaced by automation. Moreover, programmes designed for the academic domain are increasingly ineffective in building the skills required in the modern workplace. Instead, companies are turning to organizations such as Udacity, edX, and Coursera, which allow people to receive training while working full-time. Companies like GE are taking the responsibility for radical retraining and moving urgently to address it using tools like these. For many companies, incubating talent internally is more likely to pay off than depending on the marketplace. To that end, GE has introduced a mobile application that prompts employees to work on development areas and provides real-time feedback. The company expects this app eventually to replace traditional performance management (Bhalla *et al*, 2017).

Fortunately, new learning and collaboration technologies like Jive, Slack, WalkMe, GuideMe, and EnableNow, as well as innovative learning models like MOOCs are making it easier for organizations to take on more of the burden in addressing current skill gaps. Much of the change in this space is being driven by the end users themselves. Employees are demanding a more retail, consumer-type experience that allows them to acquire learning in 'the flow of work' and do so in real time by easy to access small 'micro' chunks. LinkedIn released their latest research in late 2018 (4,000+ L&D and business professionals) and asked people how their workplace learning could be improved (LinkedIn, 2018). They found that the #1 issue was that people do not have enough time. 'Getting employees to make more time for learning' was the #1 challenge they cited, and among the learners who responded, 68 per cent preferred to learn at work, 58 per cent wanted to learn at their own pace and 49 per cent wanted to learn in the flow of work (Spar *et al*, 2018).

People say they don't have a lot of spare time at work; however, recent studies show that they will set aside time to invest in building new and relevant skills if it is easy to find, applicable to the work at hand, and can be done in short bursts of time (LinkedIn, 2018). In my recent experience in SAP, for example, if learning content is presented in familiar consumer formats like Netflix, Spotify, Amazon, as 'channels', 'topics', 'recommendations', with 'featured content' and in the flow of current work it is more likely to be taken up and completed. Additionally, technology is rapidly becoming more intelligent, knows the learner, their role and their skill gaps, and serves up learning 'nuggets' at the right time and the right place.

Given these emerging models and technologies are making learning much more targeted, accessible and easy to consume, the main task left is to know what skills the organization needs today and tomorrow. The first step towards creating an effective skills management capability is to develop a competency framework to assess, maintain and monitor the knowledge, skills and attributes of people in your organization. The framework allows you to measure current competency levels to make sure your staff members have the expertise needed to add value to the business. It also helps managers make informed decisions about talent recruitment, retention, and succession strategies. And, by identifying the specific behaviours and skills needed for each role, it enables you to budget and plan for the training and development your company really needs (Mind Tools Content Team, nd (a)).

FUTURE SKILLS EXAMPLE
IBM AI Skills Academy

While the rise of AI marks many exciting opportunities, it's equally (if not more) important to make sure staff are all up to speed with its use.

This is where the IBM AI Skills Academy comes in, boasting a suite of learning tools and resources which can empower their employees with everything they require to make the most of AI technology. Executive strategy workshops help communicate and train leaders on the importance and potential of AI and help them prioritize related projects over other legacy concerns. Consulting services help with staffing and implementation of AI-related projects. An AI learning curriculum counts data science, mathematical modelling and data visualization among its modules and helps organizations bridge AI skills gaps. Finally, an AI 'Garage' allows for the development of co-creation spaces to facilitate the tailoring and customization of bespoke AI solutions.

Their overview states:

> The IBM AI Skills Academy is here to help you on your AI adoption journey; the adoption of AI isn't as simple as flipping a switch – rather there are many steps in between AI in the headlines and AI in your individual teams. Our new AI Skills Academy consists of four integrated components that guide a client through the process of identifying an AI opportunity, prioritizing AI projects to pursue based on anticipated business value, learning curriculum designed to address AI skills gaps and increase adoption of AI solutions.

Skills forecasting – aka skills anticipation

As mentioned in Chapter 1, skills forecasting is something that very few organizations have a grip on, let alone an effective capability. I often start my talks with this simple question: how many of you know what skills you have? And then, the kicker, what will you need in 18 months? Almost zero hands acknowledge the second question. Not surprisingly, like most things in business today, it's all about here and now. Without a doubt, one of the most powerful capabilities an organization can develop is the ability to look into the future and forecast skills needed 6, 12, 18 months out.

Some of the most important capabilities an organization can build are the ability to:

- match supply to current demand for skills;
- help workers and enterprises adjust to change;
- build and sustain competencies for future needs.

The good news is that a number of government organizations do some of the work for you. It's best practice to leverage these governmental organizations as part of your efforts. At the global level the OECD invests in looking at skills trends and forecasting across member countries (most of the world economy). The OECD not only measures skills in student and adult populations, it also works with countries to develop skills strategies tailored to specific needs and contexts – excellent annual research looking at global trends and forecasts out as far as 2060.

At a regional level, both in Europe and in the United States, there is a significant amount of public investment put into skills forecasting at both a macro (national economy) and micro (sector-based) level analysis – that should be your first port of call when beginning your program. In the EU, the main government body on skills forecasting is CEDEFOP (the European Centre for the Development of Vocational Training). In the United States, this research and analysis is done by The National Skills Coalition; a quasi-governmental organization dedicated to a vision of an America that grows its economy by investing in its people so that every worker and every industry has the skills to compete and prosper. On an annual basis, these organizations do massive amounts of research on skills trends and skills forecasting that should be the first input into your programme. These organizations look out 5, 10, up to 30 years in the future. The United States, one of the most capitalist economies in the world, devotes more resources to this activity than anywhere else. The approach is backed up by large investments in labour market information, including forecasting, aimed at ensuring that students, workers and employers are well informed about the choices they face.

CEDEFOP is an agency of the European Union dedicated to guidance and counselling for organizations on forecasting the demand and supply of skills; the recognition and validation of learning that takes place outside the education system; and the development of qualification frameworks for the workforce. As CEDEFOP puts it: change is ever present and knowing how the labour market will be transformed by technology, climate change and demography is to possess a powerful capability for the organization, the individual and society at large (Bakule et al, 2017). Individuals would benefit greatly from knowing what type of education and training to follow, enterprises would know the skills they need, and policy makers could adapt education and training systems to new skill needs. Labour market and skills intelligence (LMSI) that provides information on current and future labour market trends and skill needs can help people, enterprises and policy makers make informed decisions. The definition of skills forecasting is the process of producing and building on available LMSI to achieve a better balance between skill supply and demand, to promote economic development through targeted skills investments by individuals, countries, regions, sectors or enterprises.

In recent years CEDEFOP has developed an approach for skills forecasting called Skills Anticipation and Matching (SA&M). For my money, their approach is the most detailed and proven, and is one that organizations can easily leverage. For example, as they adeptly describe the approach:

> Skills anticipation offers early warning of evolving skill mismatches, allowing sufficient time for action to counteract them. Individuals, firms and education and training providers, who have to make decisions about the kinds of education and training required for the future workforce, need to assess future prospects carefully, looking to fill information deficits and avoid future imbalances and mismatches. Anticipating the future is not straightforward, yet it allows the identification of current trends and strategies and their likely implications in the future (Bakule et al, 2017).

Though SA&M was designed mainly for CEDEFOP to support governmental entities in helping specific countries to address skills gaps, the methods they outline are easily transferable to the private sector organization as well.

CEDEFOP's 2017 paper, 'Developing Skills Foresights, Scenarios and Forecasts' (Bakule et al, 2017), lays out a detailed framework as well as guidelines on how to implement it, with the main goals being:

- matching supply to current demand for skills;
- helping workers and enterprises adjust to change;
- building and sustaining competencies for the future.

The vast majority of organizations would agree that these three goals create a powerful capability. Let's take a look at a summary of the SA&M approach. The SA&M approach is made of two key parts: *foresight* and *skills forecast*.

FORESIGHT

The first step in forecasting skills, foresight is mainly a qualitative approach that sometimes can be confused with forecasting. It is a different discipline in that it is focused on systematic, future intelligence gathering combined with a medium- to long-term vision-building process aimed at understanding areas of weakness in skills required to assist present-day decision making. The key element in foresight activities is that 'they are action-oriented, in the sense that the final aim is to influence, shape and act upon the future. Foresight processes and outputs should be oriented towards contributing to, facilitating or guiding the decision-making process.'

The chain of foresight activities follows an 'activity chain': Information (reality) > Analysis (map current state) > Interpretation (understanding of the state) > Perspectives (possible future development) > Outputs (what should be done) > Strategy (what and how do we do that?)

In their SA&M paper, CEDEFOP assess a number of different 'scenario methods' that allow for analysis of data in creating foresight with each described in a 'pros and cons' format. No one method is the solution for all challenges, therefore a number of different approaches are highlighted. CEDEFOP categorizes the possible foresight analysis methods into three buckets:

- exploratory;
- normative;
- supplementary.

Exploratory methods start from the present and seek to discover where events and trends might take us if we explore 'what-if' questions. Among typical techniques in this category are the Delphi method, scenarios or cross-impact analyses.

Normative methods start with a vision of a possible or desirable future and work backwards to see if and how this future might be achieved, or avoided, given the existing constraints (skills, resources, technologies, institutions). Backcasting or morphological analyses are representative of this category.

Supplemental methods include techniques which are not directly considered as foresight methods, but in some way support them in achieving their goal. This category comprises strengths, weaknesses, opportunities, and threats (SWOT) analysis, literature and statistics reviews, focus groups, and brainstorming.

There is no right method, other than the one that suits the organization and its characteristics. The variety of foresight experiences demonstrates that no one method or structure is best: the choice must reflect both fitness for purpose and the national culture in which it is situated. According to researchers Mohamad Hammoud and Douglas Nash, any foresight exercise is neither a single approach to a single problem nor a panacea for all national problems (Hammoud and Nash, 2014). The cultural, economic, political, social and institutional contexts play a crucial role and have to be taken into consideration as well.

Once the methods of analysis have been selected, the next step to completion of the exercise is implementation. The key steps in successful foresight programmes are the following (Rohrbeck, *et al*, 2015):

- **Define foresight areas to be considered:** Defining the focus of the foresight exercise is essential before starting. It usually tackles one core issue but different types of focus may coexist (eg future skills shortage in a selected sector).
- **Clarify the purpose of the foresight exercise:** The first step when thinking about a foresight programme is to see if it can provide the kind of information sought and fulfil expectations: what role can a foresight exercise play in meeting key social and business challenges for stakeholders?
- **Clarify the programme design elements:** Once the focus of the foresight exercise is clear and the decision to proceed is taken, a number of important issues need to be planned: objectives, expected outcomes, foresight time horizon, partners, stakeholders, participants, scope, methods and formats to apply, and time and resources to allocate for the exercise.
- **Clarify the questions and way to find the answers:** Selecting an appropriate methodology should be done early in the foresight design process. The chosen methodology should be problem-solving driven and result oriented. It should also take into account feasibility of the implementation and resources needs/constraints.
- **Conduct and manage the foresight exercise:** The foresight implementation plan has to include a number of organizational issues, such as forming the implementation team and assigning roles and responsibilities to its members, setting up a steering committee, outlining a communication strategy, estimating and securing financial and non-financial resources, contracting external collaborators, and forming expert working groups if necessary.

From this foresight exercise comes the building blocks of the skills forecast. Having done this qualitative analysis on broad trends and environmental factors allows for the skill forecasting to be started in the proper context and background for the organization, as it is today and how it will be in the future.

SKILLS FORECAST

Some argue that trying to forecast future skills is pointless, that it's impossible; there are too many 'unknowables' and that looking out beyond current needs is therefore futile. Often, I have seen organizations use this as an excuse to avoid the subject; however, not only is skills forecasting very doable, it is necessary in maximizing people potential in the organization. The experience of the United States and other countries across the globe suggests that skills forecasting can provide systematic analysis of the implications of continuing past and current trends and patterns of behaviour. It can help to map out different scenarios, based on alternative assumptions, which can form a basis for intelligent and informed debate and further research, as well as helping to inform individuals making career decisions (Bakule *et al*, 2017). This approach can be readily applied at the sector and company levels. It is essentially the same thing on a smaller, more controllable scale.

The questions answered by effective skill forecasting are:

- Whom are we forecasting for – key stakeholders?
- What is the duration of the forecast?
- How is the data required found?
- What jobs and or roles will demand increase or decrease?
- What are the replacement needs?
- How will the findings be implemented?

Stakeholders The first step in skill forecasting is to define for whom we are doing the analysis and who will benefit most. Stakeholders include the senior management of the organization, trade unions, education and training institutions, careers guidance organizations and, most importantly, individuals making occupation or job/role choices.

Duration The duration of the forecast is guided by the specific goals the organization is trying to achieve. Long-term planning and insights into developments in the labour market, jobs/roles, qualification and skills demand are often best served by longer time horizons of five to ten years.

More specific questions about the make-up of the future skills can be better served with more detailed, but mid-term forecasts, every two to four years. Keep in mind that the longer the forecasting period, the less detailed and precise the forecast becomes, so finding the balance is key.

Data   It is hard to predict the future without an understanding of either the past or the present. Data, especially external labour market and internal skills data, is crucial to skills forecasting. This is why conducting a foresight exercise first can help significantly in getting good data. Many organizations augment their internal and external data by using surveys. Surveys are the most common form in which the key data about the current state of the organization skills can be understood as well as surveying senior managers for what they are looking for in the future. Data quality needs to be good for reliable forecasts. Organization skills surveys usually sample a group of respondents to generate statistics that are sufficiently reliable and robust to then extrapolate findings. However, many organizations prefer to survey all or much of the organization to gain more accurate insights.

Skills increase (and decrease)   Employer surveys usually collect information on employment within firms, qualifications, skills and/or task requirements, and firm- or sector-related information. They have the advantage that information about demand by skills or qualifications can be identified directly from the source. Matched with more macro-level data collected in the foresight step, based on the data collected, it starts to become clear what skills will be needed and which ones will need to be replaced. It is important to note this effort is not manpower planning, it is not about predicting numbers of people required. The focus should remain on the supply and demand of skills, with one of the most important, and sometimes more difficult, decisions being what skills to discontinue and replace, and with what.

The final step in the analysis of skills forecast is choosing a modelling methodology for the data gathered to create final conclusions. There are a number of methods that can be used, but a popular approach is combining the Delphi method with a SWOT analysis of the outputs. The Delphi method is a simple forecasting process framework based on the results of multiple rounds of questionnaires, or surveys sent to employees, managers and a panel of previously defined expert stakeholders. Several rounds of questionnaires are sent out to the group, and the anonymous responses are aggregated and shared with the group after each round. From these outputs the forecasting team can create a SWOT analysis, which is a strategic planning technique used to help a person or organization identify strengths, weaknesses, opportunities and threats related to business project planning. A SWOT analysis often asks and answers questions to generate meaningful information for each category to make the tool useful and identify competitive advantage. SWOT has been described as the tried-and-true tool of strategic planning and analysis (Mind Tools Content Team, nd (b)).

The findings As with any other important organizational planning activity, once the findings are collected and summarized, they need to be presented to the organization for decision making. In many cases this is the most difficult step, and is why the first step, to identify stakeholders, is so important, not only to identify the right stakeholders but to involve them in the process and ultimately in ratifying the findings. The right stakeholders are those who take the findings, make decisions and then implement successfully in an appropriate timeframe.

To sum up, the CEDEFOP approach of 'Skills Anticipation' in skills forecasting is one that really resonates and has the advantage of combining both qualitative and quantitative approaches to get a full picture. Additionally, making use of publicly available detailed governmental research to set the context for the first layer of inputs is both an efficient use of resources and puts your efforts squarely in the realm of economic realities. I highly recommend a read of the CEDEFOP 2017 paper, 'Developing Skills Foresights, Scenarios and Forecasts' (Bakule *et al*, 2017).

Right place, right time (strategic workforce planning)

So far in the PEIP journey we have outlined an approach to identifying the right people with the right skills. However, having this is all for nought if you cannot deploy them to the right job at the right time to make the most use of their capabilities – and leverage their motivation for working in your organization.

A relatively new discipline known as strategic workforce planning (SWP) is emerging as a key capability to enable greater performance and productivity. SWP is the process of analysing the current workforce, determining future workforce needs, and identifying the gap between the workforce you currently have available and your future needs. This enables the organization to more effectively accomplish its mission, goals and strategic plan. Having an ability to predict and deploy the right people to the right place at the right time is a powerful differentiator and a competitive advantage. SWP is becoming such an important topic that many top universities and other organizations, such as the Human Capital Institute, have designed and put in place degree programmes and certifications to increase the depth of skills in this space – to meet the growing demand for these skills in the marketplace.

The SWP approach has at its core a key principle: creating a proactive resource risk management approach versus a reactive resource risk management approach. The large majority of organizations, in my experience, lean heavily towards a more reactive approach to SWP than a proactive approach. To be sure, developing an SWP capability is not easy, and I see many HR organizations struggle to make the case for doing so because the approach can be likened to changing the tyres on a car going 60 mph. You can't just stop what you are doing and take stock of supply and demand. Additionally, the workforce needs to be involved in the exercise, otherwise it is 'done to them' rather than 'done with them' – a recipe for copious amounts of dissatisfaction in the ranks.

Therefore, the main purpose of effective SWP should be two-fold:

- ensure the workforce is proactively aligned to work according to business objectives;
- ensure work is proactively aligned to the workforce's personal motivations and objectives.

Let's outline some key principles high-performing organizations put in place in developing an effective SWP capability (Louch, 2014):

- Align organization strategic planning with head count and talent planning.
- Create a clear view of talent demand and supply issues by investment area, reporting relationship, and by location.
- Provide managers easy-to-use reports and tools to determine the impact of their talent decisions and prioritize future workforce investments.
- Provide leaders with the right metrics – identifying talent risk before it impacts business objectives.
- Help control unplanned talent costs and highlight issues that limit employee productivity.
- Build competitive advantage through planned versus reactive talent management.
- Give business leaders consistent reporting of results to quantify measurable and meaningful outcomes.
- Give the workforce a say in what they do and when they do it.

THREE-DIMENSIONAL SWP: A TOTAL TEAM EFFORT

One of the biggest mistakes organizations make in developing and implementing SWP is that it very often becomes more about the employer's needs and less about the employee's. One sure way to destroy employee engagement is by creating a situation where people perceive or experience a lack of say in what they do and when/where they do it. As we talked about previously, one of the biggest stressors on people is a situation where they feel a lack of control over their tasks, their time and their place of work. To avoid this situation, it is important to look at SWP as a three-dimensional model that takes into account all aspects of the work equation. Done effectively it becomes the most powerful part of PEIP – and one that can create clear blue water between your organization and your competitors.

The three dimensions (or stakeholders) are:

- senior managers
- the workforce
- HR SWP team (individuals with SWP analytics and programme management experience).

Having this three-dimensional approach to SWP is key as it involves the entire organization in this very important process. Let's have a look at this in more detail.

SEVEN KEY ELEMENTS OF EFFECTIVE SWP

There are seven key elements for an effective SWP approach:

- create an SWP charter and 3D-SWP team;
- understand historical trends (external and internal);
- pivotal jobs: segmentation;
- demand and supply analysis;
- gap analysis;
- workforce engagement analysis;
- action planning.

SWP charter and the 3D team The most successful SWP programmes have at their core a compelling reason for being – usually, in the first instance, a pressing mission-critical situation that needs to be solved. This helps to create a focus that a programme 'charter' can be built around. This charter should:

- have a compelling reason for conducting SWP;
- have a team, reporting within HR and Finance, dedicated to strategic workforce planning;
- staff the team with individuals who possess strategic workforce planning and analytics expertise, and have a good understanding of pivotal jobs and workforce needs/motivations.

The compelling reason for being is the key first step, because when the SWP effort is nebulous and not well defined, it can end up focused on something in the organization that is not high priority, and therefore will struggle to get support. Additionally, it's important to have a cross-discipline team of HR and Finance to match the plan with the financial realities of the business. Most Finance organizations have excellent data on workforce costs and productivity, and this data can be used to frame SWP on the right priorities and put real numbers of cost vs benefits. And lastly, the team should have at its core a representative from each of HR and Finance, but should also have workforce representation to layer in the workforce's objectives and motivations. Having workforce representatives from each part of the business to input into the plans according to workforce needs and capabilities helps to create a three-dimensional view and buy-in across the business.

Historical trends SWP as an internal, forward-thinking proactive process actually starts by looking backwards and outwards. To understand the future the organization needs to understand the present and the past, as well as the environment it operates in. To understand the recent past, workforce and management surveys come in very handy and are often used to get this context before getting started. As for the environment the organization operates in, often the government data is a good source of intelligence. As in the previous section on skill forecasting, organizations like CEDEFOP have a treasure trove of historical (and current) data on global and sector trends. Make use of this as the starting point for effective SWP.

Pivotal jobs: segmentation Attempting SWP for the entire workforce in the first instance, particularly in very large organizations, can dilute the exercise and its value. Understanding the priority workforces, the most value-added roles, is the ideal place to start. The truth is, some roles in the organization produce more value than others – often, orders of magnitude more than others. The pivotal roles and people in these roles differ not only industry by industry but also company by company. That's why connecting people to the firm's future strategy is critical. Before planning roles, organizations must be clear about the skills and capabilities needed to create success in their chosen models. Rather than attempt, at least initially, to do an SWP analysis for the entire organization, it's best to segment into the highest-value workforces first. This creates focus and priority right from the start. As the SWP capability becomes more mature, additional areas of focus can be brought online.

Demand analysis The demand planning component of workforce planning determines organization head count that is required in each job role for each organizational unit. There are three keys to moving beyond this demand planning challenge impasse.

The first is *cultural*. Organizations should avoid confusing planning with the plan, and should value planning as much as, if not more than, the actual plan. The plan will not happen. The future is far too uncertain. Planning, however, is a competency that helps managers deal with such uncertainty more quickly and effectively.

The second key is to move from top-down planning to *bottom-up planning*, which requires technology that allows end users to evaluate various factors and define talent demand for their business area. This bottom-up planning can be rolled up for various corporate-wide outputs, such as the corporate workforce plan, the budget feed, the real estate plan, the reforecast and more, but it also can be conducted as needed as part of a frequent recalibration of talent needs based on the state of the business.

The third is to *avoid making 'perfect' the enemy of 'good enough'*. Too often organizations look to have 'perfect' data from which to plan. This is a major mistake, as SWP is never an exact science. There are too many variables looking out into the future to take them all into account. The fact is that SWP done with reasonably good data is good enough.

According to Quinn Thompson, global director of Talent Acquisition and Diversity at International Paper, on the shift to user-defined input driving their workforce planning process: 'It starts with the benefits created by a centre of excellence (CoE), but is based on software that allows end users to create their own workforce plans and end-customers to leverage predictive analytics for their customized gap analyses' (Louch, 2014). A lower-performance organization will have managers decide in a vacuum on their need for talent. In this setting, the industry experience of managers and the amount of data available to make the decision defines the quality of the output. In a high-performance organization, managers are guided through the decision-making process.

For example, a manager may be led through a decision tree based on strategic objectives and job criticality. Alternatively, a manager may be provided with demand drivers and conduct what-if scenarios that help determine the appropriate number of workers for the workload based on a combination of historical staffing levels and productivity objectives. In the ideal situation, a manager could be provided with a detailed proforma demand plan that describes the staffing level for job roles based upon how the organization typically staffs against work volumes and other demand drivers. Then the manager can be led through decision making to ask questions such as:

- Do we typically staff against demand correctly? Specifically, do we hire too soon, too late, too much, too little? Knowing how the business is likely to behave in its staffing approach does not mean it's the correct approach. It's just a great starting point of the decision making – and not the end, as there may be a need to not only know, but also optimize staffing levels.
- When we examine our business strategies and look at the specific ways we want to create value, does that describe certain roles that should be staffed up?
- Conversely, when we look at those strategies, are there certain staff areas that are relatively low risk for understaffing? Because it is not possible to staff everything generously, where can we 'understaff' with minimal risk to the business?

In summary, a technology-enabled bottom-up approach to demand planning creates a more accurate plan and enables a planning culture where managers use data to make staffing decisions – and are more equipped to evaluate how changes to business objectives and environment should impact staffing levels (Louch, 2014).

Supply analysis   Within the internal supply analysis component of workforce planning, an organization evaluates whether it has the supply internally to meet its demand. On a quantitative basis, the process is to evaluate talent supply by job role after attrition: turnover, retirement and internal job movement. On a qualitative basis, it is important to also look at capability and performance, even within jobs that are fully staffed.

To derive a supply forecast, a lower-performance organization will simply carry forward historical turnover rates or use industry benchmarks. This approach is not sufficiently actionable – at best it is only interesting data to consider as part of workforce planning; at worst, it is incorrect.

A high-performance organization will use predictive analytics to identify the risk of turnover, retirement, and workforce mobility of specific individuals. Machine learning statistics packages allow an organization to conduct complex multivariate analysis that incorporates employee demographics, employer actions and workplace conditions, and external economic conditions.

An accurate internal supply forecast can thus be aggregated by any dimension and provide a much clearer line of sight into supply risks that need to be closed to fully meet talent demand requirements. Knowing which individuals are at highest risk for turnover provides an organization the lead time to address future workforce gaps with minimal disruption to the business, enabling the following outcomes:

- creation of targeted replacement planning and knowledge transfer for critical roles;
- understanding which talent gaps are the largest, highest priority, and/or most difficult to fill externally;
- proactive sourcing by the recruiting function based on prioritization of gaps;
- roadmap of future open positions that can be filled through promotions and developmental assignments;
- managed attrition programmes that avoid costly workforce reductions for job roles that have a reduced staffing requirement.

As with demand planning, technology is a key enabler for internal supply analysis, since it provides a forecast of attrition and movement risk on an employee-by-employee basis. Furthermore, this approach helps organizations that are not currently proficient at demand planning to move towards proficiency by highlighting problems that require consideration of the importance of that problem, ie the demand. For example, if a certain employee is known as highly likely to turnover, a manager can ask 'What's the risk to my work unit of this likely turnover event? Will we still get the required work completed? If the answer is no, is it because of the necessity of the role or the performance of the individual? If the answer is yes, is it because we are overstaffed in this role? Can we eliminate the role with the likely turnover event and hire for a more critical need?' In short, reviewing turnover, retirement, and movement risks helps this hypothetical manager conduct demand planning on a micro level, and with the right tools and training, the manager will improve talent decision making (Louch, 2014).

Gap analysis Within the gap analysis and action-planning component of workforce planning, an organization evaluates its gaps and determines what actions it can take to close those gaps. Traditionally, those actions consisted of recruiting, development and transition, but with modern predictive technology, an organization can also model the prospective impact of potential interventions in HR policies and talent management actions.

A proficient organization can combine its demand planning and internal supply analysis as described above and gain a much clearer picture of the size, type, and timing of gaps between demand and supply. These gaps will lead to a high-quality directional recruitment plan and will highlight areas where an organization may wish to beef up its developmental programmes where there are large and consistent gaps. This gap analysis will also highlight where there are job roles that are subject to career transition in one part of the business (demand less than supply) and requiring recruitment in another part of the business (demand greater than supply), so that an organization can reallocate resources and avoid some of the costly cycles of staffing up and down. Each of these responses to the demand–supply gap represents valuable organizational action planning to address gaps, but they do not go as far as making specific interventions to change and control the demand–supply gaps.

> A high-performance organization will build upon the specific quantitative plan for build-buy-lease as discussed for a proficient organization and will also use technology to conduct what-if analysis to evaluate specific management interventions. The organization will understand how a number of factors drive retention, engagement and organizational performance, including:
>
> - pay strategy and annual merit increase;
> - career ladders and working structures;
> - promotions, lateral transfers and reorganizations.
>
> By understanding these relationships, a high-performance organization can seek to close gaps not only through the traditional means of build-buy-lease, but also achieve higher retention and performance by optimizing its workforce policies around those desired outcomes.
>
> This organization will not only be creating the appropriate plans to address gaps between its forecasted demand and supply but will be selectively addressing potential retention and performance risks of critical resources and roles and will manage those risks through individual action planning measures (Louch, 2014).

Workforce engagement analysis There is no one-size-fits-all solution to employee engagement as an input into SWP, because every workforce and every employee is different. The most effective approach is to ask employees to share their input through an employee SWP engagement survey. Before embarking on the SWP survey process, the key is to choose the right tools. There are many online tools to help with the survey process, and free versions of SurveyMonkey, FluidSurveys or Qualtrics are the most popular.

Once the tool is chosen, the next step is to define the questions that best reflect the workforce view on where and how to deploy people to the right work. The power of this approach is that the people on the ground have a very detailed view on how work actually gets done and who does it. Putting this knowledge to work shows the workforce that their input is valued as well as bringing in 'local knowledge' to the process.

Action planning As with any other high-priority programme, without a plan to implement, it is just some information on paper (or a hard drive). And nowhere is action planning more important than in workforce planning. Getting your SWP up and running and embedding it in the organization is not possible if there is not an effective plan for implementation. Consider the following steps:

1 Identify and involve stakeholders to gain buy-in: to get the most effective buy-in, involve the customers (stakeholders) of the exercise right from the start. Programme stakeholders can give invaluable input on what steps are needed to achieve the SWP objectives and how best to implement them. If they are involved and bought-in early on, they are more likely to work diligently on implementation. The customers of your workforce plan are often the best and most motivated to help successful implementation.

2 Break it down: the core of the SWP action plan is a list of tasks for achieving your objectives. Break down the strategic plan into manageable steps that are easily understandable and assignable.

3 Set a timeline: now establish a timeframe for achieving each action.

4 Designate resources and responsibilities: name who will be responsible for each action. Also outline what other resources (money, equipment, personnel) you'll need to carry out the SWP plan.

5 Establish a follow-up and measurement process: spell out how you will follow up on SWP to ensure the steps are carried out. This can include internal reporting and regular meetings held to discuss the plan's progress.

Also specify the measures you will use to track implementation. These can include both milestones, such as the completion of certain tasks, and quantifiable measures, such as revenue or market share.

6 Communicate the plan: make sure all stakeholders are aware of the action plan, including their role in implementing it. Explain how the plan fits into the overall business strategy and 'what's in it' for them.

7 Keep SWP alive: in addition to regular communications and follow-up, it's critical to maintain the energy around the programme. Demonstrating and making a big deal of the key successes to both stakeholders and the workforce helps keep the 'buzz' going about the efforts and how it is helping management as well as employees.

RECENT EXAMPLE
Implementing an effective SWP capability – what do they do?

APQC (American Productivity & Quality Center), one of world's foremost authorities in benchmarking, best practices, process and performance improvement, and knowledge management, partnered with several organizations, including IBM, to put together an excellent paper on recent best practice case studies for SWP: 'Strategic Workforce Planning: Best and next practices report' in March 2017 (Tucker *et al*, 2017). I highly recommend purchasing this report from the APQC online store as a great starting place for your SWP project. The following are some of the implementation examples they offer.

Phillips 66 embedded HR business partners have primary accountability for implementing the plan. The senior HR business partners have their own leadership teams to take on implementation and pull support from appropriate HR centres of excellence as needed.

Kaiser Permanente – the business units are primarily responsible for the successful implementation of the workforce plan. Taking a less visible role in implementation, the workforce planning team collaborates in a supportive role, such as preparing cost-benefits analyses and assessing the appropriate investments associated with each intervention.

At MITRE, embedded HR business partners have primary responsibility for implementing the plan with involvement from HR areas of expertise such as recruiting, learning, and succession and career planning. The strategic workforce planning team is only involved as technical advisers upon request. This partnership reflects the strategic workforce planning team's advisory role among the centres. That is, it works to ensure the pertinent functions are well informed and then tracks results based on those functions' decisions and changing circumstances.

USDA Farm Service Agency – the state-level executive directors who create the plans are accountable for ensuring interventions from the plans are implemented. The agency's action plan template uses the RACI model for defining roles and responsibilities, outlining who is *r*esponsible, *a*ccountable, *c*onsulted, and/or *i*nformed. The six HR business partners who make up the centralized strategic workforce planning group track each organization's status on the completion of its human capital initiatives, as do the organization's executives.

At US Geological Survey, the deputy director is responsible for the oversight of the workforce plan implementation. Meeting monthly, the implementation team is responsible for implementing the strategies and associated action items identified in the workforce.

RECENT EXAMPLE
An emerging strategic workforce planning and engagement tool: Optunli

(Full disclosure, I am an investor and a non-executive director on the Board of Optunli).

In 2018, I came upon a software solution that was something that I had not seen before, and it struck an immediate chord. It's a solution called Optunli, developed by two clever women entrepreneurs in the UK. They worked in a large corporate organization that had a reactive approach to SWP, and certainly did not involve the workforce in resourcing decisions. The organization also lacked a capability in planning for people's future development into roles further down the road – a one-dimensional approach to resourcing. They decided to take matters into their own hands and have a go at solving this challenge themselves. In 2016, they outlined a design for a tool that would be like a company 'matchmaking' service; matching people up to not only current roles, but roles they would aspire to in the future. Successfully implemented, this tool allows both the organization and the employee to take a look into the future to 'Know, Plan and Engage', getting right people, right place, at the right time and, most importantly, aligned to people's motivations. Essentially this solution is PEIP codified into software, giving the organization a 3D look into the present and future of SWP. They acquired some seed funding and set about finding the right software designers and engineers to bring the idea to life; creating a number of clever algorithms and design features, a new 3D approach to SWP emerged.

> Optunli is a software as a service (SaaS) platform that helps organizations change the way they understand, plan and engage their current and future workforce, and helps people build and manage their careers. Powered by a new approach to workforce AI, Optunli enables the individual to represent the totality of who they are and what they wish to achieve, their preferences and priorities. This, in turn, provides organizations with unprecedented insight that informs selection processes as well as planning processes, eliminates bias from the match and supports organizations in their Diversity and Inclusion agendas. Organizations using Optunli can benefit from a dramatic impact on internal mobility, reduced attrition, a self-motivated workforce, increased engagement and productivity, as well as greater insight and speed in planning decisions and competitiveness.
>
> Needless to say, this was a solution after my own heart. I agreed in 2018 to join the board as a non-executive director. Optunli is the tool that most closely captures the essence and the power of PEIP, so it was an easy decision to join forces.

In summary, the key to making the case in shifting workforce planning from a top-down strategic idea to one that is geared towards provoking thought and action is:

- creating a mindset of proactive workforce planning risk management versus reactive risk management;
- developing the right metrics – perhaps the most crucial levers to drive support for workforce planning;
- shifting workforce planning from a top-down strategic idea that is only geared towards thinking about the future to an operational exercise designed to manage talent risk, with specific financial implications;
- providing metrics to quantify the risk, giving something even more concrete for leaders to manage;
- outlining the cost of not doing SWP; if we do nothing, what will happen?

By taking this approach, a high-performance organization will be able to conduct gap analysis on the work unit, business unit, and on the organization as a whole. At the work unit level, managers will be better at planning and responding to changes in the business. Managers will also be able to make data-driven decisions that move gradually from blanket HR policies to targeted HR interventions based on the importance of a role or the performance of the individual. Business units and the total organization will also reap the benefits of the workforce planning programme. Finance and real estate will have the information needed to construct their budgets. HR will be able to make better high-level decisions about recruitment, development, redeployment, and transition programmes. And senior leadership will be able to monitor the people health of the organization and the organizational capacity to meet present and future business objectives.

The benefits of SWP:

- reducing labour costs in favour of workforce deployment and flexibility;
- responding to the needs of their customer base;
- identifying skills gaps and areas of succession risk;
- relevant strategies for talent management and people development;
- targeting specific and identified inefficiencies;
- employee retention initiatives;
- improving the quality of outputs;
- improving work-life balance;
- recruitment and training responses to changes in the education system.

Right motivation

Now we arrive at the keystone of PEIP: motivation. This is the dimension that pulls all the pieces together and makes it all hum. Imagine all the other dimensions are primed and ready to go, so when you tap into people's purpose and motivations in working for you, the engaged workforce can execute with remarkable energy, focus and effectiveness. In Chapter 2 we covered the topic of motivation extensively. Now let's put it in the context of PEIP to show the true power of the engaged workforce.

Coming back once again to our friend Rumi: 'Everyone has been made for some particular work and the desire for that work has been put in every heart' – the true power of PEIP comes in that 'desire' for a certain type of work. Matching desire, motivation, to the type of work that gets one out of bed in the morning raring to go, should be the goal of all employers – and employees. Yes, that is correct. Like much of PEIP, it is a two-way discussion between the employer and the employee. PEIP does not work effectively in one-way traffic. It is up to employer *and* employee to articulate the meeting point on desire/motivation. Does one's personal motivation always match to the work at hand? No. However the overall goal, on a day-to-day basis, should be to attempt to match the work required to the right person and their desire. The act of both employee and employer working together in good faith to balance work and desire as often as possible will create the engagement required to make PEIP hum.

THE MANAGEMENT

Collectively as managers, it should be an important part of the job to recognize and to tap into employees' deeper motivation. Ask them: Why are you doing this work? What drives you about this particular work? What gives you the gratification of a job well done? What makes you feel great about yourself?

Whenever I come to this point in managing a team, managing individuals, I always recall a great article by Peter Bregman, of Bregman Partners, in *Harvard Business Review* back in 2010 (Bregman, 2010). Peter tells the story of five strangers in Manhattan helping a man in a walker who was struggling against a raging storm to get across a busy street to a Metropolitan New York disabled access van. As Peter describes it, the driver of the van was warm and dry inside watching the group of five struggle in the pouring rain to lift the man across the street to the van. The driver seemed content to sit and watch as the team of people eventually got the man to the van. Once inside, onlookers mouthed 'thank you' to the group of five, while the driver simply waved at them and drove off. What's interesting is that the person being paid to help the man gain access to the van did very little to help, while five complete strangers happily helped the man for free – which generates a lot of different questions around people's motivations for doing something. There are enough questions to fill an entire book, so we will not have the time to delve into it here. However, there is one key question that *is* relevant here: Why did five people, who were not being paid, act quickly and successfully, when the one who was being paid did not? I am not suggesting we ask people to work for free; however, this story illustrates a powerful truth about people aligned to a certain task that fits their personal values; they don't think about the money, they just act. But how can this story help a manager of a team tap into people motivation?

As Peter puts it, the answer is fairly simple (Bregman, 2010):

> People tend to think of themselves as stories. When you interact with someone, you're playing a role in her story. And whatever you do, or whatever she does, or whatever you want her to do, needs to fit into that story in some satisfying way. When you want something from someone, ask yourself what story that person is trying to tell about himself, and then make sure that your role and actions are enhancing that story in the right way.

> We can stoke another person's internal motivation not with more money, but by understanding, and supporting, his story. 'Hey,' the driver's boss could say, 'I know you don't *have* to get out of the van to help people, but the fact that you do – and in the rain – that's a great thing. And it tells me something about you. And I appreciate it and I know that man with the walker does too.' Which reinforces the driver's self-concept – his story – that he's the kind of guy who gets out, in the rain, to help a passenger in need.

This idea of understanding your employees' personal stories is a powerful one. It tells you most of what you need to know to tap into a person's desire, and their desire for a particular kind of work.

THE EMPLOYEE

One of the most interesting features about working in Andersen Consulting back in the '80s and '90s was the overall ethos of the employee-employer relationship. The firm employed an 'up or out' model, which today probably seems archaic and vaguely unfair. The model was, once you reached a plateau of capability and performance, it was time for you to look for another job, elsewhere. Everyone knew this – it was not a bug in the system, but a *feature*.

I remember my first meeting on the first day on the job – the local HR director sat the 10 of us 'new starters' down to have a talk. The first thing she said was:

> Take a look around you, at your fellow colleagues. Ten or twelve years from now, only one of you will still be here, having been promoted to partner and completed a successful journey in the firm. The rest of you will have moved on to successful careers in other organizations, having had the benefit of being developed by one of the top firms in the world… It's up to you to make the most of this opportunity. We will provide you with globally recognized, award-winning personal development; however, you must make your own plan in navigating the roles available to you and the learning that comes with that.

This was a shocking reality check, to say the least. However, this model had been employed since the 1920s and was very successful for both the firm and for former employees, who did, indeed, go on to successful careers elsewhere. The key here was that the firm would make available excellent development opportunities and interesting projects to work on, but it was up to the employee to make the most of this. This is an important point, and is a critical success factor in making PEIP work effectively. The employer (manager) should put in the effort to understand your motivations and the type of work that fits best for you, and give you the opportunity to flourish;

however, in the end, it is really up to the individual to make known their desires and development needs. As the Andersen HR director put it to us, 'create a plan' to take advantage and communicate this plan to your manager. Help the organization understand 'your story' to provide the best roles and development opportunities, and see where this leads.

This two-way communication and understanding are the keystone for PEIP to work its magic. Expecting the employer to always do for you in your career is not realistic or recommended.

PEIP – bringing it all together

Hopefully by now, the power of PEIP is becoming evident and intriguing. Additionally, it should be clear that it is not a theoretical idea but is one that has worked successfully in the recent past and will work again in the near future – if we take it on board. PEIP is as much a mindset as it is a set of working principles and processes. It forces us to think differently but *not* counter-intuitively. Much of it should be common sense: from the need for an integrated human capital lifecycle to the importance of understanding human motivations, the human *story* for why people do what they do.

Now that we have established the idea, the concepts and the principles of PEIP, the next step is to turbo-charge it – make it even more powerful. In the first chapter we looked at the challenges facing organizations today with some unprecedented trends washing over us as we try to come to terms with the 21st-century workplace. These trends can seem daunting, and downright scary in some respects. However, in the context of PEIP, they may become exciting *opportunities*. If we harness these trends in our favour and then use emerging technologies, from SaaS HR systems to AI and machine learning, we can turn PEIP into an unprecedented engine for growth for organizations, for people and for society at large. The potential is great if we ride these trends and harness the technology.

References

Bakule, M, Czesaná, V, Havlíčková, V, *et al* (2017) Developing Skills Foresights, Scenarios and Forecasts: Guide to anticipating and matching skills and jobs, volume 2, CEDEFOP/International Labour Office. Available at: http://www.cedefop.europa.eu/files/2216_en.pdf (archived at https://perma.cc/7QJZ-BFC5) [Last accessed 16 August 2019]

Bartash, J (2018) U.S. job openings hit a record 7.1 million, exceed number of unemployed Americans [blog] *MarketWatch*, 16 October. Available from: https://www.marketwatch.com/story/us-job-openings-jump-to-record-71-million-2018-10-16 (archived at https://perma.cc/D4RB-EQS2) [Last accessed 16 August 2019]

Bernmar, D (2017) Ignore the headlines: A six-hour working day is the way forward, *Guardian*, 6 January. Available from: https://www.theguardian.com/commentisfree/2017/jan/06/ignore-headlines-six-hour-working-day-swedish (archived at https://perma.cc/KGZ2-W33V) [Last accessed 16 August 2019]

Beyer, J (2019) How to build an internal employer branding team [blog] *Built In*, 25 July. Available from: https://builtin.com/employer-branding/how-build-internal-employer-branding-team (archived at https://perma.cc/56RN-WD68) [Last accessed 16 August 2019]

Bhalla, V, Dyrchs, S and Strack, R (2017) Twelve forces that will radically change how organizations work (The new new way of working series) [blog] *Boston Consulting Group*, 27 March. Available from: https://www.bcg.com/en-us/publications/2017/people-organization-strategy-twelve-forces-radically-change-organizations-work.aspx (archived at https://perma.cc/3VF4-A9T8) [Last accessed 16 August 2019]

Bregman, P (2010) A story about motivation, *Harvard Business Review*, 3 February. Available from: https://hbr.org/2010/02/a-story-about-motivation.html (archived at https://perma.cc/V4J4-D3VR) [Last accessed 16 August 2019]

Bucy, M, Finlayson, A, Kelly, G and Moye, C (2016) The 'how' of transformation [blog] *McKinsey Insights*, May. Available from: https://www.mckinsey.com/industries/retail/our-insights/the-how-of-transformation (archived at https://perma.cc/MT67-BY44) [Last accessed 8 August 2019]

Dembe, A (2016) A four-day workweek could be hazardous to your health [blog] *CNN*, The Conversation, 15 September. Available from: https://edition.cnn.com/2016/09/15/health/four-day-workweek/index.html (archived at https://perma.cc/Y3WL-M4WK) [Last accessed 16 August 2019]

Downs, L (2012) Integrated talent management: Building a strategy one block at a time, *TD Magazine*, August. Available from: https://www.td.org/magazines/td-magazine/integrated-talent-management-building-a-strategy-one-block-at-a-time (archived at https://perma.cc/GF8M-7YX4) [Last accessed 16 August 2019]

EURES (2019) Skills for jobs: How to get the most out of the OECD's database [blog] *The European Job Mobility Portal*, 24 January. Available from: https://ec.europa.eu/eures/public/news-articles/-/asset_publisher/QOSmqQGuvdnC/content/skills-for-jobs-how-to-get-the-most-out-of-the-oecd-s-database? (archived at https://perma.cc/LNK4-V3D5) [Last accessed 16 August 2019]

Eurostat (2019) Job vacancy statistics, June [blog] Eurostat Statistics Explained. Available from: https://ec.europa.eu/eurostat/statistics-explained/index.php/Job_vacancy_statistics#Job_vacancies_between_2017_and_2019 (archived at https://perma.cc/9DYQ-9WTB) [Last accessed 16 August 2019]

Gerstner, L (2003) *Who Says Elephants Can't Dance? Inside IBM's historic turnaround*, HarperCollins, New York

Goodman, C and Mance, S (2011) Employment loss and the 2007–09 recession: An overview, US Bureau of Labor Statistics. Available from: https://www.bls.gov/opub/mlr/2011/04/art1full.pdf (archived at https://perma.cc/T8GM-GDTF) [Last accessed 16 August 2019]

Graham-McLay, C (2018) A 4-day workweek? A test run shows a surprising result, *New York Times*, 19 July. Available from: https://www.nytimes.com/2018/07/19/world/asia/four-day-workweek-new-zealand.html?smtyp=cur&smid=tw-nytimesbusiness (archived at https://perma.cc/593U-QUHN) [Last accessed 16 August 2019]

Hammoud, M S and Nash, D P (2014) What corporations do with foresight, *European Journal of Futures Research*, 2, p 42. Available from: https://doi.org/10.1007/s40309-014-0042-9 (archived at https://perma.cc/DAR3-VQBB) [Last accessed 16 August 2019]

Jorgenson, D, Ho, M and Stiroh, K (2008) A retrospective look at the U.S. productivity growth resurgence, *Journal of Economic Perspectives*, 22 (1), pp 3–24

Kleinbard, D (2000) The $1.7 trillion dot.com lesson [blog] *CNN*, 9 November. Available from: https://money.cnn.com/2000/11/09/technology/overview/ (archived at https://perma.cc/2LSL-26SQ) [Last accessed 16 August 2019]

Kotecki, P (2018) Companies are shortening the 40-hour workweek to increase employee productivity: Here's how it's going around the world [blog] *Business Insider*, 26 July. Available from: https://www.businessinsider.com/employee-productivity-experiments-companies-shortening-the-workweek-2018-7?r=US&IR=T (archived at https://perma.cc/99ZK-ZNXQ) [Last accessed 16 August 2019]

LinkedIn (2018) 2018 workplace learning report: The path to opportunity is changing [online report] *LinkedIn*. Available from: https://learning.linkedin.com/resources/workplace-learning-report-2018 (archived at https://perma.cc/8Z6R-YCCC) [Last accessed 13 August 2019]

Loftin, J (2011) Utah ends 4-day workweek experiment, but Provo says it still works for them, *Deseret News*, 5 September. Available from: https://www.deseretnews.com/article/705390321/Utah-ends-4-day-workweek-experiment-but-Provo-says-it-still-works-for-them.html (archived at https://perma.cc/T977-BPNZ) [Last accessed 16 August 2019]

Louch, P (2014) Workforce planning is essential to high-performing organizations [blog] *SHRM*, 3 October. Available from: https://www.shrm.org/resourcesandtools/hr-topics/technology/pages/louch-workforce-planning.aspx (archived at https://perma.cc/6272-F8LN) [Last accessed 16 August 2019]

Mind Tools Content Team (nd (a)) Developing a competency framework: linking company objectives and personal performance [blog] *MindTools*. Available from: https://www.mindtools.com/pages/article/newISS_91.htm (archived at https://perma.cc/NWJ7-UD9P) [Last accessed 16 August 2019]

Mind Tools Content Team (nd (b)) SWOT analysis: How to develop a strategy for success [blog] *MindTools*. Available from: https://www.mindtools.com/pages/article/newTMC_05.htm (archived at https://perma.cc/D8M4-5USK) [Last accessed 16 August 2019]

MSNBC (2016) The Pets.com Phenomenon [blog] *MSNBC*, 19 October. Available from: https://www.msnbc.com/msnbc-originals/watch/the-pets-com-phenomenon-789155395746 (archived at https://perma.cc/T2H9-LNP2) [Last accessed 16 August 2019]

OECD (2017a) Getting skills right: United Kingdom (Getting Skills Right series), OECD iLibrary, 22 August. Available from: https://doi.org/10.1787/9789264280489-en (archived at https://perma.cc/CFM6-QP25) [Last accessed 16 August 2019]

OECD (2017b) Executive summary, in Getting Skills Right: Good practice in adapting to changing skill needs – a perspective on France, Italy, Spain, South Africa and the United Kingdom, pp 7–10. OECD Publishing, Paris. Available from: https://doi.org/10.1787/9789264277892-2-en (archived at https://perma.cc/T6ND-JK4K) [Last accessed 16 August 2019]

Osborne, J (2016) A CEO has come up with a brilliant way to help his workers sleep better, *Independent*, 12 April. Available from: https://www.independent.co.uk/life-style/health-and-families/health-news/a-ceo-has-come-up-with-a-brilliant-way-to-help-his-workers-sleep-better-a6981571.html (archived at https://perma.cc/XZ5E-JUCE) [Last accessed 16 August 2019]

Pang, A S-K (2017) *Rest: Why you get more done when you work less*, Penguin Books, UK

PwC (2017) The talent challenge: Harnessing the power of human skills in the machine age. Available from: https://www.pwc.com/gx/en/ceo-survey/2017/deep-dives/ceo-survey-global-talent.pdf (archived at https://perma.cc/P685-S38G) [Last accessed 16 August 2019]

Richtmyer, R (2000) Pets.com at its tail end [blog] *CNNMoney*, 7 November. Available from: https://money.cnn.com/2000/11/07/technology/pets/ (archived at https://perma.cc/3B6W-9TCN) [Last accessed 19 August 2019]

Rohrbeck, R, Battistella, C and Huizingh, E (2015) Corporate foresight: An emerging field with a rich tradition, *Technological Forecasting and Social Change*, 101, pp 1–9. Available from: https://doi.org/10.1016/j.techfore.2015.11.002 (archived at https://perma.cc/RW6U-CPRZ) [Last accessed 19 August 2019]

Saad, L (2014) The '40-Hour' workweek is actually longer – by seven hours [blog] *Gallup News*, 29 August. Available from: https://news.gallup.com/poll/175286/hour-workweek-actually-longer-seven-hours.aspx (archived at https://perma.cc/ZLF4-LBVL) [Last accessed 19 August 2019]

Schmidt, L (2013) This IS NPR recruiting: An employment branding case study [blog] *The SHRMBlog*, 2 July. Available from: https://blog.shrm.org/blog/this-is-npr-recruiting-an-employment-branding-case-study (archived at https://perma.cc/43H8-WWFY) [Last accessed 19 August 2019]

SHRM, https://www.shrm.org/resourcesandtools/tools-and-samples/hr-qa/pages/cms_023007.aspx (archived at https://perma.cc/U4ZE-NWYV)

Shinal, J (2005) Netscape: The IPO that launched an era [blog] *MarketWatch*, 5 August. Available from: https://www.marketwatch.com/story/netscape-ipo-ignited-the-boom-taught-some-hard-lessons-20058518550 (archived at https://perma.cc/YST7-TW2U) [Last accessed 19 August 2019]

Smith, A (2015) Searching for work in the digital era [blog] *Pew Research Center*, 19 November. Available from: https://www.pewinternet.org/2015/11/19/1-the-internet-and-job-seeking/ (archived at https://perma.cc/8BDL-EPGY) [Last accessed 19 August 2019]

Snyder, B (2016) Arianna Huffington's next disruption: Your sleep patterns [Online] *Stanford Business Press*, 29 April. Available from: https://www.gsb.stanford.edu/insights/arianna-huffingtons-next-disruption-your-sleep-patterns (archived at https://perma.cc/KG7X-W3WF) [Last accessed 19 August 2019]

Spar, B, Dye, C, Lefkowitz, R and Pate, D (2018) 2018 Workplace learning: The rise and responsibility of talent development in the new labor market [Online] *LinkedIn Learning*. Available from: https://learning.linkedin.com/content/dam/me/learning/en-us/pdfs/linkedin-learning-workplace-learning-report-2018.pdf (archived at https://perma.cc/U7PL-K3AV) [Last accessed 19 August 2019]

Tucker, E, Collins, R and Mobray, P (2017) Strategic Workforce Planning: Best and next practices report, American Productivity & Quality Center, Houston, TX. Available from: https://www.apqc.org/knowledge-base/documents/strategic-workforce-planning-best-and-next-practices-report (archived at https://perma.cc/RAB4-W9VW) [Last accessed 19 August 2019]

Universum (no date) Future of employer branding [blog] *Universum Global*. Available from: https://www.socialtalent.com/blog/recruitment/2020-outlook-the-future-of-employer-branding-infographic (archived at https://perma.cc/F7PD-XCM3) [Last accessed 19 August 2019]

van Ark, B, O'Mahony, M and Timmer, M (2008) The productivity gap between Europe and the United States: Trends and causes, *Journal of Economic Perspectives*, **22** (1), pp 25–44

Yang, C (2000) Commentary: Earth to dot com accountants [blog] *Bloomberg L P*, 3 April. Available from: https://www.bloomberg.com/news/articles/2000-04-02/commentary-earth-to-dot-com-accountants (archived at https://perma.cc/U49N-KLTC) [Last accessed 13 August 2019]

04

Turbo-charging the future

Five trends to ride, now

Now on to what may be the most exhilarating potential of the PEIP story: turbo-charging the future. A new way of living and working makes for a better person, better organization and better society. There is a quiet revolution going on in the background where science, technology and advanced research are combining to change the world as we know it to an almost unfathomable degree. For example, our understanding of the nature of the Universe at the microscopic level (quantum mechanics, or the unobservable, elementary particle level) to the macroscopic, (classical mechanics, or the very large things we can observe relatively easily in the world and in our galaxy and beyond) has come on by leaps and bounds in only 50 years.

Take the weird world of quantum mechanics for example, where almost everything we know or perceive in the observable world around us breaks down and behaves in unimaginable, weird and paradoxical ways. Our deepening understanding of these strange properties is presenting new and fantastical opportunities in areas like quantum computing which will create machines with incredible abilities to process information in size and speed, that the human brain will struggle to comprehend.

Similarly, in the biological sphere, our understanding of the human body has accelerated tremendously over just the last 10 to 15 years. Mapping the human genome, at the end of the 20th-century, has led to all-new fields of research and discovery that are bringing us within reach of curing diseases that have plagued humans for thousands of years. Deeper understanding of life at the genetic level is helping us understand the process of ageing, and the possibility of stopping or reversing many of the ravages of time. We may even be able to grow replacement parts for our bodies in the not too distant future.

The one area of biological science that has seen probably the fastest increase in understanding is in the study of the human brain. There are two main areas that research is focused on: first, simulating the human brain in digital computing (artificial intelligence), and second, understanding neurodiversity – conditions such as dyspraxia, dyslexia, attention deficit hyperactivity disorder (ADHD), dyscalculia and autistic spectrum. Both of these areas of research require detailed understanding of how the brain is wired; how the synapses (and other biological processes) connect and function. Research in these areas is yielding some startling findings that are making their way into mainstream medical science, today.

However, before we go too far afield into material for another book, we need to put these scientific trends into the perspective of *this* book. So, to bring us back to earth, and our day jobs, if we assume the PEIP principles and operating model described in Chapter 3 are in place, it is possible to reimagine the world of work by embracing and harnessing five key trends that are emerging on the back of these broader scientific trends:

1 **The ageing workforce is not ageing so fast anymore:** one of the most powerful trends to help reverse declining human productivity is leveraging the effort, experience, and skills of our senior population, who are, thanks to science and research, healthier and more able than their predecessors. Easier said than done, so how do we do this?

2 **Gender balancing and the power of female/male co-leadership:** the modern workforce is steadily increasing in female participation (Sancier-Sultan and Sperling, 2018). This should be a welcome trend in the workplace as not only is it good for society in general, it increases the productivity of the workforce. Gender-balanced teams make better decisions and get better results, and are also more engaging and interesting places to work (Sodexo, 2018).

3 **Create innovation with 'different brains':** recent developments are creating a better understanding of neurodiversity and the unique characteristics that come with different brains; this new understanding has triggered a complete rethink about how these unique traits benefit individuals, organizations, and society at large to drive more innovation and productivity.

4 **Harness the intelligence of the machines:** it is a fact that with mechanization people lose their livelihoods, and the misery this causes is real and should not be discounted. However, data shows that at every technological inflection point in history (the point where a new technology development

disrupts the status quo) within a relatively short period of time, people find new and often better jobs by either creating a new role (or business) or learning to *harness* the technology to their benefit.

5 **Digital at home, digital at work:** the digital home has crept up on us steadily over recent years. If you think back to digital technology you used in your home in, say, 1990, you realize just how much has changed in a relatively short period of time. However, how much has work changed, relative to your home? Think about the digital gadgets you have at home, then compare them to work. Not the same, right?

Let's take a look at each of these trends in turn.

The ageing workforce is not ageing so fast anymore

One of the fastest-changing areas of work is the make-up of workforce age demographics. The elongation of a healthy human lifespan is continuing at a pace, creating the situation where in 2020, we will have six full, healthy and productive generations in work at once. Imagine a workforce aged from 19 to 90, creating a surplus of diverse talent which presents a significant opportunity to improve global people productivity.

It might seem counterintuitive, but in the United States for example, the labour participation rate for older workers is steadily increasing. The data shows that since 2016, the older the worker the greater the labour participation rate growth; similar rates are recorded globally. For example, the 70–74 age group was in decline from 2013 through the end of 2015 but saw a striking uptick in 2016 that has continued (Mislinski, 2019). The growth rate is even more prominent for women aged 70–74. Baby boomers are not retiring in anywhere near the numbers that were predicted in the early 2000s. This is not the scenario that would have been envisioned a generation ago for the 'golden years' of retirement. Consider: today nearly one in three of the 65–69 age group and one in five of the 70–74 age group are in the labour force; more than double the number of only five years ago (Mislinski, 2019).

Setting aside baby boomers for a moment, astoundingly we see similar increases in labour participation rate for the generation *before* the boomers, known as the 'silent generation' (born 1927 to 1945). It's a generation we rarely hear much about (thus 'silent') as they are sandwiched between two better-known generations. They were born just too late to be World War II participants and just too early to be New Age, Summer of Love cohorts.

The US Bureau of Labor Statistics shows that the percentage of workers over the age of 75 will increase from 6.4 per cent of the workforce in 2019 to 10.4 per cent by 2026 (US Bureau of Labor Statistics, 2017). This trend, which was somewhat unpredicted, is one that organizations should be preparing for now, to take full advantage. Suddenly, the predicted talent shortage has turned into a talent surplus, and those in a position to take advantage of this trend stand to gain handsomely from it.

If you think about it, the number of people in their late 70s, 80s and early 90s still in work and having an impact on our lives today is astonishing: people like Sir David Attenborough, who, in his 90s, has started a worldwide revolution to combat plastics pollution that is killing sea life in record numbers. He has inspired countless millennials in particular in this regard. He did not start this revolution from his comfy chair; he spent a year travelling the world's seas filming his *Blue Planet* TV series for the BBC to show people directly the impact of plastics pollution in a highly poignant and persuasive manner. Warren Buffett, in his late 80s, continues to be the guru of the investment world. And, again, not from his comfy chair; he travels the world speaking, advising and researching. He keeps a full schedule, as he always has. Dick van Dyke, at the age of 93, appeared in the recent sequel to the 1964 *Mary Poppins* film, *Mary Poppins Returns* (2019), delighting a whole new generation of film goers (he began his career in 1947!). He let loose an impressive and extended dance scene on the top of a table that even those in their 50s would be loath to attempt. Sir David, Mr Buffet and Mr van Dyke are great examples of how the older generation (many years older than baby boomers) are still passing on what they have learned during their long lives and are having a significant impact on emerging generations.

According to OECD projections, the number of people in the 90+ age range is expected to quadruple by 2050; from 2.8 per cent in 1980 to over 10 per cent in 2050 (OECD, 2016). Interestingly, and somewhat paradoxically, one of the key reasons people are living longer is that they are working much later into life, apparently because it is good for you. More and more evidence shows that working, in some meaningful capacity, into your 70s actually elongates lifespan; the UK Chief Medical Officer recently concluded a study that proves this. The data shows that 'staying in work, volunteering or joining a community group can make sure people stay physically and mentally active for longer. The health benefits of this should not be underestimated' (Spencer, 2016). In fact, a study in 2016 showed early retirement may be a risk factor for mortality and prolonged working life may provide survival benefits among US adults (Wu *et al*, 2016).

Working later in life is only one of the reasons we see human lifespan increasing. A quiet revolution in biomedical science is a driving factor for the elongation of a healthy lifespan. Sure, reductions in smoking and an increase in exercise have helped; however, it has mainly been advances in treatments and medicines to address fatal conditions of old age. Strokes, heart attacks and cancer have all been drastically reduced in recent years from better understanding of the causes and use of preventative medicine.

The theoretical lifespan for a human being is about 120 years. The process of 'senescence', or biological ageing, refers to the general deterioration of an organism's physiological functions, leading to increased susceptibility to diseases and ultimately death. It is a complex process that involves many genes. Lifespans vary greatly across different animal species. Thus, for example, flies live for four weeks, horses for 30 years, whereas some species of tortoises may live for up to two centuries. Why is the range of lifespans in nature so broad? This is one of the basic and most intriguing questions faced by biologists (Muntané *et al*, 2018). Solving for senescence is where most of the focus is being placed in research and developing solutions to slow or stop ageing. Breakthroughs in tissue rejuvenation, stem cells, regenerative medicine, molecular repair, gene therapy, pharmaceuticals, and organ replacement (such as with artificial organs or xenotransplantations) will eventually enable humans to have much longer lifespans; we are starting to see some of the benefits of this research, even today.

Hip replacement, knee replacement and heart valve replacement surgeries have all become commonplace, even routine, and have a significant impact on our quality of life well into our later years; and all contribute to our ability to work later into life. But this is just the beginning of what is to come. One of the most exciting developments in recent years is regeneration of damaged human cells. Most human organs and tissues cannot regenerate themselves once damaged. Unfortunately, we are not like salamanders that regrow damaged body parts as needed. However, in 2018, a research team from Tongji University in China made a breakthrough in human lung regeneration technology. For the first time, researchers regenerated patients' damaged lungs using autologous lung stem cell transplantation in a pilot clinical trial (Ma *et al*, 2018). For patients suffering from chronic pulmonary diseases, lung stem cell transplantation could be their biggest, if not last, hope. 'Both patients and researchers need great courage to step forward from benchside to bedside, to test the new therapeutic strategy. Now the good news is that the strategy looks quite promising,' said author of the study, Professor Wei Zuo. Only five years previously, the team were only doing this treatment in tests with mice, which demonstrates how quickly this very promising field of biomedicine is progressing. Professor Wei Zuo predicts that within the next five years, degenerative lung diseases could be completely curable.

When I read about these amazing advances, I am reminded of my grandparents who, when they hit their mid-50s in the early 1980s, were physically challenged in their ability to continue to do any meaningful work. Both of my grandfathers had had multiple heart attacks by this age, and their overall physical fitness was not great. They had circulatory issues that made just the basic act of walking difficult. However, they retired at this age (normal practice in those days) with a nice pension and medical cover and lived another 20 to 25 years, enjoying a very pleasant lifestyle. This was great for them, but not so great for their employers, who rather suddenly lost the benefit of their experience and skills. The employers had to rely on training up younger staff to take their places and hope for the best. This was normal practice back in those days and just seen as a cost of doing business.

Fast forward to today, and we see a very different situation. People in their 50s and 60s are not only healthy and able to contribute at a very high level, they *enjoy* the opportunity to continue leveraging their skills and experience, and in many cases, even developing *new* skills in *new* careers; and smart employers have spotted this. Take Barclays Bank in the UK, for example. Barclays was seeing a shortage of appropriately skilled young people coming out of education, and in 2015 took matters into their own hands by setting up apprenticeships for over 50s to fill the talent shortage. They offer a new career, where they can work their way up after completing the apprenticeship where candidates will be completely retrained for this new career. The programme has been a huge success, being practically over-subscribed since inception, and with Barclays' competitors copying the approach. What Barclays found is that the longer we have older, highly experienced people in the workforce alongside the next generation, the more knowledge capital and human potential we have to increase productivity overall to help us reverse the trend of declining people productivity.

This has led to the popularizing of the idea of 'pro-tirement': the act of early retirement from one career with the positive idea of pursuing another career, or similar, that can be even more fulfilling in the future. Apparently, the term has been around for some time, and was coined by Arthur Godfrey in 1961, according to the article 'Let's Protire' (*The American Mercury*, January 1961). Some people call it 'Life 3.0,' where 1.0 is your early years in education (lasting up to the mid-20s), where 2.0 is your 'starter' career (lasting up to your mid-50s) followed by your 'fun' career where you do something more fulfilling than before and pass on your experience to the next generation. The benefits for the employee are clear, but the benefit to the employer is not very well understood or taken advantage of.

Ask any HR professional if their organization is prepared and capable to recruit both 19-year-olds and 70-year-olds, and the vast majority will just chuckle: 'no way'. Understanding how to recruit, let alone retain, someone in their 70s or 80s is really not something that many organizations have thought about. They are missing out, big time. Just think of the power of combining diverse generations at work and seamlessly deploying them to mix according to their experience and skills; this is what can turbo-charge the next generation and, more importantly, turbo-charge PEIP. The time to start figuring this out is now. The amount of talent out there to scoop up and put to work is mind-boggling, and the amount of value in doing so is almost incalculable.

Gender balancing and the power of female/male co-leadership

While women's participation rate in the workforce rose globally from 44 per cent to 47 per cent from 2000 to 2017, it is still below their 51 per cent share of the global population. Europe, in particular, has lagged behind other regions in making progress in this area; however, there have been significant strides in improving female representation in company board rooms. For example, from 2013 to 2017, women's share of seats on private sector corporate boards in France rose from 26 to 40 per cent; in Germany, it rose from 20 to 33 per cent. In the same period, the share of women on French and German executive committees of companies in the CAC40 and DAX30 rose from 9 and 7 per cent to 17 and 14 per cent respectively (Sancier-Sultan and Sperling, 2018). However, while women account for 51and 55 per cent of graduates of secondary and tertiary education, globally, they represent less than 20 per cent of executive committee members in leading companies across the globe (Sancier-Sultan and Sperling, 2018). So while progress is being made, there remains a significant amount of work left to be done. The question becomes: Why is this important? What difference does this make to improving people productivity? We are bombarded with statistics about female representation in work, but very often the meaning and the *importance* of the data get lost.

How we got here and how to increase female leadership in the executive ranks of organizations is a topic for an entire library of books. We won't solve this one here. However, explaining how a more gender-balanced workforce, both in the middle ranks and in leadership, is good for people engagement, innovation and performance is a more focused area in which to potentially help define how this topic contributes very positively to PEIP. The sheer fact that it is a hot topic that most organizations are, at minimum, aware of and, at most, have achieved substantial, measurable progress to address, demonstrates the importance of addressing gender balancing. Bottom line: organizations are learning it's good for business.

Having worked for and with a number of organizations as both an employee and a consultant, one thing has really struck me over and over again: there is a conspicuous difference in individual and team performance when a group of people working together has something approaching a gender balance. I admit it is difficult to put a finger on exactly what factors create this dynamic, but with a reasonably sizable sample, the following seems to almost always ring true in my experience: a team made up as close as possible to 50 per cent men and 50 per cent women tends to create more effective team dynamics in reviewing and debating operations and organization data, forming conclusions, conducting decision making and carrying out action plans. Additionally, I am struck by how gender-balanced teams take on a more empathetic and egalitarian outlook on business; the idea of 'fair play and fairness' comes to the fore more often in a gender-balanced team. Discussions tend to be more far ranging and have more consideration of different points of view. Sure, these teams have their conflicts, cross-purpose agendas and rivalries just like male- or female-dominated teams, but gender-balanced teams overcome these challenges more effectively than a single-gender-dominated team, and the results bear this out.

Altogether the gender-balanced dynamic strongly tends towards producing results that have higher probability of being accurate, are more sustainable, and more predictable than those of unbalanced teams. Additionally, collaboration improves, and more innovation comes from bringing more diverse skills and experience together. Let's look at some examples where engagement, innovation and performance improved with gender-balanced teams.

In one of the most detailed, long-term and large-scale studies (they have over 425,000 employees) of the benefits and measurable results achieved from gender-balanced teams, from 2011 to 2016 Sodexo undertook a global, multi-year study of 50,000 managers and found that teams managed by a balanced mix of men and women were more successful in areas including employee engagement, brand awareness, client retention, productivity and financial metrics. In 2017, the Sodexo CEO summarized their findings from over 90 company entities around the world and the results were compelling. They clearly show that teams with a male–female ratio between 40 and 60 per cent (or better) produce results that are more sustained and predictable than those of unbalanced teams. For example, gender-balanced management reported an employee engagement rate that was 14 per cent higher than other entities. Client retention rates were 9 per cent higher, and the number of accidents decreased by 12 per cent. Similar findings showed a correlation between gender diversity and other business metrics, including operating profit (Sodexo, 2018). Sodexo CEO Michel Landel said:

> We wanted to go one step further and demonstrate how gender balance drives results at all levels of the organization. Moreover, we are convinced that more women in the middle ranks increases the pipeline of candidates for these top positions. Our case study has confirmed what we have always known: gender balance can only deliver results if it is systematically addressed throughout the organization.

Additionally, Sodexo found that gender-balanced teams also produced more innovation. 'We believe that gender balance fosters creativity and innovation, and ultimately drives better business results. When women reach their full potential, business and society are stronger and more successful,' said Sophie Bellon, chairwoman, Sodexo board (Landel, 2015).

In another recent study of 1,069 leading firms across 35 countries and 24 industries, researchers found that gender diversity relates to more productive companies, as measured by market value and revenue. Interestingly the research found that these results were largely found in contexts where gender diversity is viewed as 'normatively' accepted. By normative acceptance, they mean a widespread cultural belief that gender diversity is important. In other words, beliefs about gender diversity create a self-fulfilling cycle. Countries and industries that view gender diversity as important capture benefits from it, while those that don't, don't. The researchers outline three main reasons why opinions about the value of diversity matter so much to the actual value it brings, and these may provide lessons for managers who wish to capture the benefits of gender diversity (Turban *et al*, 2019):

- First, they found industries that are inclined towards gender-balanced teams tend to have organizations that lead in gender balancing. For example, they found that the percentage of women in telecommunication companies in Western Europe, historically a relatively gender-inclusive context, was significantly tied to a company's market value – specifically, a 10 per cent increase in Blau's gender diversity index related to a roughly 7 per cent increase in market value. However, in the energy sector in the Middle East, which has historically not been gender-inclusive, firms' gender diversity was unrelated to company performance.

- Second, the research found that countries and local cultures that value gender balancing also have organizations that value it as well. They found positive effects of diversity in societies with *normative acceptance* of working women.

- Third, however, they found that societies with only regulatory support do not necessarily lead to gender-balanced organizations. Though regulatory support of working women is correlated with normative acceptance, they are not the same. Some countries have strong cultural support, but few legal structures in place. Others have established legal structures, but cultures that are strongly male dominant.

- Another promising outcome for organizations and societies that focus on achieving gender balancing is that, in numerous studies, research has shown that employees in pro-diversity regions, like the United States and Western Europe, prefer diverse work environments: in a survey of 1,000 respondents, the jobsite Glassdoor found that 67 per cent of job seekers overall look at workforce diversity when evaluating an offer (Glassdoor Team, 2014). Top female candidates, in particular, care about gender-diverse work environments; a recent report by PwC found that 61 per cent of women look at the gender diversity of the employer's leadership team when deciding where to work (Flood *et al*, 2017).

The takeaway is that the most talented individuals go to places that do better with diversity, and this may be what is driving diverse firms in certain contexts to outperform their peers (Bernstein and Raman, 2015). So, achieving gender balance in organizations (and societies) is a good selling point in your employer brand for attracting top talent. Yet another reason that gender balancing can help turbo-charge PEIP.

Create innovation with 'different brains'

Somewhere between 66 and 86 per cent of adults who are on the autistic spectrum are unemployed or significantly underemployed (Rudy, 2019). While the exact number varies based on the research and survey parameters, there's little doubt that employment is not readily available for adults on the autistic spectrum. There is a long-held stigma around people with autism – they are often considered to be highly rigid and moody, possessing poor communication and social skills. But when we go below the surface we learn that there is a much more intricate and nuanced reality from what we see on the exterior. Namely that this condition is not stand-alone but actually a broad spectrum of characteristics that are better described using the term 'neurodiversity': those with autism, ADHD, and other learning or neural processing differences. Note the word 'differences' because the more we understand the origin of these conditions, the more we learn that they are a normal part of human brain evolution. Neurodiversity is a term that's been around since the 1990s, when it was first coined by the Australian sociologist Judy Singer (Singer, 1999). What Singer was looking to describe was a group of conditions such as ADHD and autism which aren't 'abnormal' or 'diseases', but simply variations of the human brain that are a natural part of the tapestry of human variety. The trick, and the opportunity, is to learn how to leverage neurodiverse individuals' unique talents to everyone's benefit.

These recent developments are creating a better understanding of neurodiversity and the unique characteristics that come with different brains. This new understanding has triggered a complete rethink about how these unique traits can benefit individuals, organizations and societies as we move away from the idea that these conditions are *disabilities* and recognize that, in many ways, they are *gifts* which should be put to use to drive more innovation and productivity.

In this context, a new model has emerged to look beyond the traditional deficit view of neurodiversity; to instead understand and harness the unique abilities of neurodiverse individuals to create systems of mutual benefit in education, research, and the private sector. Indeed, if we can understand and leverage the unique capabilities of neurodiverse individuals to fuel innovation in the 21st-century economy, we will have a new reservoir of talent and ideas to turbo-charge the PEIP into the future.

Neurodiversity in the workplace is beginning to have a major impact on organizations. In just the past few years a number of the world's top companies have put in place active and targeted programmes to recruit neurodiverse individuals. Why are they doing this, and what do they stand to gain?

The advent of the information economy and the data-intensive nature of work in the 21st-century workplace has opened up entirely new opportunities for meaningful engagement of individuals with innate talents uniquely well suited to detailed, quantitative, data-immersive employment. Around the world there is a recognition that there is an urgent and unmet demand for talented, highly skilled and capable individuals in sectors such as technology, finance, cyber-security, healthcare analytics, and others. In London, for example, high-tech companies frequently cite the limited employment pool and the fact that this situation is impairing their ability to create innovation and new products/services. The good news is there is an untapped pool of talent to fill these roles if we just think differently about what 'normal' means in the context of who we hire.

Many companies have learned how to tap into the thought patterns and work ethic that are common among neurodiverse individuals. For example, autistic adults are, in general, dependable, routinized, focused, detail oriented, and passionate about their work. Many have outstanding technical and/or math skills. And quite a few are able to find unique solutions to problems that have eluded their more conventional colleagues. This is why companies such as German-based software giant SAP have had, for more than three years now, a programme specifically recruiting people who have autism or related differences. SAP is, as they put it, tapping into a pool of talented people who can bring innovation and new ways of working that drive new notions and ideas for products and services that do not exist today (Phillips, 2019). Other companies that have joined SAP in putting in place similar programmes with similar goals are:

- Microsoft
- Google
- Freddie Mac
- Ford Motor Company
- Ernst & Young
- Walgreens

The list keeps growing as the benefits of having a workforce that brings new thinking, unique capabilities and innovation, that are not usually available in a traditional workforce, are felt.

There is a great example of just how powerful and innovative neurodiversity can be – the far-reaching impact that can be achieved when these unique talents are put to good work. It is an example that is over 100 years old, and one that 21st-century companies are looking to replicate in a workforce that features people with different brains. In 1892 in Dayton, Ohio, Orville and Wilbur Wright founded their bicycle repair, rental and sales business. By 1896 they had begun manufacturing and selling bicycles of their own design, the *Van Cleve* and the *St. Claire*. These were the most innovative bicycles available: they invented the self-oiling bicycle hub and created the machining of the 'crankarm' and pedal on the left side with left-hand threads to prevent the pedal from coming unscrewed while cycling. Seems like a small thing today, but these innovations completely changed the experience of riding a bicycle. Their Wright Cycles became all the rage across the US and Europe, becoming a fashionable device to own by the wealthy and even the royalty of the age. These two brothers from rural mid-west America became world famous for their new product.

However, all was not always great for the brothers. They had had a difficult time in school while trying to pursue a formal education. They were both considered 'odd' and 'eccentric' and were frequently bullied. Wilbur was purposefully smashed in the face with a hockey stick, knocking out most of his front teeth, after which he became housebound and withdrawn, never returning to school.

Orville also decided that he had had enough of formal education and the constant threats of physical harm; he also left school and the brothers decided to educate themselves at home. Unfortunately, they lost their mother to tuberculosis when they were relatively young, and as a result were mainly looked after by their slightly younger sister, Katharine. Their father was a travelling preacher and was mostly away while the boys grew up. He was a highly educated man who had an extensive library at the home in Dayton. The boys read everything they could find of interest in their home library and took to home education very enthusiastically. They also tinkered endlessly, developing exceptional engineering and design skills in a local tool shop.

Early in their twenties they opened their bicycle company and became increasingly adept at designing and building not only bicycles but other devices in their busy shop. They were extremely hard working, focused intensely on creating new engineering designs, and did not have much of a social life. Many young ladies in the town were interested in the successful and highly eligible bachelor brothers, but they remained focused on their work, and in fact never married. This focus on their business meant they quickly became relatively well-off, financially. However, it was not long before they lost interest in their bicycle manufacturing business, becoming bored with doing the same thing every day. They offloaded most of the running of the business to a trusted childhood friend, Edward Sines, and began to think about their next adventure.

Initially, Wilbur took the most interest in the idea of putting their refined engineering skills towards the problem of flight. In the early 1890s, he saw newspaper and magazine articles with photographs of the dramatic glider flights by Otto Lilienthal in Germany. Lilienthal's flights led to an immense amount of interest and activity around the world in figuring out why all previous attempts to build a 'heavier than air' motorized flying machine, failed – in some cases, spectacularly. The efforts had captured the public imagination in both the United States and in Europe, and had certainly captured Wilbur's imagination as well. Then, in 1896, three highly publicized events happened in quick succession that caught Wilbur and Orville's attention:

- In May, Smithsonian Institution Secretary Samuel Langley successfully flew an unmanned steam-powered fixed-wing model aircraft.
- In mid-year, Chicago engineer and aviation authority Octave Chanute brought together several men who tested various types of gliders over the sand dunes along the shore of Lake Michigan.
- In August, Lilienthal was killed when his glider crashed.

These events lodged in the minds of the brothers, especially Lilienthal's death, and spurred them to start to think about doing something new. After a year or so, they decided that this was the next adventure for them, and the brothers went all-in, packed up their bags, with Katharine in tow, and took the train to Washington DC to set up a household near the Smithsonian Institution. The substantial earnings from their bicycle company allowed them the freedom to afford to live in DC and the free time to completely dedicate themselves to learning about all things to do with flight. The Smithsonian library was a treasure trove of data and information going back to the 15th century, including drawings and designs by geniuses such as Leonardo Da Vinci. They pored over the materials, taking copious notes, and conducting nightly debates with Katharine (also a very bright Wright sibling). After months of completely immersing themselves in the concepts of flight, they started to draw some unique and startling conclusions that were very different from the current modes of thinking on the subject.

Essentially, the vast majority of the thinking at the time focused on solving the physics of 'lift' (which allows an aeroplane to get airborne and stay there) and creating engines powerful enough to attain sufficient lift. However, the brothers came to a different conclusion that no one else had thought of. They were convinced that the problem of lift had been solved, and that combustion engines that existed at the time were both small enough and powerful enough to propel an aeroplane into flight. What they concluded was the problem was one of 'control of the aircraft' once airborne. They theorized that the reason all previous attempts at flight had been unsuccessful was because once airborne, the pilot could not control the aircraft.

They resolved to focus on this aspect of flight and find a way to fix it. So, once again, they packed up their bags and took the train to the beaches of North Carolina to make extensive observations of birds in flight. Once again, they became completely immersed in the idea, to the point of not having thought through how they might live on a cold, windy, isolated beach in Kitty Hawk, North Carolina. All they brought with them was a tent, a few pots and pans and some less than appropriate clothing to keep them warm enough.

The few locals that lived near the beach were, initially, completely baffled by these two newly arrived 'oddball' Daytonians, who had obviously never lived near the sea. In a matter of days, the brothers were suffering from exposure, a lack of food and appropriate shelter. Luckily, the locals rescued them, helping them build a wooden shack with a stove and beds, so that they could properly live out the rest of the spring on the beach. To the locals, they clearly lacked the 'common sense' that most humans have, but nonetheless, their antics on the beaches endeared them to the locals. They would marvel at the brothers as they ran around on the beach replicating the movements of the seagulls above them. They sat drawing sketches for hours on end of the shape of the wings of seagulls and also their operational flying capabilities.

After a few months or so of extensive observations of seagulls, they realized the unique capability that the birds (all birds, for that matter) had that human flying machines had not replicated: opposable wings. Birds can move their wings independently of each other and can create a 'wing warping' effect that allows them to control flight – one wing in an up position, while the other wing is locked in a down position, allowing them to perfectly control flight in all wind conditions. This was it! They were sure that they had cracked the problem, so packed up, and caught the first train back north to Dayton. Their innovation was about to be tested.

Once back to their Ohio workshop, they began creating models of aeroplanes that had this 'wing-warping' capability and testing them in rudimentary wind tunnels. Sure enough, they found that this was the key to keeping aircraft airborne. The problem of lift had been solved, but the control of the aircraft once airborne was the key to success. To finalize their conclusion, they built full-scale gliders (effectively very large kites) that were early prototypes of their Wright Flyer, that had the 'wing-warping' innovation as the key feature.

They packed up once again and headed back to their shack on the beach in Kitty Hawk, with large crates that contained their disassembled glider. Once back in Kitty Hawk, they re-assembled the gliders and did hundreds of test flights, recruiting the locals to help them. They were able to achieve exceptional control of the unmanned aircraft and keep them aloft and under control for as long as their (and their neighbours') arm strength held up. Soon followed manned flights using long wooden handles to create the wing-warping effect that was required to fly the gliders.

Not long after this, they strapped an engine to the first model of a Wright Flyer and the rest was history. These two 'oddball' engineers went from knowing next to nothing about flight and engineering an aeroplane to within three years solving the problem, once and for all. Their 'different brains' allowed them to come to conclusions that no one else had to date. An extraordinary feat in human history, and the first major win for 'neurodiversity'.

So, it is a similar feat that many organizations are trying to replicate when they look to hire and put to work people with different brains. They are curating the next 'Wright Flyer' idea that will give them competitive advantage by the creation of innovative products or services, or by solving thorny problems. A capability that people with different brains can bring, that others cannot – to turbo-charge PEIP and take an organization (and society) to a whole new level of productivity. Who are the next Wright brothers? Well, whoever they are you want them in *your* organization.

Harness the intelligence of the machines

In 1965, Wernher von Braun, one of the fathers of rocket-assisted space flight, purportedly said the following when asked if man will be completely replaced by machines in space flight:

> The best computer is a man, and it's the only one that can be mass-produced by unskilled labour.

In other words, humans are ultimately the most cost-effective high-performance machines in the universe and, even better, they are easily and cheaply mass-produced (ha-ha). At the very least, the economics favour the human machines over the man-made machines as far out as anyone can see. Thank goodness for that, right?

To further the point, one can regularly find headlines in the press about how 'machines are taking our jobs'. In fact, the first instances of these types of headlines began appearing in the press in the late 18th century, when new machines called 'stocking frames' were coming online to increase production of textiles. In fact, this machine led to the advent of the cotton gin, which in turn led to the formation of the Luddites in 1811. The Luddites were a group of textiles workers who violently rebelled against the cotton gin. Workers were already becoming restive during this period as there were many challenges coming to fore in the early Industrial Revolution; for example, the increasingly adversarial relationship between owners/management and the workforce. However, this new machine came along and was a step too far. The workers were so upset about the threat this technology represented to their livelihoods, they planned and executed regular attacks, sneaking into factories at night to destroy the machines they perceived were taking their jobs. As we know, this was to no avail, as the textiles industry remains highly mechanized today. In fact, the term Luddite is still used to describe people who refuse to accept that technological advances are potentially a good thing in the long run.

To be clear, without a doubt, the machines we invent create large-scale disruption to individuals, organizations, industries and whole societies. It is a fact: people lose their livelihoods and the misery this causes is real and should not be discounted. However, data shows that at every technological inflection point (the point where a new technology development disrupts the status quo) within a relatively short period of time, people find new and often better jobs by either creating a new role (or business) or learning to *harness* the technology to their benefit. The challenge and the hardship are more often working through that period of disruption and getting to the other side where new opportunity awaits.

Let's look at an example. If you have ever been to London, you will have seen, and probably taken, a black cab (officially known as a 'hackney carriage'). They are ubiquitous across this vast capital city. The thing you may not know about the black cab driver, is that they spend around three years doing a training course called The Knowledge. The Knowledge is literally the memorization of every street in central London and using this information to decide the quickest route to the destination. The examination to become a London cabby is possibly one of the most difficult tests in the world – demanding years of study to memorize the labyrinthine city's 25,000 streets and any business or landmark on them.

Over three years, a student will have logged more than 50,000 miles on motorbike and foot across London, the equivalent of two circumnavigations of the Earth, to build the knowledge required to become a certified London taxi driver. The student will need a thorough knowledge, primarily, of the area within a six-mile radius of Charing Cross station. They will need to know all the streets, housing estates, parks and open spaces, government offices and departments, financial and commercial centres, diplomatic premises, town halls, registry offices, hospitals, places of worship, sports stadiums and leisure centres, airline offices, stations, hotels, clubs, theatres, cinemas, museums, art galleries, schools, police stations and headquarters buildings, civil, criminal and coroner courts, prisons, and places of interest to tourists. In fact, anywhere a taxi passenger might ask to be taken.

Successfully completing this challenge earns the cabbie their coveted 'green badge' and puts them in a position to buy (or lease) their first vehicle and hit the streets in one of the city's famous black taxis. This is an immense personal investment in one's career. And for this dedication, for decades, the black cab driver's job was mainly safe from any real competition. In fact, they are the only taxi drivers licensed to pick people up, curb side; all other taxis must be booked in advance. They had an enormous advantage over any other mode of car-bound transport. Unfortunately, it's a phenomenal achievement that is quickly becoming undermined by GPS technology.

On 2 July 2012, Uber was launched onto the streets of London. Uber was a big success in cities like San Francisco, where it was first launched in 2009. Suddenly, in London, you could summon within minutes a driver from an app on your phone, and this driver was around 25 per cent cheaper than a black cab. Sure, this driver did not have The Knowledge – not even close. However, this driver had the next best thing: GPS and Google Maps. This driver was harnessing the intelligence of the machines to compete very effectively with the black cabs. Within months, Uber was having a massive impact on the revenue and profits of black cab drivers. The black cab drivers mounted protests in London, blocking the main thoroughfares around the city, bringing it to a standstill during rush hour. Unfortunately, like the Luddites before them, this backfired badly. Essentially, they were giving Uber free publicity and as a result the number of people downloading the app and 'taking an Uber' increased four-fold in the one month after the strikes – an 'own goal' as the football-mad British public call it (ie accidentally scoring a goal for the other team). Suddenly, they were faced with an existential threat to their livelihoods, and it was not going away any time soon.

Unfortunately, this is just the first wave of disruption for black cab drivers. Given the pace of technological improvements, it will not be long before the development of a Sat Nav algorithm that works better than the most ingenious cabbie, before a voice-activated GPS or a driverless car can zip a passenger from Piccadilly to Putney more efficiently than any Knowledge graduate. In late 2018 the UK Government announced plans for the first driverless transport services by 2021, including a driverless bus service crossing the Forth Bridge to Edinburgh, Scotland, and self-driving taxis in four London boroughs.

London is classed as one of the few 'mega-cities' in Europe and has some of the most challenging driving conditions in the world, caused by a combination of its complex historic road layout, congestion and well-travelled road surfaces. This has made the city ideal for developing and testing driverless cars. Blue Vision Labs, a London-based firm that specializes in mapping street layouts using car-mounted smartphones, is a fast-growing company recently bought by Uber rival, Lyft. So, it is pretty clear that the next wave of disruption is about to wash over the traditional black cab drivers.

However, is this the end of the story? That's it, no more black cabs? Is it inevitable that all black cab drivers are going to lose their jobs in the near future? No. As with other technology inflections over the past 200 years or so, this is the beginning of a new adventure for those that have invested in The Knowledge. First of all, a number of enterprising black cab drivers have been selling their innate understanding of London's streets and driving patterns to companies like Blue Vision. Many others are either augmenting their taxi work or going to work full-time for the companies that are developing the software for driverless cars in London – helping the intelligent machines become even more intelligent, using human intelligence to do this. The other bonus? These jobs are better paying and much less stressful than driving the streets of London!

Second, many black cab drivers are planning to harness the new driverless car technology to give them economic leverage (more revenue/profit). Most black cab drivers either own their taxi or lease it from a third-party company. Once driverless cabs come online, a cabbie can buy or lease one or more of these new cabs, and instead of driving only one cab themselves, they can own and manage a business of multiple black cabs that drive themselves! They can literally be in two, three, four places at once. Again, making more money with less stress!

This is what we see throughout history: humans harness the machines to eventually create better jobs for themselves, often making more money. Research published over the past decade by two eminent MIT professors of economics, Erik Brynjolfsson and Andrew McAfee, details the many instances where this has been the case. Brynjolfsson is a professor at the MIT Sloan School of Management and co-director with McAfee of the MIT Initiative on the Digital Economy; McAfee is also the associate director of the Center for Digital Business at the MIT Sloan School of Management. Both have for years been studying in detail the ways information technology affects businesses, business and people as a whole. They have co-written two best-selling books, *Race Against the Machine* (2011), and *The Second Machine Age* (2014), which are highly readable and expertly researched/written.

Brynjolfsson and McAfee have been looking to answer some pretty big questions around the widespread belief that 'machines, it seems, can do almost anything human beings can'. They have been providing their expertly researched views on what this premise means for business, workers and society at large. Will there be any jobs left for people? Will machines take over not just low-skilled tasks but high-skilled, high-paid ones too? If a man and a machine work side by side, which one will (or should) make the decisions? What will this automation do to people's incomes? These are some of the questions facing people, companies, industries, and economies as digital technologies transform business. For sure, these questions are not about the far-off future; this is the reality today, and a reality that is accelerating as we head towards 2020, 2030 and beyond (Bernstein and Raman, 2015). In other words, the questions they are posing and attempting to answer are here now, and most of business and society are not fully ready to tackle them. And most importantly, they also look at the reasons why, with all the fantastic technology, we are not increasing our productivity at work.

In a widely read and shared 2015 interview in *Harvard Business Review*, Erik and Andrew summarized some of their findings. For example, they observed that the United States enjoyed a jump in labour productivity growth in the mid-1990s; economic research by them and others concluded that IT drove that growth in productivity. However, it didn't last long. By the mid-2000s labour productivity growth had slowed down to pre-1996 levels, and it has stayed relatively low since then; thus, why we are where we are today (Bernstein and Raman, 2015). They also agree that there has been a loss of innovative organizational thinking and, as they say, a loss of business 'dynamism' in making best use of and organizing themselves to take full advantage of emerging technology. As Brynjolfsson put it:

> Technologies continue to race ahead, but there has unfortunately been a drop in business dynamism. This is an opportunity for entrepreneurs to think of ways of using humans in new applications, combining them with technology. We call that racing with machines as opposed to racing against them. For some reason, business hasn't been creating new jobs as effectively as in the past (Bernstein and Raman, 2015).

Sound familiar?

McAfee adds that, despite technology racing ahead:

> Let's be clear about one thing: digital technologies are doing for human brainpower what the steam engine and related technologies did for human muscle power during the Industrial Revolution. They're allowing us to overcome many limitations rapidly and to open up new frontiers with unprecedented speed. It's a very big deal. But how exactly it will play out is uncertain (Bernstein and Raman, 2015).

They believe that, despite the challenges, the coming second machine age will be better for us all for the simple reason that, thanks to digital technologies, we'll be able to produce more: more health care, more education, more entertainment, and more of all the other material goods and services we value. And we'll be able to extend this bounty to more and more people around the world while treading lightly on the planet's resources. McAfee said: 'We haven't experienced anything quite like this before. Even though machines did more and more work and the population grew rapidly for almost 200 years, the value of human labour actually rose. You could see this in the steady increase in the average worker's wages' (Bernstein and Raman, 2015).

Brynjolfsson and McAfee bring together a range of statistics, examples, and arguments that employment prospects are grim for many today not because technology has stagnated, but instead because we humans and our organizations aren't keeping up. The problem is, as they put it, we have hit a wall of 'the Great Decoupling' (Bernstein and Raman, 2015), where the rate of increase in people productivity has slowed alongside a stagnation of labour value and wages – the first time in history we have seen this. Until around 2005, there was a long-held (and accurate) notion that technology inflections eventually help everyone and increase wages – all boats float on this incoming tide. However, since the Great Decoupling, we have for the first time found that this kind of success is not automatic or inevitable. *It depends on the nature of the technology, and on the way individuals, organizations, and policies adapt.* And therein lies the problem – a challenge that we have been looking at (and offering solutions for) in this book.

So, as Brynjolfsson and McAfee have found, we are in a different period where the laws of economics and the impact of technology are not holding true any longer. As they put it, if we increase business dynamism and focus on aligning people to technology (PEIP?), workers will do as they always have done: harness the technology to make themselves, organizations and society better than before (Bernstein and Raman, 2015). They go on to describe how, if we align people to the new technologies, we are on the cusp of reinventing the laws of economics and creating productivity levels that have never been seen before – not only will we be better than before, we will 'turbo-charge' (Brynjolfsson and McAfee, 2014) the future. For example, they point out the 'uber-efficiencies' (Bernstein and Raman, 2015) that can be created by digital technology. At its most elemental level, digital technology redefines the productivity and the value equation.

McAfee says:

> For example, digital technologies allow us to make copies at almost zero cost. Each copy is a perfect replica, and each copy can be transmitted almost anywhere on the planet nearly instantaneously. Those were not characteristics of the Industrial Age, but this is standard for digital goods, and that leads to some unusual outcomes that we are only beginning to understand how to harness, and more importantly quantify. Products like the iPhone are just 11 years old. Autonomous cars first drove on American highways nine years ago' (Bernstein and Raman, 2015).

In 2014, Baylor College of Medicine in Houston announced that it had used IBM's Watson technology to generate hypotheses about proteins and cancer growth, many of which proved to be correct (Saporito, 2014). The point is, we are only at the beginning of humans harnessing intelligent machines to make us better.

Additionally, humans still have a big lead on the machines, in terms of our capabilities versus theirs. Brynjolfsson and McAfee point out three areas in which humans still, and may always, lead machines:

- 'One is high-end creativity that generates things like great new business ideas, scientific breakthroughs, novels that grip you, and so on. Technology will only amplify the abilities of people who are good at these things.

- The second category is emotion, interpersonal relations, caring, nurturing, coaching, motivating, leading, and so on. Through millions of years of evolution, we've got good at deciphering other people's body language and signals, and finishing people's sentences. Machines are way behind there.
- The third is dexterity, mobility. It's unbelievably hard to get a robot to walk across a crowded restaurant, bus a table, take the dishes back into the kitchen, put them in the sink without breaking them, and do it all without terrifying the restaurant's patrons. Sensing and manipulation are hard for robots' (Bernstein and Raman, 2015).

Contrary to what we read or see in the media, according to those who research this space, there is much to be optimistic about, if we change our thinking and look to make more dynamic use of the technology.

Organizational and institutional innovations can recombine human capital with machines to create broad-based productivity growth. When these things are digitized – when they're converted into bits that can be stored on a computer and sent over a network – they acquire some weird and wonderful properties. They're subject to different economics, where abundance is the norm rather than scarcity. As we'll show, digital goods are not like physical ones, and these differences matter.

Erik and Andrew conclude that 'We're encouraged by the emerging opportunities to combine digital, organizational, and human capital to create wealth: technology, entrepreneurship, and education are an extraordinary opportunity' (Bernstein and Raman, 2015).

However, too often, the intellectually lazy thing to do is to look at an existing, traditional organization structure, a long-held process and a 'certain way' of doing things, and say, 'If it ain't broke, then why fix it?'; there it is – we lose the power of harnessing the machines. If we just look at something and say, 'How can we get a machine to do that work?', we miss the point. It does take a certain amount of creativity and a little bit of work to think and do differently, but we do see that every time people think differently, and choose the path of innovation augmented with machines, we create value where there was little to none before. It is true, it takes a lot more courage to say, 'How can we have this machine and this human work together to do something never done before and create something that will be more valuable in the marketplace?' However, if we embrace the machines and *harness* them, we will turbo-charge our world.

Digital at home, digital at work

The digital home has crept up on us steadily over recent years. If you think back to digital technology you used in your home in say, 1990, you realize just how much has changed in a relatively short period of time. In 1990, you may have had a cordless home phone and a CD player – a couple of new gadgets that foretold what was coming – but that was about the extent of it.

At work, there wasn't much more digital technology to speak of either. Virtually no PCs, no PowerPoint, no Excel, no mobile phone. In 1990, in the Andersen Consulting office in Columbus, Ohio, where I had just started working, telephone calls came into a main switchboard, and announcements were made over a loudspeaker across the entire office for you to pick up your call from the nearest phone 'on line one'. We did have one new tool to use: the Octel voice mail service (which I believe was an analogue system). It was the forerunner of email, in that you could use it to send a message to one (or many), send a message to a distribution list, and could easily reply to messages. Company communications were sent out over Octel as well. Friday social gatherings after work were regularly coordinated using Octel, just like we use Facebook or similar today. Octel was the 'cool' new technology of the day.

Fast forward to 2019, and we are awash in digital technology, particularly in our home lives. Many of us have an Amazon Echo or Google Home device. Most people have at least one PC or laptop (or both) in the home. Additionally, it is not uncommon that there are several tablet devices in the family, and of course everyone in the house has a smartphone, and many more still have a smart watch on their wrists. Some households control heating, lighting, security cameras and even home alarms from their tablets or smartphones or watch. I don't know about your home, but our Amazon Echo is in constant use. In the morning Alexa lets us know the latest news headlines, the weather and, most importantly, when the next train or bus is coming along, and whether there is any disruption to the service. In the evening, Alexa is put to work choosing music playlists and dimming dining room lights for dinner time. Many homes are connected to the IoT, whereby home appliances such as the refrigerator are always connected to the internet and can order basic food staples like milk, eggs, etc. when it detects that these items are running low. In 1990, we would have thought this was the stuff of sci-fi movies, rather than our reality today.

Also fast forward to 2019 in the workplace – much has changed here as well. Gone is the Octel system, though voice mail is still used to a certain extent, but has mainly been replaced by email, messaging or texting. Most employees have access to a desk-based PC, or a laptop if they are on the go. Many employers also provide a smartphone to their employees, and a few even provide a tablet or smartwatch.

The first PCs and laptops were rolled out in many offices around 1992. Compaq, IBM and Apple provided some of the first models to be mass produced and bought/deployed by companies to improve people productivity. Microsoft provided the first graphical interfaces for these new machines in the late 1980s and from about 1991 it started to become ubiquitous, with the release of Windows 3.1 in 1992. This MS DOS-based operating system made it possible for non-techie types, like most employees at the time, to relatively easily interact with these new desktop machines. Around the same time, Microsoft began including a bundled 'Office' package of PowerPoint, Word and Excel programs to turn the desktop (and laptops) into powerful people productivity tools. Around the same time, they launched versions of Windows NT which began the networking of PCs to each other and/or to servers. In parallel, companies like SAP and Oracle developed sophisticated on-premises software called Enterprise Resource Planning (ERP) to automate much of an organization's back office.

Within a couple of years, technology at work took a great leap forward. People were using email to communicate (the death knell of the internal paper-based memo), PowerPoint to do whizzy presentations, Excel to do sophisticated spreadsheets, and Word to write memos or letters to be faxed or physically posted. Most big (and medium-sized) companies bought an ERP to automate the back-office functions to reduce costs and improve organization productivity, and create access to real-time data for decision making. The implementation of these technologies was big business for software and consulting firms. Firms like Andersen Consulting, Deloitte, E&Y and Price Waterhouse set up global practices of thousands of consultants who performed business process analysis to streamline work and then configure these ERP powerful systems to run the back end of large global companies more efficiently. Another area of investment was to ensure employees were taught how to use these systems effectively. Millions of dollars were invested in training programmes and change management to align people to the new technology to get the most return on investment. Steadily throughout the 1990s more and more companies (big and small) invested in the hardware and software to create efficiencies and make best use of the internet and increasingly powerful computing technology. The zenith of this investment in technology and change was in 1999 when there was a rush to address the perceived Y2K challenge; warnings were raised because many long-standing computer programs represented four-digit years with only the final two digits – potentially making the year 2000 indistinguishable from 1900; yet more business for software makers and consultants!

From 1990 to 2000, technology-driven change at work was unprecedented and transformational. On our desks were PCs more powerful than anything NASA had during the Apollo programme. The software became easier and easier for humans to interact with, and improvement in people productivity, particularly in the United States, hit all-time highs. Then in the mid-1990s the flip mobile phone became ubiquitous. Technology at work went mobile! In less than 10 years, the workplace had been transformed. At this point, home was changing as well, but not at anywhere near the pace that was observed at work. True, the PC became a must-have device in the home, and laptops were also appearing, but the consumer market for home-based software and computing was just getting started. Work technology was pretty cutting edge and significantly more advanced than anything we had at home.

Then, as we have seen in earlier chapters, 9/11 happened. A geopolitical and economic shockwave was unleashed that effectively stalled, for a time, the unprecedented level of investment in technology at work and, more importantly, aligning people to the technology. Hardware and software developers, as well as implementers, were forced to find revenue elsewhere. This accelerated the bringing forward of a whole host of new consumer digital electronics, such as the smartphone, as well as applications or 'apps'. The year 2001 became an inflection point where the focus moved from being almost completely about digital technology for work to more of a focus on the individual consumer and their homes.

Which brings us to 2020. Have a look around next time you are in the office. Digital technology at work has not really changed that much since 2001. We still have a desktop or laptop, we use a mouse and keyboard to interact with it, and the operating system is still Microsoft Windows or Apple Mac. The printer/copy machine may be hooked up to the Wi-Fi, and probably breaks down a bit less (or not?). I bet your office coffee machine has become much more sophisticated than it was in 1990. The space you work in is probably more comfortable and relaxed than 29 years ago, with sofas, coffee tables, even 'quiet spaces' for a quick nap. Your main device may be a tablet, but those have been around for 10 years now. You will certainly use some apps on your device, but the operating systems and user interfaces are largely the same as 1990. The systems you access, like SAP or Oracle, are still rather clunky but certainly less so than 10 years ago. They will have some applications that are 'software as a service' cloud applications, but you will have to frequently move from one antiquated system to another, maybe even have to do multiple different sign-ins on your keyboard, with different passwords that you may have forgotten and have to look up. You probably have to go to fairly regular training courses to learn the next version of the systems you use, and take a day or two out per year for your trouble.

Yet, when you are in your home or car, many of the devices and apps you use you don't need a keyboard or a mouse. In many cases you actually speak to them, and they quickly do your bidding. The software you use is almost all cloud-based apps that work seamlessly across all of your devices with log-ins remembered by the device after it scans your thumb print or your face. Even better, these apps require zero training to learn how to use them effectively. All your home data, including pictures, music and videos, resides in the cloud and can be accessed from most of your devices. In fact, the whole family can access this digital data and services easily and you did not have to hire a consultant to set it all up for you.

Penn Schoen Berland (PSB), a market research, political polling and strategic consulting firm based in the United States, ran a global study of individuals working in a variety of different industries to capture what they expect from their employers as we move into the future. They uncovered some compelling findings (Twele, nd):

- Employees are generally happy in their jobs, but as communications and productivity technology advances, they are becoming increasingly dissatisfied with workplace tools and capabilities.
- Though they will make do with the use of analogue equipment, like landlines and desktops, if they have to, they're ready for a workplace that can accommodate their changing lifestyles and how they consume technology at home.
- In addition, 44 per cent of those surveyed didn't feel their workspace was 'smart enough', and their biggest time wasters at work were related to technology, including slow or glitchy software and devices.
- One in three individuals said the technology they had in their homes was more advanced than that at work. Unless addressed, this number will likely increase in the coming years.

- It's often thought that employees, particularly millennials, seek out things like ping pong tables and free food, or low-tech perks, in a workplace. However, the study found that just 29 per cent of respondents prefer low-tech perks compared to 58 per cent who would choose high-tech perks, like virtual or augmented reality and the IoT.

So clearly there is a gap in expectations of technology at home and work, which has developed over recent years and is growing as fast as the next clever app or gadget comes along that people have at their disposal. But how to fix this? Surely this must mean massive new investment in software, hardware and gadgets to bridge the gap. Most organizations are still trying to get value and cost savings from the last implementation (probably not fully completed) of an ERP and new hardware. You can imagine the look on the CFO's face when HR and the CEO come knocking for the cash to close the gap. Yeah, that is not a conversation that anyone wants to have. In the next chapter, we will outline how to prepare for and handle this conversation. However, first we need to understand how we got here and what the roadmap looks like for the way forward. To do this we need to look at the history of human capital technology to see how we got where we are today.

An (abbreviated) history of the human resource information system (HRIS)

The first instance of HR processes and 'technology' goes back to the mid-1800s as workers began to flood into factories from the rural farms on which they used to work – see Figure 4.1. This created a volume of people that became overwhelming for most companies. To handle this and manage the costs effectively for paying and deploying people, factories had rather large offices with row after row of desks manned (and yes, they were all men) with giant ledger books for entering costs and payroll, and index card drawers with the name, address, age and basic info on the employee. These were the first instances of 'white-collar workers'; young men in suits and ties with some academic qualifications, given the title of 'clerk'. These were prestigious and well-paid jobs and ideal for starting out on one's professional career.

And thus it was for over 100 years, until just after World War II when the first mainframe computers started to come online and help companies store and process large volumes of data, including personnel records and rudimentary payroll systems. This was a major leap in automation of the back office,

FIGURE 4.1 The evolution of HR technology

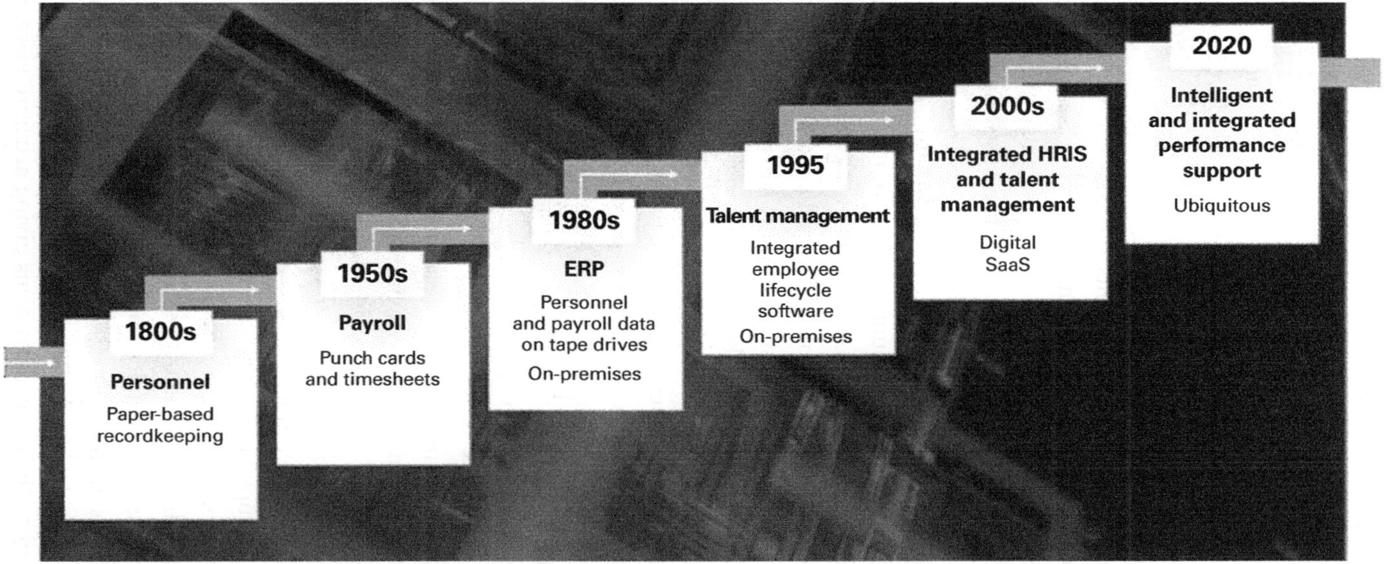

1800s
Personnel
Paper-based recordkeeping

1950s
Payroll
Punch cards and timesheets

1980s
ERP
Personnel and payroll data on tape drives
On-premises

1995
Talent management
Integrated employee lifecycle software
On-premises

2000s
Integrated HRIS and talent management
Digital
SaaS

2020
Intelligent and integrated performance support
Ubiquitous

using technology to create significant costs savings (and unemployment for white-collar clerks). This was the 'punch card' and 'tape drive data' era, which allowed organizations to use timesheets to track employee time and effort, and then pay accurately, by the hour, or salary in a much more efficient manner. This also provided real-time data to the finance department and managers to help manage costs and to measure productivity of the workforce. It also allowed the 'personnel department' to hold basic data on employees and pay them with automated checking or directly into their bank accounts. These were important developments for both the worker and the organization, and offered increasing efficiencies, which was all the rage in the 1950s.

Next, in the early 1980s, software companies like SAP and PeopleSoft developed versions of ERP software that focused on the back office of the 'human resources department'. HR, as it was now known, could automate not only payroll but other aspects of the HR function as well. During this period many large and medium-sized international organizations began to set up 'HR service centres' to handle the increasingly large volumes of HR transactions, including payroll and benefits like health insurance, expenses management, pensions and similar. These software platforms also included employee 'self-service' capabilities, allowing individuals to handle many basic transactions themselves by accessing the HR system.

This period was a major inflection point for HR organizations, as the number of things they became responsible for expanded rapidly. Fortunately, these software programs gave them leverage to handle what the business was asking for. The challenge was that these systems were complex, clunky to use and required small armies of expensive consultants to configure and train the workforce to use them. The vogue at the time was taking these 'on-premises systems' (licensed commercial models where the software resided on the organization's premises), SAP HR or PeopleSoft, and creating highly customized versions to fit the organization's HR processes. These programs often took two or more years, with costs running into the tens of millions. Major investments were required, and the disruption to the businesses while implementing these platforms was equivalent to having years of major roadworks on the main highways of a nation. It was costly, often painful, and the return on investment was often difficult to measure.

Nonetheless, once implemented and online, these HR platforms were powerful tools for the organization to manage large (and small) numbers of internationally deployed workers. Real-time data became available and was often linked to the financial systems giving accurate views on the cost and productivity of the organization.

In the 1990s, once the automation of the back office of HR was underway, attention shifted to the idea of better managing talent through creating an integrated talent management lifecycle. As we outlined in earlier chapters, the integration of goals, recruiting, learning, deployment, succession, etc, was a major strategic shift in the role of HR, which was made possible by the evolution of HR platforms from a 'system of record' to a full suite of talent systems. In 1997, Dave Ulrich's idea of putting in place HR business partners to support the business in better managing talent was one that resonated in this new era of HR and was adopted by organizations, globally.

In a 1998 *Harvard Business Review* article, Ulrich laid out a new paradigm for the HR role. He was answering the question, 'Should HR be abolished?' as a non-value-add drag on the organization performance (Ulrich, 1998):

> The question for senior managers, then, is not should we do away with HR? but what should we do with HR? The answer is: create an entirely new role and agenda for the field that focuses it not on traditional HR activities, such as staffing and compensation, but on outcomes. HR should not be defined by what it does but by what it delivers – results that enrich the organization's value to customers, investors, and employees.

More specifically, HR can help deliver organizational excellence in the following four ways:

- First, HR should become a partner with senior and line managers in strategy execution, helping to move planning from the conference room to the marketplace.
- Second, it should become an expert in the way work is organized and executed, delivering administrative efficiency to ensure that costs are reduced while quality is maintained.
- Third, it should become a champion for employees, vigorously representing their concerns to senior management and at the same time working to increase employee contribution; that is, employees' commitment to the organization and their ability to deliver results.
- And finally, HR should become an agent of continuous transformation, shaping processes and a culture that together improve an organization's capacity for change.

The question of whether HR should be abolished was being driven by the new reality that many HR transactions and operations were being automated by ERP technology, putting a focus on HR of 'What now?' and 'Do we need HR anymore?' Ulrich argued that if HR were to remain configured as it was in 1998 – transactional and the 'policy police' – he would have to answer the question with a resounding, 'Yes – abolish the thing!'

What he was outlining was the future role of HR: a focus on 'achieving organizational excellence'. Become a strategic adviser focused on building organization engagement, innovation and performance. A new era of HR had begun – one that was facilitated by a new era of HRIS, which put in place an integrated human capital lifecycle – and, largely, HR answered the call for change.

Fast forward to the modern HRIS of the 21st century

The 21st-century advent of 'cloud computing' created the next era of HR: 'HR on demand'. Cloud computing is the on-demand availability of computer system resources, especially data storage and computing power, without direct active management by the user. The term is generally used to describe data centres available to many users over the internet typically accessed by easy-to-use applications that reside on a smartphone or tablet (Ulrich, 1998). Immense computing power was literally at the fingertips of individuals. Amazon was one of the first to recognize the power of cloud computing and set out to base its entire retail sales and operations on the idea: create a networked, easy-to-use online store where you could buy just about anything. Cloud computing, unlike previous technologies, was all about the end user, the consumer, and creating the ability to shop 24/7, from the comfort of your tablet, while sitting on the sofa.

Suddenly, complicated and clunky software became intuitive (did not require training to use) and available 24/7 on PCs and hand-helds alike. This development saw a number of new HRIS startups established to take on SAP and Peoplesoft, with HR technology that was vastly simplified, much easier to implement and focused more on the end-user than on the HR and IT teams. Companies like SuccessFactors and Workday were born in the early 2000s, and both grew rapidly. They sought to compete directly with SAP and PeopleSoft (which was now owned by Oracle, who bought PeopleSoft from Workday founders Aneel Bhusri and Dave Duffield) using this new on-demand, consumer-oriented model for HR.

With cloud computing, HR transactions and operations for both manager and employee could be 'self-serve' with little more than high-level support from HR and IT. Managers could conduct most of the key talent management activities for their teams, such as recruiting, goals, learning, deployment, compensation and succession, using relatively simple apps and hand-held devices such as tablets or smartphones. Managers had access to sophisticated people analytics and unprecedented amounts of information to help increasingly virtual teams across widespread geographies. Employees could get direct access to all of their personal information and could easily download a pay stub or other information they might need. No longer did they need to talk to an HR person to get pay information and a reference for getting a mortgage, for example. So, by 2020, most companies around the world are either putting in place a programme or concluding a programme to transform HR on the back of these new technologies, changing the role of HR yet again.

Digital at work, finally!

The net-net of these developments in the latest HRIS technology is to put businesses and employees on track to be as digital at work as we are at home. I am surprised how often I hear C-level executives say they want people's interactions with the organizational technology 'to be like Facebook' (or other similar cloud application). I have seen large, successful organizations make very large investments in moving off their legacy on-premises PeopleSoft or SAP HR systems with the value case for doing so nothing more than 'improved user experience and engagement'. I often get to see C-level executives' reactions when they first see cloud HRIS technology, and it is one of 'amazement' and 'possibilities' when they see that they can create a consumer-like online experience for their employees. These meetings very often turn into action, as creating this kind of experience for employees becomes a strategic imperative. Let me give an example of the power of this approach.

In SAP, we have undergone a programme of shifting most talent management activities to the manager by using SuccessFactors. In December 2011, SAP bought SuccessFactors, which was one of SAP's first big moves into the cloud computing business. One of the main reasons for buying SuccessFactors was to use the platform to transform SAP's HR organization. SAP wanted to push the centre of gravity for managing employee engagement and performance down to the manager and employee and away from it being an HR-run set of processes.

When I joined SAP in 2014, I quickly learned how successful this approach was. By 2016, I was responsible for most of the talent management activities for my direct reports as well as their direct reports. One area that I was particularly concerned about having the skills for was around compensation for my teams. It had been an area that, throughout my career, HR did for me with my input. Now I was responsible for deciding, actioning and concluding people's salary increases, bonuses, long-term incentives, etc. This was new ground for me. However, I quickly discovered when I went into the SuccessFactors app, into the Compensation tile on the portal, that it was clear what I needed to do. I had all the data I needed to take a meritocratic approach to dividing up my budget for each individual's compensation. I also had data on compa-ratios and other key indicators that were required to help me with my decisions. Additionally, it was a simple interface that was easily understandable. I completed the job across 14 direct reports in about 45 minutes. It was not much more complicated than buying some clothes online.

Operationally, HR was there to review my work and suggest changes (all in the Compensation workflow), and I could make adjustments as needed. Behaviourally, it completely changed my views on fair and balanced compensation. I knew that I was not going to be able to blame HR if someone was unhappy with my decisions; I had to be very deliberate and fact-driven in all of my actions, and be able to explain those decisions to my team. This is the mindset that is created when the centre of gravity of HR decisions is pushed out to the manager and employee.

What was most evident, though, was not only did the system make me look like a compensation expert, it was very easy to do and required no training. In fact, I could have done the entire exercise from my sofa on my iPad, if I'd chosen to. The experience matched my digital experience at home. *Digital at Home, Digital at Work.* Finally.

References

Bernstein, A and Raman, A (2015) The great decoupling: An interview with Erik Brynjolfsson and Andrew McAfee, *Harvard Business Review*, June, pp 66–74. Available from: https://hbr.org/2015/06/the-great-decoupling (archived at https://perma.cc/X8ZS-KLVU)

Brynjolfsson, E and McAfee, A (2011) *Race Against the Machine: How the digital revolution is accelerating innovation, driving productivity, and irreversibly transforming employment and the economy*, Digital Frontier Press, Lexington, MA

Brynjolfsson, E and McAfee, A (2014) *The Second Machine Age: Work, progress, and prosperity in a time of brilliant technologies*, W W Norton & Co, New York and London

Flood, A, Terry, J, Johnson, S, et al (2017) Winning the fight for female talent: how to gain the diversity edge through inclusive recruitment, *PricewaterhouseCoopers LLP*, March. Available from: https://www.pwc.com/gx/en/about/diversity/iwd/iwd-female-talent-report-web.pdf (archived at https://perma.cc/UX4U-DHPV)

Glassdoor Team (2014) What job seekers really think about your diversity and inclusion stats [blog] *Glassdoor for Employers*, 17 November. Available from: https://www.glassdoor.com/employers/blog/diversity/ (archived at https://perma.cc/7XDR-WZTR)

Landel, M (2015) Gender balance and the link to performance [blog] *McKinsey & Co*, February. Available from: https://www.mckinsey.com/featured-insights/leadership/gender-balance-and-the-link-to-performance (archived at https://perma.cc/7CHF-MS4X)

Ma, Q, Ma, Y, Dai, X, Ren, T, et al. (2018) Regeneration of functional alveoli by adult human SOX9+ airway basal cell transplantation, *Protein & Cell*, 9 (3), pp 267–282. Available from: https://doi.org/10.1007/s13238-018-0506-y (archived at https://perma.cc/3338-HR7B)

Mislinski, J (2019) Demographic trends for the 50-and-older work force [blog] *Advisor Perspectives*, May. Available from: https://www.advisorperspectives.com/dshort/updates/2019/04/10/demographic-trends-for-the-50-and-older-work-force (archived at https://perma.cc/DPB2-469Q)

Muntané, G, Farré, X, Rodríguez, J A, Pegueroles, C, Hughes, D A, de Magalhães, J P, Gabaldón, T and Navarro, A (2018) Biological processes modulating longevity across primates: A phylogenetic genome-phenome analysis, *Molecular Biology and Evolution*, 35 (8), pp 1990–2004. Available from: http://dx.doi.org/10.1093/molbev/msy105 (archived at https://perma.cc/ADJ8-64AQ)

OECD (2016) Historical population data and projections (1950–2050) [Online data set] *ODCD.stat*. Available from: https://stats.oecd.org/Index.aspx?DataSetCode=POP_PROJ (archived at https://perma.cc/RN2J-M6MR)

Phillips, S (2019) Autism at work: Why it works for SAP, *Telegraph*, 4 April. Available from: https://www.telegraph.co.uk/business/autism-in-workplace/why-it-works-for-sap/ (archived at https://perma.cc/WB2F-L5V4)

Rudy, L J (2019) Top 10 autism friendly employers: Options are growing for autistic job-seekers [blog] *VeryWellHealth*, 30 March. Available from: https://www.verywellhealth.com/top-autism-friendly-employers-4159784 (archived at https://perma.cc/5HDF-B6QG)

Sancier-Sultan, S and Sperling, J (2018) Women and the future of work: A window of opportunity in Western Europe? [blog] *McKinsey & Co*, November. Available from: https://www.mckinsey.com/featured-insights/gender-equality/women-and-the-future-of-work-a-window-of-opportunity-in-western-europe (archived at https://perma.cc/SX8B-D95T)

Saporito, B (2014) IBM Watson's startling cancer coup, *Time*, 28 August. Available from: https://time.com/3208716/ibm-watson-cancer/ (archived at https://perma.cc/82BX-NNBK)

Singer, J (1999) Why Can't You Be Normal for Once in Your Life? In *Disability Discourse*, ed M Corker, Open University Press, p 64

Sodexo (2018) Sodexo's gender balance study 2018: Expanded outcomes over 5 years, Sodexo Operations LLC. Available from: https://www.sodexo.com/files/live/sites/sdxcom-global/files/PDF/Media/2018_Gender-Balance-Study_EN.pdf (archived at https://perma.cc/5XSE-MFMB)

Spencer, B (2016) About to retire? Carry on working into your 60s if you want to stay healthy, says medical chief [blog] *Mail Online*, 8 December. Available from: https://www.dailymail.co.uk/news/article-4011700/Dame-Sally-Davies-chief-medical-officer-advises-60s-working-stay-healthy.html (archived at https://perma.cc/Z2E9-7C69)

Turban, S, Wu, D and Zhang, L (2019) Research: When gender diversity makes firms more productive [blog] *Harvard Business Review*, 11 February. Available from: https://hbr.org/2019/02/research-when-gender-diversity-makes-firms-more-productive (archived at https://perma.cc/WJC8-446A)

Twele, C (nd) What do employees want the most? Modern technology that lets them excel in their work [blog] *The Hartman Blog*. Available from: https://hartmanadvisors.com/employees-want-modern-technology-lets-excel-work/ (archived at https://perma.cc/R4KQ-TDXB)

Ulrich, D (1998) A new mandate for human resources, *Harvard Business Review*, Jan/Feb. Available from: https://hbr.org/1998/01/a-new-mandate-for-human-resources (archived at https://perma.cc/3QDP-7KVL)

US Bureau of Labor Statistics (2017) Table 3.3. In: Employment Projections Program, USBLS, Washington, DC. Available from: https://www.bls.gov/emp/tables/civilian-labor-force-participation-rate.htm (archived at https://perma.cc/HL5D-PY7R)

Wu, C, Odden, M C, Fisher, G G and Stawski, R S (2016) Association of retirement age with mortality: A population-based longitudinal study among older adults in the USA, *Journal of Epidemiology and Community Health*, 70, pp 917–923. Available from: http://dx.doi.org/10.1136/jech-2015-207097 (archived at https://perma.cc/G85C-TMPR)

05

Making the case for change

The optimists' case: it's a strong one

Hopefully, by now, you are leaning more towards optimism than pessimism about the future of people engagement, innovation and performance, as well as for our future economic prosperity. Clearly there are formidable challenges, but we have outlined ready solutions there for the taking if we think and act differently. The Pessimists say that organizations will not make the structural change required to take advantage of new digital technologies and management thinking. They say organizations will continue to work in a traditional 20th-century, post-Industrial Revolution operating model, including hierarchical management structures that tamp down innovation and sap motivation through a more command-and-control approach to managing the workforce.

What we have seen in earlier chapters tests the Pessimists' point of view. In reality, increasing numbers of organizations *are* addressing these challenges and making the investments required to drive change. There is, in my experience, widespread understanding that there is significant value in driving people engagement and that this drives innovation and improved performance. As we saw in previous chapters, there is strong evidence emerging that organizations are changing the way they think about their workforce. So why is there a case for optimism?

First of all, people performance improvement is now widely seen as a 'final frontier' for creating organizational value. More and more company boards, government organizations, executives and politicians are beginning to address the significant untapped value that people create when in the right place, right time, with the right skills and right motivation. The talk that 'people are our greatest asset' has been replaced with action and new thinking that just saying so is not enough.

Second, creating an environment where people flourish by engaging them in their work is, today, seen as good business. Enough data and evidence exist to demonstrate that engaged employees produce better outcomes. They treat your customers better, they come up with new products and services, they create new and better ways of doing things, and they stay with your organization longer. Engaged workplaces are also a lot more fun.

Third, time and money are being invested in implementing new HR operating models. The benefits of an integrated human capital lifecycle, where employees enjoy an end-to-end and consistent employee experience, are revolutionizing people performance. Additionally, many organizations are moving the centre of gravity for talent management out to the line management and away from HR, making it a more strategic and less transactional process. Looking after their talent directly puts managers at the centre of building trust and ultimately more engagement in their people's work lives.

Fourth, cloud HRIS technology has significantly improved the employee and manager experience. These platforms are simple and intuitive to use, requiring very little training. They give a consumer-grade online experience and are available 24/7 on a PC or even a smartphone. They are also cheaper to maintain, and significantly reduce the amount of hardware and other IT spend that older generations of HRIS incurred.

Next, organizations are changing their structure to take advantage of digital technology. They are flattening hierarchy and removing levels of management that are no longer needed, given the level of automation and intelligence of the software. Organizations are instilling new management disciplines around virtual working, digital skills, and reducing organizational drag by getting rid of processes and policies that do not add value, as well as driving down the number of emails, and utilizing collaboration technologies instead. Technology is simplifying our home lives and the same ideas and approaches are being brought into work. Digital at home, digital at work.

Lastly, the post-baby-boomer generations are demanding that organizations rethink the world of work. Contrary to current thinking, these generations have similar desires and requirements to the boomer generation (they also want financial and job security). However, they are demanding more control over their workplace, their working hours and, more importantly, their careers. They want more flexibility in when and where they work and have an intuitive grasp of what makes them more productive. Many organizations are tapping into these new work attitudes and this reality is driving substantial change in the make-up of the 21st-century workplace.

Recall from earlier chapters that the OECD, leading the Pessimist camp, argues that people productivity will continue to be a challenge for decades to come as they predict that organizations (Guillemette and Turner, 2018):

- will not change structure to adapt to technology and ways of working;
- will not adapt to how people are motivated in the 21st century;
- will not make investments in making work as digital as home;
- will not make the investments in aligning people to new technology and a digital workplace.

However, the reality is turning out to be much different, and as we have seen, change is happening at a pace, and the benefits are measurably positive in both people performance and organization performance. Therefore, there is one last piece to the PEIP story: how to make the case for change and get started implementing it. Let's tackle this next.

What is an effective 'case for change'?

In previous chapters we outlined real examples of organizations changing the way they think and act, seeing real benefits in improving engagement, innovation and people performance; so there is a lot to be optimistic about. So, what next?

To embark on any change of the magnitude of PEIP, your organization is going to want to know 'why now, what are benefits, the risks, how do we get from here to there, and how much will it cost?' An effective case for change captures the rationale for initiating a programme of change and provides the data and story that helps convince decision makers to take action.

A well-structured, formal document, the case for change tells the story of an initiative from beginning (what problem or situation triggered the initiative) to middle (what benefit, value or return is expected) to end (how do we get there from here). These cases are typically written at the project or initiative level as a way to secure funding and commitment. However, before putting fingers to keyboard, it's important to take a look at three key high-level starting principles for the ideal case for change:

- the human point of view;
- technology;
- economic viability.

The human point of view

The human point of view is *the* jumping-off point for the PEIP case for change. It is easy to lose sight of the human element of these change programmes, as, often, they become very quickly caught up in the process and technology change. Being connected to the workforce right from the start, and understanding what they are looking for, is critical to gaining buy-in. Make sure your programme starts with their point of view first.

Technology

Even though you should be very careful to avoid making your change programme all about the new technology, it still has a very important place in driving change. The technology should be considered foundational to the change programme, but is not the overriding element. It's the enabler of the change, not the change itself.

Economic viability

Once the first two elements are established, the justification for the investment in time, resources and money is usually where the final decision is taken. This is where the return on investment must be defined, and a payback period established. Often, because these change programmes are seen as highly strategic, a case that 'breaks even' can be enough to consider it viable. However, given the amount of money that can be saved by just simplifying and reducing the costs for the technology, this can also make these cases attractive, with compelling returns, in reasonable paybacks. But, at a minimum, the programmes need to be viable to get the 'green light'.

A compelling case for change is a powerful vehicle for presenting the rationale and approach for implementing PEIP because, if well constructed, it will address many of the most common objections or challenges to driving change. It also becomes a guide for the programme, to keep it on track, and feeds into your programme roadmap: how to get from here to there.

Simply put, your case for change is the documented answers to the following typical questions the organization will ask.

What do you want to do? Articulate your case for 'why now?'

Articulate the vision and mission of the effort and describe what it is that the organization wants to do and compelling reasons for doing it immediately.

This should be a statement put together in collaboration with others on the team, and those who are key stakeholders for the programme. The fewer words the better as you set out to explain the rationale. It should be a punchy statement that gets to the heart of what exactly needs to change and why it is a strategic imperative now. It should be an inspirational call to action that is linked to the organization's overall business objectives and how the programme will support those objectives.

What outcomes are you seeking?

Develop a shortlist of the top five to ten (no more!) high-level key outcomes that you are confident that your PEIP programme can achieve. They should, again, align to and support the overall business objectives. These are usually statements of action, rather than specific numbers, but each should have quantifiable benefits. For example:

- improved workforce engagement (with targets);
- simplification (processes and technology);
- people insights (actionable data);
- reduced IT spend (cloud HRIS replacing expensive legacy system);
- improved employee experience (integrated digital HCM).

Keeping these outcomes at a high level helps everyone understand what to expect and sets the stage for the business case analysis that will then back up these outcomes with cost vs benefit and ROI (return on investment) calculations (more on this in a moment).

What are the pros and cons? Risks, challenges, opportunities

Every programme has its pros and cons. It is important not to oversell what you are trying to accomplish and be clear-eyed with everyone involved on what the potential downsides may be. Creating an agreed list of pros and cons helps you to identify the risks, the challenges and the opportunities that exist. It's impossible to look into the future and get these all right, but decision makers will want to see that you have done your due diligence on what may happen down the road, and created plans to mitigate the downsides while at the same time planning to capture the benefits of the upsides.

What is the business case? Qualitative and quantitative benefits

The business case is your forecast of financial and other benefits for your PEIP programme. It is the justification for when the business asks: 'What happens if we take this or that action?' The case answers in business terms: business costs, business benefits, business risks. A strong business case combines forecasts for both financial (quantitative) and organizational (qualitative) benefits. It includes business costs, business return on investment/pay back calculations and business benefits. It answers the questions: Does the programme earn enough to cover its costs ('pays for itself')? Is it more profitable than other available options? Is it the lowest-cost solution available?

Who are your stakeholders? The decision makers

Stakeholder engagement and stakeholder management are arguably the most important ingredients for successful programmes, and yet are often regarded as an afterthought. Transformation programmes depend on people to respond to the outputs and benefits that they deliver. People will only respond if they are engaged. The phrase 'stakeholder management' implies that these people can be made to respond positively to a project, but the truth is that a programme manager frequently has no formal power of authority and therefore has to rely on engagement to achieve his/her objectives. Stakeholders should be identified and *persuaded* to join the transformation; they cannot be *told* to do it. Therefore, successful programmes recognize that they live in an 'influence model' situation, and behave accordingly. Successful programmes create a map of key decision makers and influencers and use the case for change to persuade them to join the programme as supporters and approvers of business decisions. Ideally, these stakeholders become part of the programme board, who meet regularly to discuss, debate and decide the way forward.

What is the cost of doing nothing? The monetary and opportunity costs of no change

Forecasting the cost of doing nothing can be one of the most important parts of the case for change. On the face of it, this statement might seem counterintuitive. However, the death knell of many strong cases for change is, 'We don't have time to do this right now, other initiatives are more important.'

This is why it is just as important to quantify the cost of doing nothing and the opportunity costs as well, so decision makers understand that, transformation or no transformation, there are costs to the organization. For example, attrition of top talent can take place when an organization still looks like 1997. The best talent wants to work in the 21st century, not the 20th. Another example is the cost of staying on legacy IT systems; quite often the costs of maintaining the status quo in your HRIS can be very expensive. An example of opportunity costs is the productivity lost in staying in the status quo; again, this can be very expensive as well. This is why the *best* cases for change make a clear statement on the cost of doing nothing.

What is your roadmap for change? Proposed options and scenarios to get from here to there

A roadmap for change is a visualization of what actions are needed to help your organization achieve short-, to mid-, to long-term goals for your PEIP programme. It connects the dots for people in your organization by showing everyone how their everyday actions fit with the PEIP vision of where it wants to be in the future.

A well-designed PEIP roadmap is like a GPS for your transformation. It not only tells you where you are and the quickest way to get to your destination, it can even shorten the route as less time is wasted with team members trying to figure out things on the go. It's one of the best tools to lift the fog and make your vision clear for everyone on the team. If you want to pinpoint the choices to make today that will affect your future, a good strategic roadmap can be your ally. More on this later in this chapter.

Identifying the benefits of PEIP

Implementing PEIP is very different from almost any other programme you will attempt. It has a broad range of different 'value drivers' (buckets of quantifiable benefits) because it is a programme that, by definition, will touch all parts of the organization. Nevertheless, despite its 'broadness' it still needs to be sharply defined with a depth of details, or the programme can get overwhelmed by trying to be all things to all people. Best practice in the development of a PEIP case for change typically focuses on five high-level areas of overall impact on the organization (see Figure 5.1).

FIGURE 5.1 The high-level benefits of PEIP

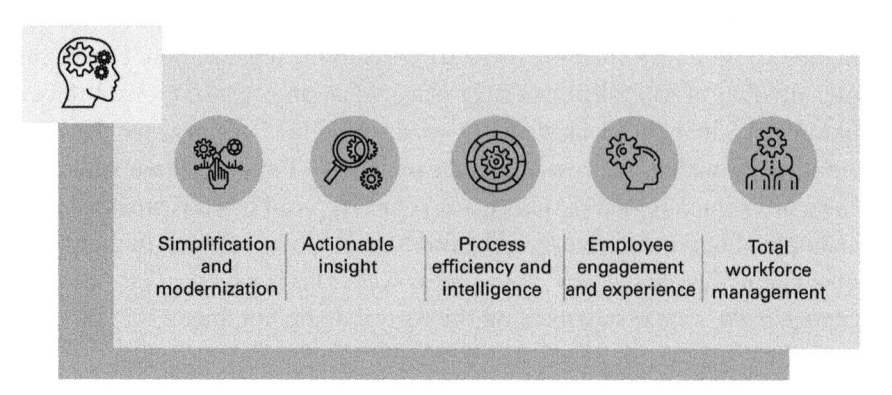

| Simplification and modernization | Actionable insight | Process efficiency and intelligence | Employee engagement and experience | Total workforce management |

Simplification and modernization

Adopting a new HR operating model and processes to support PEIP, will, by definition, create an HR organization that is streamlined, more focused on performance and will drive a more modern mindset. Additionally, becoming as digital at work as we are at home significantly updates the organization's technology and creates a more 'digital' mindset and outlook.

Modern digital HRIS platforms come with ready-made best practice processes that force the organization to adapt to these simpler and more agile ways of working. This is both a blessing and a challenge. The best practice processes that come with the platforms are market tested over many years and are constantly being improved and streamlined, but fitting the organization to these platforms is not an easy task. For example, in the 1990s and early 2000s any organization that implemented an on-premises installation of PeopleSoft or SAP HR created a highly customized version of the software to fit to the *organization* (not to the software). Modernizing your HR organization by adopting a cloud HRIS will overhaul how you work in the future and, if followed through, will significantly streamline your processes. Simplifying and modernizing HR may seem like a 'soft', qualitative benefit, but as we will see later in this chapter, it is more substantial than you might think. It also ticks a checklist item on a CEO's to-do list; many are under pressure from their boards on the subject of simplifying and modernizing the organization. Same goes for the public sector; taxpayers expect that their government services are more modern, streamlined – and cheaper.

Actionable insights

We hear repeatedly about the importance of 'big data'. Everyone should have access to big data, right? As we touched on in previous chapters, big data is the enemy of PEIP. What we need is bite-sized, relevant chunks of data to make PEIP provide maximum value. Getting lost in an avalanche of data does not help anyone. What's important is a situation where the data brings us easily understood *insights* rather than just large amounts of unintelligible numbers. Just having the data, and a lot of it, does not bring much value. In fact, being able to provide actionable insights is the most important emerging new job for the HR organization: becoming *people insights salespeople*.

One of the most powerful advantages of modern cloud HRIS platforms is that they have almost completely automated the analysis and presentation of actionable insights. These platforms have become very powerful people data analysis machines. The HR organization does not need to worry about becoming 'data scientists' who do complex stochastic modelling or detailed regression analysis; the machines do this for us. The skill that the modern HR organization needs to develop is one of being able to persuade and convince the organization decision makers to do something different based on the insights that the HRIS provides. Not only is this an important skill to develop, it's one of the most powerful value drivers that PEIP brings to the organization. Having the ability to take more accurate decisions based on real-time actionable insights can help an organization avoid very costly mistakes. Additionally, the speed with which these actionable insights can be developed is ideal for the agile organization. The real-time, 24/7 nature of the insights that these platforms provide are at the heart of the truly agile organization. The value in both risk avoidance (from making poor decisions with bad information) and the ability to speed up the decision making in an organization, in many cases, provides enough benefit on which an entire value case can be made.

Intelligent processes and technology

As discussed previously, today's cloud HRIS systems come with best practice HR processes built in. Increasingly these processers are enabled further by intelligent software algorithms and matching learning. They significantly improve the productivity of HR and the workforce by automating areas like employee or manager self-service. For example, many of these platforms have chat bots that can guide an employee on just about any aspect of self-service. Very similar to when you call a contact centre and speak to a bot, they can guide you to the right person, product or service with very little human intervention. These bots learn about teams and individuals and become more effective and, most importantly, more efficient over time. There are potentially significant cost savings and productivity improvement that can change the role, size and shape of the HR shared service centre as a result. This is an area that will continue to grow in value and make the case for change stronger and stronger in the very near future.

Employee engagement and experience

Ensure every employee has access to what they need when they need it, to manage careers, teams and productivity. Leverage mobile, social collaboration across all HR processes – digital at home, digital at work. Creating a consumer-style experience at work is proven to build employee engagement and very often is listed as a top priority by the most senior decision makers. Sometimes engagement is thought of as a 'soft benefit'; however, in recent times the sophistication in engagement tracking and measurement allows for direct measurable benefit to be attributed in terms of people retention and improved productivity. Both can have hard dollar value contribution to the case for change.

Total workforce management

Visibility across the full pool of human resources is a clear competitive advantage. Right people, right place, right time is critical for your internal talent, but also for externals. The ability to dip into external pools onboard and align exceptional outside talent can improve productivity as well as reduce overall costs of labour. The value in gaining visibility into your total workforce across your organization to effectively manage all contributors for maximum business impact can be a major driver for value in your case for change.

Quantifying the value of PEIP: the business case

Businesspeople everywhere are losing patience with management error leading to poor financial outcomes for the organization. They also demand real accountability for decisions and plans to mitigate risks. And the competition for scarce funds is increasing everywhere, particularly for people programmes. No surprise, then, that many organizations now *require* business case support for project, product, investment and capital acquisition proposals.

Even though everyone talks about the business case, surprisingly few really know what that means. The business case is an analysis, meant to produce three key outcomes:

- **Forecasts:** The business case asks, 'What happens if we take this or that action?' The case answers in business terms: business costs, business benefits, business risks.
- **Proof:** Reasoning and evidence make the case for choosing one action over another. The case proves in compelling terms why the chosen action is the better business decision.
- **Financial justification:** The justification case demonstrates that an action meets one of three criteria. The proposed action:
  - earns enough to cover its costs ('pays for itself');
  - is more profitable than other available options;
  - is the lowest-cost solution available.

Additionally, a compelling business case produces two key capabilities in executing on change programmes:

- **Decision support:** Given two or more possible courses of action, the business case provides objective, quantitative measures for deciding which action is the better business decision. The case also shows whether or not the business risks with possible actions are acceptable. Capital review committees, for instance, rely on business case analysis to help prioritize and choose from incoming funding proposals.
- **Business planning:** The business case can deliver accurate forecasts of future spending needs and incoming revenues. This is key as, over time, the profile of change, well, changes. Being able to predict and then act on these changes is key to keeping momentum and sustaining the change programme.

The PEIP business case: what does good look like?

Value definition for PEIP should be balanced across the two value agendas we discussed in Chapters 1 and 2. There are two high-level areas of monetary value: *Strategic*, all about improving productivity, and *Foundational*, reducing costs from effective and efficient HR back office (see Figure 1.1). Improving productivity is where the most value can be found (worth as much as 10 × cost savings); however, the most powerful cases for change also include money saved from being more efficient, so both are important.

Benefits such as process efficiency, labour productivity and cost reduction due to full-time-equivalents (FTE) and time savings are usually all readily measurable, down to the dollars and cents; all measurable, as long as you can identify and track the data points. Most finance organizations have this data available and it should be a key part of the programme team when quantifying the case for change.

On top of these quantitative and tangible benefits, there are also benefits to be found in reducing risk in the organization. These risks could be related to project risks, such as lack of resources, interdependency with other ongoing projects/prerequisites, business-related risks (ie economic downturn and budget cuts), as well as regulatory exposure, and so on. These can also be identified and calculated so that we have strategies in place to mitigate these risks when we encounter them, which adds to the overall value of the case.

Additionally, there are qualitative benefits that we cannot always put a monetary figure on, that are just as important. Employee wellness is a prime example, yet we can still calculate a number for it based on benchmarks from the value of enhanced health and better attendance; but many still categorize this as a 'soft' benefit. However, once again, the level of sophistication around the benefits from wellness programmes is increasing and the ability to measure in hard dollars is improving as more benchmark data is developed.

Finally, we have innovation which creates additional value for the business. Implementing change that creates an environment where new products and services, or new ways of working, are regularly being generated can be worth a tremendous amount to an organization. *It* is critical for all stakeholders in the organization to understand the potential.

Figure 5.2 shows the four main categories for quantifying, in detail, your case for change and provides a structure on which you can organize the detailed statement of benefits: the business case. At the highest level, your business case value should be categorized or structured according to these four buckets. These are the four areas of change that senior decision makers are usually looking for to support their business imperatives. If you map

FIGURE 5.2 Main areas of business value of PEIP

Efficiency/simplification
Simplify processes to improve handling of business complexity

Cost-effective
Reduce HR cost per employee

Decision quality
Provide accurate, real-time, relevant information to enhance business decisions

Agility
Improve agility, while decreasing time to and cost of responding to business changes

Operational optimization

Strategy enablement

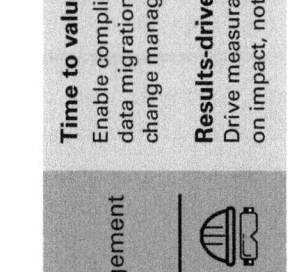

Business value

Risk management

People experience

Time to value
Enable compliance/security, data migration, integration, change management, adoption

Results-driven
Drive measurable change, reporting on impact, not just activity

Engaging experience
Deliver modern user experience, via mobile, for better adoption

Strategic HR
Shift HR focus on purposeful, strategic work, (total rewards, diversity and inclusion, well-being)

your business case to these four areas, you are well on your way to getting the management attention required to justify your programme.

- **Operational optimization:** every strong business case has, at its core, reducing costs through optimizing operations. Often, this is the area that gets the most immediate attention. Every CEO and CFO, every government minister or secretary, wants to know what you are doing to help them demonstrate to shareholders or taxpayers that they have their cost base under control and are constantly looking for areas to do better. This area often is called the 'basic hygiene' of operations. If your business case cannot pass the most basic test of cost effectiveness, the other three areas of value quickly become irrelevant. Demonstrating cost savings from simplification and operational efficiencies is 'low-hanging fruit' and is a recommended starting place for your case. The good news is that the PEIP business case is ripe for creating and capturing cost efficiencies. More on this in a moment.

- **Risk management:** similar to cost savings from efficiencies, a case that demonstrates how risk can be reduced is very welcome to senior decision-makers. Since the Great Recession, demonstrating compliance to regulatory bodies is a major part of doing business. Many CEOs, half-jokingly, will say this is the 'keep me out of jail' or out of the news part of the business case. However, more seriously, avoiding major fines or other penalties is a major financial benefit of a PEIP programme. Flattened organization hierarchies increase visibility to risk, and new cloud HRIS technology automates reporting to regulatory bodies, significantly reducing costs, improving compliance and generally helping senior leaders sleep better at night. A very valuable part of your business case.

- **Strategy enablement:** as you may recall from previous chapters, one of the most challenging parts of being the leader of an organization, big or small, public or private, is when you hand over your business strategy to the organization to execute. Most senior leaders plan for this and assume that much of what they designed in the strategy will be diluted in execution. It's just a cost of doing business. However, PEIP, once implemented, gives the organization an advantage in execution. First of all, business objectives can be better cascaded to individuals in personal objectives that match to the individual's contribution to execution (and results). Second, the organization becomes more agile and able to deal with and manage change during execution. Response times improve and, given real-time data is available to all that need it, errors or challenges in execution can be picked up quicker and more accurately. This saves time and money, as well as grief as complex programmes of change are implemented. It is akin to an airline pilot having accurate instruments and real-time information to fly by when in heavy fog – a powerful capability when in the throes of change.

- **People experience:** on the surface, this would seem to be a 'soft benefit'; however, as we have seen, this is, first, a major driver for senior decision makers in today's change programmes and, second, has measurable value. A modern user interface is simple to use and makes people more productive on the job. It allows people to do complex tasks when not at their desk, as mobile applications allow work to be done almost anywhere, creating additional measurable value.

Quantifying PEIP

Now to the heart of the business case: quantifying the value. Figure 5.3 gives a helpful guide on how to organize specific financial benefits. Similar to the HR Value Model from Chapter 1, the model here is split into two main parts. On the left are the 'foundational' aspects of saving money and improving efficiencies. This is the bottom part of our HR Value Model. On the right is the value from strategic change. It is the improvement in organizational and people productivity. It is the 'strategic' or top part of the HR Value Model. It shows that there are two value agendas that we are quantifying and outlines examples of detailed items for quantification. This is a typical value 'tree' that you can take to your finance organization as a starting point for quantifying your business case. These are areas that, often, the finance organization has the data for and can accurately calculate financial value to support the business case. This is where, working across operations, finance and HR, the case starts to take shape and gain buy-in from the organization. Across the bottom is the split of overall value: 30 to 35 per cent of the value comes from efficiencies, whereas the majority of value in your business case, 65 to 70 per cent, comes from improvements from more productive people.

In your partnership with operations and finance, the value tree can then be formatted into the one-page ROI and pay-back model that most senior decision makers are looking for (see Figure 5.5). They want to know total investment and then the 'pay-back' period for their investment. Figure 5.4 is an example and is the anchor page for your overall case for change. From here, the last step is your roadmap for change. How do we get from where we are today, to where we need to be?

FIGURE 5.3 The PEIP value tree

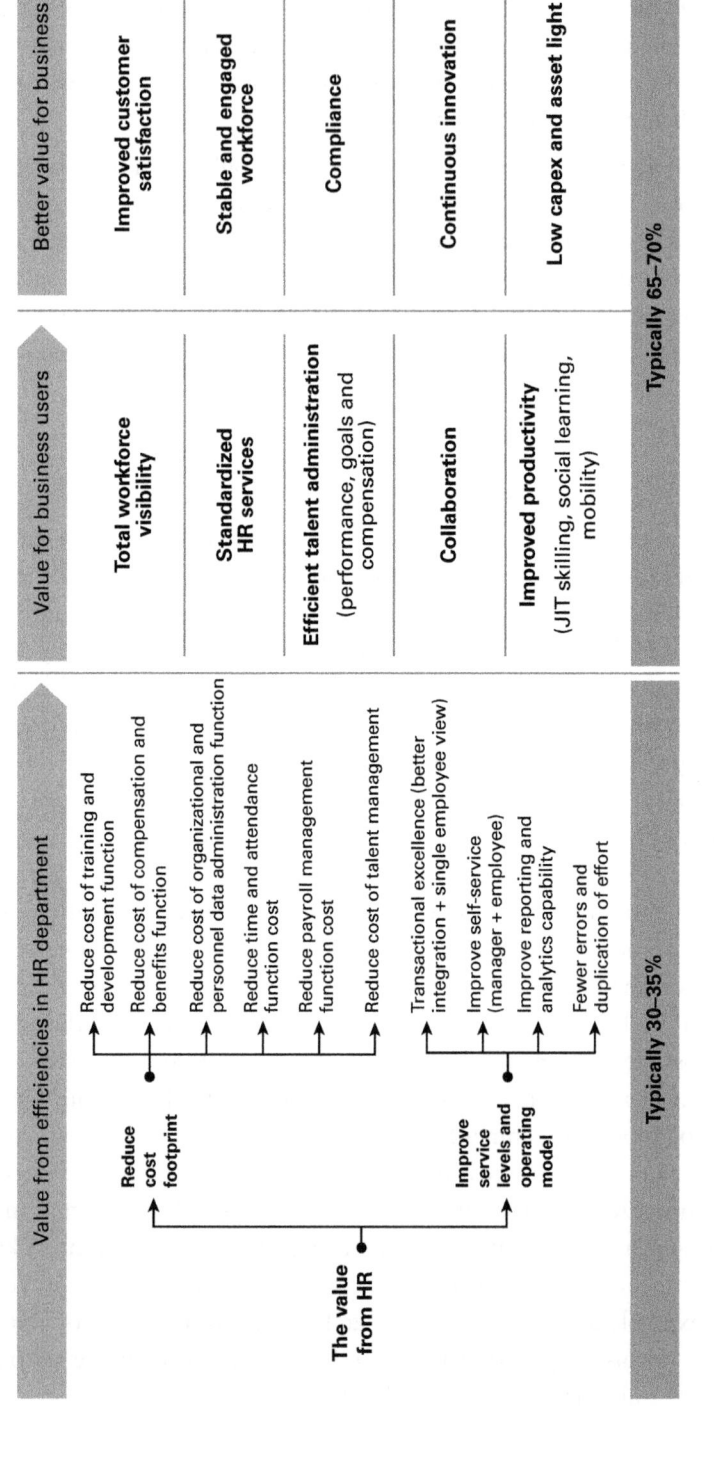

Value from efficiencies in HR department (Typically 30–35%)

The value from HR

- **Reduce cost footprint**
  - Reduce cost of training and development function
  - Reduce cost of compensation and benefits function
  - Reduce cost of organizational and personnel data administration function
  - Reduce time and attendance function cost
  - Reduce payroll management function cost
  - Reduce cost of talent management

- **Improve service levels and operating model**
  - Transactional excellence (better integration + single employee view)
  - Improve self-service (manager + employee)
  - Improved reporting and analytics capability
  - Fewer errors and duplication of effort

Value for business users (Typically 65–70%)

- Total workforce visibility
- Standardized HR services
- Efficient talent administration (performance, goals and compensation)
- Collaboration
- Improved productivity (JIT skilling, social learning, mobility)

Better value for business

- Improved customer satisfaction
- Stable and engaged workforce
- Compliance
- Continuous innovation
- Low capex and asset light

FIGURE 5.4 A typical return on investment summary

Compelling economics
Benefits significantly exceed cost

Cash flows
$ Millions

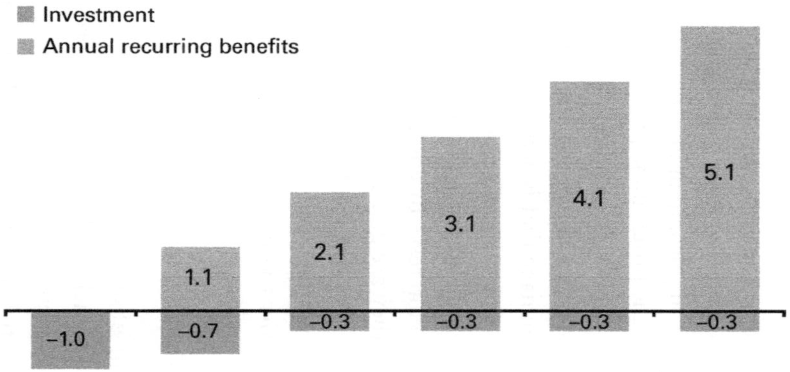

■ Investment
■ Annual recurring benefits

-1.0	1.1 / -0.7	2.1 / -0.3	3.1 / -0.3	4.1 / -0.3	5.1 / -0.3

Note: The numbers on this slide are for conservative scenario.

5-years project economics

Net present value (NPV)	**6.02 M**
ROI	**226.99%**
Internal rate of return (IRR)	**98.93%**
Payback (in Years)	**1.56**
3 months cost of delay	**0.14 M**

Analysis based on the annual recurring savings minimum

Benefit ramp-up (conservative)

Yr1	Yr2	Yr3	Yr4	Yr5
20%	40%	60%	80%	100%

Developing a roadmap: getting from here to there

The change roadmap does what it implies: it describes how we get from where we are today to the future state. A change roadmap is a time-based plan that defines where a business is on its transformation journey, where it wants to go, and how to get it there. The most effective roadmaps are a visual representation that organizes and presents important information related to future plans.

Add the change roadmap to the case for change and you have the culmination of how the people strategy and HR operating model will support the business strategy; an end-to-end programme that is tied to the overall business imperatives.

Step 1: Programme vision

The first step is key. It is essentially setting out your stall and letting everyone know what it is the programme is about. It should be simple, pithy and something that everyone can understand on reading. It should also become the clarion call for the organization to rally around from start to successful finish. This statement of your vision should be at the top of the very first page. This is the important guiding post that everyone should continually be reminded of as the programme progresses.

A clear and effectively communicated vision can prevent a lot of difficulties and misunderstandings for the organization. The vision you create should have language that is action oriented and follows an approach similar to this: (action) a (deliverable) that (criteria). An example could be (develop) a (compliance programme) that (prepares the workforce to recognize conflicts of interest). By comprehending the vision statement, your team knows where they are going, why, and what kind of action is expected. It is recommended that you use writing tools such as Revieweal or ViaWriting for help with writing your statement. This saves time and can help make your vision easier to understand and more impactful.

Step 2: The critical goals

Goals are an observable and measurable end result having one or more objectives to be achieved. Goals can be broad in scope; for example, a goal might be to 'increase profits'. Or they can be quite specific: 'achieve a payback on return of investment of 18 months'. Additionally, goals need to have a dimension of prioritization. In other words, not everything can be a goal. In fact the fewer the better, and the way to make this happen is to have a clear view on what is critical to the programme, and what is not.

When setting up a program, it can become easy to get lost in the details and lose sight of the critical things you want to achieve. Therefore, a balance needs to be struck between the scope of the goals (broad or specific) and the priorities of the goals (what is important to success, and what is not). Typically, on the scope it is most effective to define your goals more to the specific side of the things, otherwise, if too broad, they can come across as generic and not meaningful to the programme. Likewise, when it comes to deciding the goals to focus on, or what is in and what is out, it is most effective to be somewhat ruthless about what is included, sticking to what is critical to the programme. That which, if not achieved, will lead to failure – known as critical goals.

Step 3: The implementation strategies

List the various strategies for achieving the goals. The age-old framework for establishing strategies, pioneered by Robert Kaplan and David Norton, is the Balanced Scorecard approach (Kaplan and Norton, 2007). This involves looking at the achievement of the overarching goals through four major perspectives: Financial, Customer, Internal (Processes), and Learning and Growth. The Financial and Customer strategies focus on the outcomes you want to achieve. The Internal Process and Learning and Growth perspectives focus on how you plan to achieve these outcomes. A well-constructed roadmap links the objectives in the four perspectives. For example, what are the key financial strategies that should be in place to support the achievement of the overarching goals or objectives? What customer strategies should be established that will yield the desired financial results and achieve the overarching goals or objectives? What internal processes will support the customer strategies that yield the desired financial results and achieve the overarching goals? Finally, what learning and growth processes should be pursued to support the internal strategies that will result in superior customer service, desired financial results and achieve the overarching objectives or goals?

Step 4: The tactics

Now list all the key actions or tactics under each of the strategies. This is a crucial part of the roadmap. It's what makes every component of the map a reality. So, spend some time here to carefully list all the actions that are required, implementable and trackable. Who is going to do what and by when? These answers move your strategic imperatives to operations. Strategies often fail because not enough attention was paid to this part.

Step 5: Potential roadblocks

Outline potential risks in each of the strategies you plan to pursue and the actions you might take.

Step 6: The milestones

Plant a small flag on your map to indicate the spot where important milestones for the achievement of the goals will happen. For example, let's say your company goal was to create an app. Milestones might be set at completion of beta testing and release of the various versions of the product. Milestones are important for team members working on projects, especially longer-term ones where it's easy to become discouraged and overwhelmed. They're opportunities for leaders not only to track progress, but to celebrate progress and recognize the team efforts – and they can oxygenate the team to persevere. The strategic roadmap is an ongoing journey. As the business climate changes and markets evolve, the paths you draw in your strategic map may need to be adjusted. Make strategic mapping an integral part of the way you run your business, on an ongoing basis, and not just a one-time process. The map can guide you to continually find the shortest distance between where you are and where you want to go. Done right, it can also help you find the less risky route. Ultimately, the strategic roadmap can be one of the best weapons in your communication arsenal. It's the one tool that can continue to remind everyone of your vision and keep everyone on the same page, and on your side.

Step 7: Management and accountability

For programmes and programme managers, the case reveals critical success factors and contingencies they must manage to target levels. For business investments of all kinds, the business case provides practical guidance for minimizing costs, maximizing returns, and mitigating risk. A solid case shows directors, regulators, and government authorities that decisions were made responsibly, with sound judgement, conforming to laws and policies.

Once the above are summarized into the case for change, the next step is to summarize into a visual representation: literally a roadmap for change.

FIGURE 5.5 HR transformation roadmap – an example

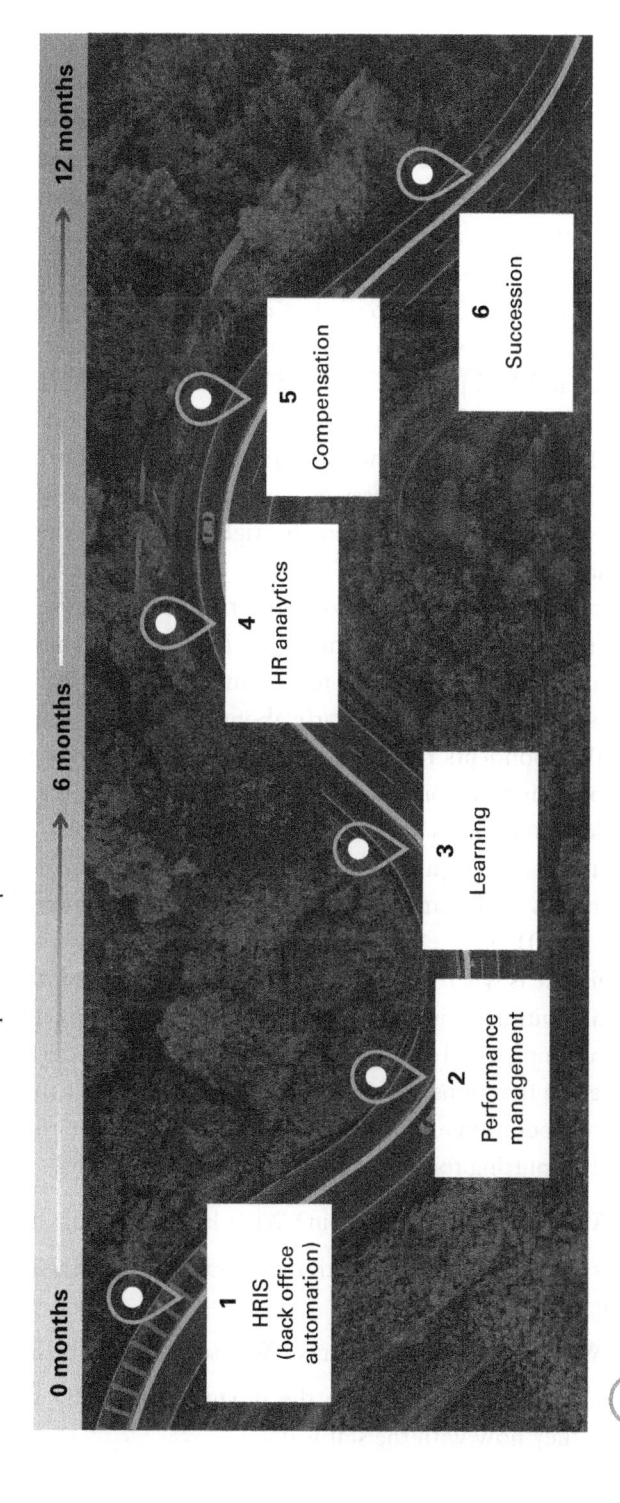

0 months → 6 months → 12 months

1
HRIS
(back office automation)

2
Performance management

3
Learning

4
HR analytics

5
Compensation

6
Succession

◯ Milestones

Beating the transformation odds: key success factors

Once these high-level operating principles are in place and understood, the basic pieces are in place to develop the details of the case for change.

First of all, it is always wise to set out on the PEIP journey with eyes wide open and with realistic expectations. McKinsey & Co put forward a sobering statistic in 2018: years of research on transformations has shown that the success rate for these efforts is consistently low – less than 30 per cent of programmes succeed (de la Boutetière *et al*, 2018). Success would mean, specifically, that these programmes were successful in creating measurable change benefits and had proven an ability to sustain the change for more than two years. Keeping this rather low rate of success in mind as you plan and execute should help make the programme vigilant about the pitfalls; measuring and celebrating the successes (and addressing the failures) as you go will help keep the programme on the right track. Nothing ever goes precisely to plan.

Second, successful programmes avoid a particular blind spot: a failure to involve frontline employees and their managers in the effort. Transformations have their truisms. Successful ones, for example, require visibly engaged C-suite leaders who communicate clearly about the changes at hand. A vast majority of all respondents report these characteristics at their companies, whether or not their transformations have worked. But the results suggest that while C-level support is necessary, it is not by itself sufficient. A transformation's success also requires that people across the organization have a specific role to play and that everyone knows how to carry out his or her part (Maor *et al*, 2017).

An early mistake is where one of either the HR or IT organization tries to develop the case within their own team, leaving out other stakeholders. For best results and improved buy-in, it's imperative that the programme team represent different functions within the organization (project management, IT, HR, finance, operation and the executive team). There are four elements to consider when putting together this multidisciplinary team:

- **Interests:** What do people care about? What keeps them up at night?
- **Analysis:** Is it a broad-based collection of data that can be mined to tell a compelling story?
- **Influence:** Who has the most influence? Whose voice will be listened to?
- **External relationships:** What does the organization really want? How satisfied are they now with the status quo?

As with every significant change, it's key to get decision and/or policy makers involved in helping to develop the vision and roadmap for the future – particularly the investment and the return the organization can expect once we get from where we are to where we know we need to be. A strong programme is clear what the future looks like and is backed up with a plan with accurate estimates of the costs and benefits, including opportunity costs and 'soft' benefits alongside the actual costs, value and 'hard' benefits. The main decision makers need to be briefed and involved in this aspect of the programme right from the beginning. Presenting a *fait accompli* case to them will very often not succeed in getting approval or funding.

Third, once it is decided that the organization is going to take the challenge on to implement PEIP, the next step is to define the cost vs the benefits. To turn talk into action we need to clearly make a compelling case for the time, resources and fiscal investment required to move forward. The good news, at the moment, is that many senior decision makers who are looking to embark on the PEIP journey get the value of the approach intuitively. Often their reaction is one of 'no-brainer' or 'this is what I have been looking for all along'.

References

de la Boutetière, H, Montagner, A and Reich, A (2018) Unlocking success in digital transformations, McKinsey & Co. survey, October. Available from: https://www.mckinsey.com/business-functions/organization/our-insights/unlocking-success-in-digital-transformations (archived at https://perma.cc/77YA-LZSX)

Guillemette, Y and Turner, D (2018) The long view: Scenarios for the world economy to 2060, OECD Economic Policy Papers, 22. OECD Publishing, Paris. Available from: https://doi.org/10.1787/b4f4e03e-en (archived at https://perma.cc/827A-7TYC)

Kaplan, R and Norton, D (2007) Using the balanced scorecard as a strategic management system [Online] *Harvard Business Review*, July/August. Available from: https://hbr.org/2007/07/using-the-balanced-scorecard-as-a-strategic-management-system (archived at https://perma.cc/JWA5-FFY6)

Maor, D, Reich, A and Yocarini, L (2017) The people power of transformations, McKinsey & Co. survey, February. Available from: https://www.mckinsey.com/business-functions/organization/our-insights/the-people-power-of-transformations (archived at https://perma.cc/P9NM-NZMK)

06

A workplace revolution – are you an optimist or a pessimist?

Seize the moment – or let it pass?

In Chapter 2 we introduced a broader definition for the term *productivity*, very simply:

> getting stuff done that measurably improves the economic and human interests of organizations and society at large.

This idea is one where we expand on the classical definition of the word with a broader view, more inclusive of what people really do and how they do it; one that challenges us to think and do differently.

Gone is the idea that humans are machines who just produce widgets. Also gone is the idea that if you put the carrot out there for motivation and use the stick to change behaviours, so the organization gets more of what it needs – debunked.

The expanded definition goes from being one-dimensional to three-dimensional:

- **Value** – the fiscal side of productivity: inputs, outputs, labour which drives GDP.
- **Engagement** – a workplace that is purpose driven, gives employees the opportunity to flourish.
- **Innovation** – more productivity leads to more innovation, and vice versa: a virtuous cycle.

It could be argued that this three-dimensional workplace is more human and less machine-like. A workplace that is more engaging than it is drudgery.

The type of workplace that has greater, broader goals than just producing more, faster or getting more for less. It is about *society at large* and how we *live in it* versus only about how we work. In short, what is being called for is a workplace revolution unlike any that has happened since the first wave of farm hands left the fields to work in factories at the dawn of the Industrial Revolution.

Like the beginnings of the Industrial Revolution, we stand at another inflection point in history where, if we seize the opportunity, we can produce a great leap in human progress, prosperity and living standards for ourselves and our descendants, the likes of which has never been seen before. Or, we could also let it go by, and continue on the path originally set for us back in the late 18th century.

This book has been about outlining the challenges, but not just leaving them there to be pondered (or to fester). I have attempted to lay out a set of proven solutions, a set of examples of those organizations making change work, and a roadmap for defining the value of change and a way forward. Ernest Hemingway said, 'don't mistake motion for action', and he is right. Going through the motions at this point in history is letting the moment go by – not seizing it.

This is where you get to choose. As a business leader, a government policy maker, an academic researcher, or one of the humans who are getting stuff done that measurably improves the economic and human interests of organizations and society at large, *you* are the most important variable in the PEIP equation, the modern worker that is at the heart of a workplace revolution. So, what is your role in the revolution? Let's have a look.

The role of small to medium-sized organizations

Very often, when I conduct a talk or a workshop on the topics in this book, I get asked, 'But what about small organizations, does PEIP work for us, too?' This is a great question. The fact is, the 'small to medium-sized enterprises' (SMEs) that exist all around the world are where the majority of the world's population are employed. It would be easy to conclude that because the very big organizations are, well, very big, that they are where most people work, but the opposite is true, by a long way.

SMEs outnumber large companies by a wide margin and also employ many more people. For example, SMEs make up 98 per cent of all Australian businesses, produce one-third of the total GDP and employ 4.7 million people (SBAA, 2015). In Chile, in the commercial year 2014, 98.5 per cent of the firms were classified as SMEs (OECD, 2016). In Tunisia, the self-employed workers alone account for about 28 per cent of the total non-farm employment, and firms with fewer than 100 employees account for about 62 per cent of total employment (Rijkers *et al*, 2014). In developing countries, smaller (micro) and informal firms have a larger share than in developed countries. SMEs are also said to be responsible for driving innovation and competition in many economic sectors. Although they create more jobs, this is also where a majority of job destruction/contraction occurs (Aga *et al*, 2015)

It may be that the mega-companies, the large enterprises (LEs), get the attention, and I have probably been guilty of this bias in this book, but it really is the SMEs that are going to drive change. In many ways, their role is of leaders in the workplace revolution.

So to the question 'what about small to medium-sized organizations?' Will PEIP work for them too? The answer is a resounding 'yes'. In many ways SMEs have a distinct advantage over LEs in implementing PEIP. Most SMEs, in my experience, have very little in the way of legacy processes and technology. Their HR operating models are fairly simple and effective, as they are serving far fewer people than a large enterprise. So, when it comes to making change happen, they do not have to deal as much with the 'old ways of doing things'. They can move faster and are more agile.

Nonetheless, there are some differences between LEs and SMEs and, in my experience, organizations of 300 people or fewer people are a dividing point. Most organizations of this size have interesting dynamics that affect the implementation of PEIP, or any other change for that matter.

First, in this size of organization, the 'everyone knows everyone else' rule usually applies. They are just the right size where the level of knowledge of the workforce is actually 'common knowledge'. This is a huge advantage in the day-to-day running of the company. It is possible for leaders in the organization to have detailed knowledge of the entire workforce, and therefore getting the right person, with the right skills, with the right motivations in the right job at the right time can be done in a fairly 'manual' manner. Through regular management meetings, backed with spreadsheets, it is possible to run the entire organization in a very 'hands-on' manner. But is this the right way to do things?

In 2014, I was market leader and director for the UK office of an SME consulting firm based in Atlanta – we were about 300 consultants, located in one office in London. Every week, the leadership would meet to look at resourcing projects. HR would come with a spreadsheet of the projects that needed people and the list of those available or about to become available, and we would conduct a lengthy discussion around getting the right person, with the right skills, with the right motivations in the right job at the right time. It was about as 'hands-on' as you could get.

Our ability to do this, with a detailed knowledge of our workforce and, more importantly, a detailed knowledge of our clients, was a unique selling point (USP) of our firm to both employees and clients. It had the double effect of first, our employees knowing that we were taking a holistic view of their work and careers into account on an almost weekly basis, and second, our clients knowing that we took such care to resource their projects. Larger consulting firms were too big to do this as effectively.

True, this was a USP for both our talent and clients, but there was also a significant downside to it. The meetings took a great deal of time, effort and, often, emotional energy. These meetings regularly became quite contentious as managers were competing against each other for the best talent for their projects. The room often felt like a courtroom, where adversaries made their case to the judge (the managing director), who made the final call. This was the disadvantage of an 'everyone knows everyone else' culture, producing a lot of behind-the-scenes shenanigans that sometimes created poor outcomes for the people and the client. There was almost too much knowledge, and therefore biases.

I was recently talking to my successor at the firm, describing the PEIP concept to him, and, like his peers at large enterprises, he was immediately intrigued. He lamented how the weekly resourcing meetings were a drain on time and energy, and, as they were growing in numbers, a new approach was needed; one that was more dispassionate, less adversarial and more 'professional', without losing the focus on the client and deploying to them the right people.

We talked about how attractive it would be to have HR go from being spreadsheet-manning policers of the resourcing process to using more automated technology to do this, and freeing HR up to focus on the more strategic aspects of resourcing (and people engagement) would be highly desirable. Having new technology to match people to roles and leave the management and HR to take final decisions would reduce the dependence on weekly resourcing meetings; the adversarial aspect would be mostly eliminated, and employees would have more say in what projects they worked on by using the technology to input their desires into the process.

This firm does not have legacy technology or a legacy HR operating model; they could start from scratch and implement PEIP relatively quickly.

In addition, the cloud HRIS technologies are first, relatively affordable for a small firm and second, come with HR best practice processes and operating models built in. A win-win, and yet another advantage that this upstart Atlanta-based firm would have over their large consulting competitors, who have decades-old technologies and operating models, legacies that they will have to undo.

Another consideration is that almost all SMEs would like to be bigger someday; to go from 300 to 3,000 to 30,000 people, with requisite growth in revenue and income. It's best not to wait until the organization gets too big and set in its ways; it's best to instigate a programme of PEIP sooner rather than later. Secure the advantage, the agility of being an SME organization, before that edge is lost as the firm grows.

The public sector role

The public sector has a unique, dual role in cultivating PEIP. The public sector role is to:

- Engage and develop public sector employees to drive productivity and improve public services, while being more efficient with taxpayer funds.
- Incentivize and encourage private sector organizations to invest in the workforce; play a positive political role in creating change in the economy and society.

The public sector role is the point where the debates on growth, living standards and deficit reduction converge. As we covered in previous chapters, in the long run, living standards and productivity are closely linked, and our political leaders as well as administrative leaders have a critical role in driving change and creating the environment for the private sector to flourish.

Additionally, the public sector is a massive employer in almost all countries around the world. It is a high-profile workplace, with a unique position in society and the power to set the workplace agenda – for good or for ill. For example, in the UK, one-sixth of workers in the country work in the public sector. This is not an unusual ratio of public versus private sector numbers of workers (O'Boyle *et al*, 2016).

Like most countries, the demand for public sector services in the UK, including healthcare and social care, is increasing, making the public sector one of the fastest-growing parts of the global workforce. Unfortunately, government organizations generally score low in people engagement and development relative to the private sector. It has been relatively tough to build a career in government service in the past decade or so. Like the private sector, the pressure to do more with less is a constant theme, but in the public sector the pressure only increases with time and the next budget round. The austerity of the 2010s continues in many countries, where there is a continued focus on debt and deficit reduction; all necessary things to do. The constant fiscal pressures suck up all the oxygen and it is therefore not a conducive environment for building engagement in the workforce. This can radically alter the environment where driving engagement and innovation becomes a distant daydream while improving the cost base is the perennial focus.

Engage talent to join 'the mission'

However, when it comes to attracting and retaining talent, the public sector usually has one unique advantage: a strong societal purpose. Most people who take up government service do it for 'the greater good' of society at large; they want to serve the community.

Take for example the UK's GCHQ (Government Communications Headquarters), which is an intelligence and security organization responsible for providing signals intelligence (SIGINT) and information assurance to the government and armed forces of the United Kingdom. It was the secret intelligence unit that cracked the German Enigma code during World War II, which many believe shortened the war considerably. Founded in 1919 at the end of World War I, its very existence was not even acknowledged by the UK government until 1994 (talk about a recruitment challenge!). This highly secretive organization has been in the midst of a rapid transformation of focus from analogue communications to digital communications and artificial intelligence. They are increasing recruitment of top talent on a year-on-year basis, competing for the same talent that Google, Apple and Twitter are looking to attract. They need the full range of digital, cyber and mathematical skills to do the highly complex and important security work they perform. GCHQ offer a competitive starting package for graduates, at about £29,000 per year with attractive benefits, but after that the rewards begin to pale when compared to experienced talent in the private sector. As a senior recruitment officer said in a 2019 *FT Magazine* article, 'We just can't compete with Apple or Amazon [in terms of pay]. So, a lot of our focus is on recruiting people with the right motivation' (Bond, 2019); and the GCHQ director, Jeremy Fleming says, 'I don't have all the levers that a private sector organization has. But I have loads of levers that they don't have. People come here because they want the mission, to feel a part of something special.'

GCHQ has another lever that it is using far better than most private sector organizations: diversity. The organization has had a policy for several years to actively seek out the LBGT community along with the black and Asian community. GCHQ has led the way for a number of years in recruiting 'neurodiverse' individuals; people on the autistic spectrum, or those that have dyslexia, dyspraxia, or dyscalculia. They have found that top talent comes in many different forms and have been very successful in putting this talent to work on some of the most complex challenges that an organization can offer its workforce. After all, they have an illustrious alumnus: Alan Turing, who cracked the Enigma code. He was a gifted mathematician, known for being on the autistic spectrum. He was a model for what made GCHQ so successful: brilliant, but also not in the mainstream of recruits; he had a different type of intelligence than others. Turing probably would have struggled to find a career back in the day, but GCHQ thankfully saw past his quirkiness, and deployed him to the most important, most secret mission of his day.

GCHQ officials have found that people with such diverse conditions are able to tackle difficult challenges by putting to best use their 'different brains'. Additionally, they have found that people in this pool of talent are highly motivated by purpose and 'the mission' and become singularly dedicated to the job and the cause – ideal for creating the best conditions for diverse people to thrive at work.

In a similar example, I was recently invited to a dinner with a senior leader in the HR department of a large Canadian city. During our highly engaging discussion, this HR leader talked about the advantage of having a broader purpose to serve in public sector roles, and how it can be a powerful motivator. She told me a story about 'waste water engineers', who are very important to the hygiene and smooth running of the city, and how this team of engineers take special pride in their role. It's unique in that it is not a role they can find in the private sector, as all waste water utilities are run by the city. She explained that they have no problem recruiting and retaining these engineers; as long as they are paid a reasonable salary (and state pension) that allows them to live a middle-class existence, they are completely devoted to their work. They thrive on finding new and better ways to deal with the waste water of this large city. Striking it rich in the private sector does not particularly motivate, so they stay and work the long hours required in this public sector role – a major advantage over private sector work. However, this can sometimes be taken for granted by public sector leaders at the expense of a broader, more strategic approach to managing a public sector workforce. Beware the limits of relying solely on a person's desire to serve. There are many other factors to consider, which we covered in Chapter 3.

PEIP for public sector roles

People engagement, innovation and performance – getting right people, right skills, right place, right time, with the right motivation – is as necessary and beneficial in the public sector as in the private sector; both public sector and private sector individuals and leaders in the workforce value and gain value from the approach equally. Additionally, to compete with the private sector, it helps the public sector tremendously to demonstrate to potential talent that the public sector workplace is as innovative and engaging as any private sector organization.

However, there are key differences between the two types of workforces that need to be considered. As described earlier, what motivates public sector workers can be somewhat different than how private sector workers are motivated. Additionally, in many cases, the types of skills required in a public sector organization can be somewhat different than you will find in the private sector. For example, being a tax accountant in the taxation authority of the government is very different from a being a tax accountant in a private sector firm. A public sector accountant's skills are focused on compliance of organizations to tax regulations through audit, whereas a private sector tax accountant would focus on minimizing the firm's tax exposure and maximizing profit from a thorough understanding of tax laws and their application. The same qualifications are required for the role, but different skills are needed to carry out the job.

Additionally, deploying public sector workforces, 'right people, right place, right time', can also have a different profile than in the private sector. Many public sector roles have a 'long runway', meaning that people often will stay in particular roles for long periods of time compared to the private sector. Take, for example, the Canadian waste water engineers; they have a particular skillset and role that will see them working in this same department for many years, even decades. The same would apply to healthcare workers, like doctors or nurses, who will spend an entire career in one, maybe two roles in one location, or one country. Strategic workforce planning for public sector roles can require a potentially longer time horizon than in the private sector. Often the term 'bureaucrat' is used to describe government workers (often in the pejorative!), but it does capture the essence of much of public sector work, which is often administrative in nature and has a different pace of change than is sometimes found in the private sector. Therefore, overall, PEIP in the public sector has some key differences.

Having made the point, however, it should not diminish the fact that when one is employed in the public sector, people are people, no matter where they work. They have the same desire to have clear objectives, opportunities to develop, opportunities for advancement, leadership that allows them to flourish, as well as a say in the type of work they do and when they do it. The differences between public sector and private sector workforces are, overall, not that big. Nonetheless, it is key to not think of the PEIP model as a 'one size fits all' but to understand the nuances of different workforces and the jobs they fulfil.

Political will to drive PEIP in society

The public sector has a unique role to play in the PEIP story. As we have seen previously, the power of PEIP is that it can not only drive change for organizations but can also create change in society at large. When a nation, or group of nations, has a goal to encourage the development of working places that allows people to flourish by engaging them, allowing them to develop new skills, and giving them the time to come up with new products or services, the knock-on effect for society is a new level of prosperity. As we saw in earlier chapters, in the United States during the 1990s there was an unprecedented level of people productivity driven by exciting new technologies, new management thinking, and a government that helped put in place the right conditions for citizens and the country to thrive. The Clinton administration was known for being particularly business friendly relative to previous Democrat administrations. The Clinton team also implemented an ambitious programme, led by Vice President Al Gore, to make government more efficient by adopting best practices from the private sector.

The private sector and the public sector were working together to take advantage of new technologies, and a focus on getting right people, right skills, right place, right time, with the right motivation. It was a powerful combination that paid off handsomely in creating eight or so years of high levels of people productivity by investing in technology and engaging/aligning people to this new technology to improve the workplace.

The role of the manager in today's public sector workplace is therefore not just to set clear objectives and facilitate ongoing professional development, but to engage staff as service designers and problem solvers in their own right. Giving employees a sense of control and autonomy can be the key factor in delivering higher performance and coping with higher demands when austerity or other major difficult initiatives are under way.

This has important implications for:

- **Policymakers:** to think differently about what productivity means in the public sector – and how to measure it. This means building on recent efforts by many countries to put in place base measures around the achievement of outcomes that are important to governments and service users.
- **Leaders and managers:** to engage staff by connecting them to the organization's purpose; empowering and enabling staff to co-design improvements to processes and jobs, not just as a motivational tool, but as a key source of information about how services, productivity and outcomes could be improved; and strengthening two-way communications with staff to improve collaboration in the workplace.
- **Human resources departments:** to consider the core capabilities required to work in a more dynamic and innovative public sector. These capabilities should include specialist expertise, but also the appetite and capacity to work with the public in redesigning services for improved outcomes and productivity. HR departments must have the technical capability to advise on the construction of roles and organizational structures to ensure that these elements encourage the overall design of good jobs and effective organizational management.
- **Providers of learning and development:** to coach and develop public sector staff to enable more adaptable talent and more collaborative ways of working within and outside the public sector.
- **Remuneration committees:** that think creatively around public sector rewards packages and implement effective programmes of remuneration.

However, do we have to wait for government to see the opportunity? Would it not be better for government to be driving the PEIP agenda in the public and private sector spheres? Proactive government that advocates for and puts in place the right conditions to encourage all organizations to put in the ability to get right people, right skills, right place, right time, with the right motivation, both in the public sector (being a leading example) and the private sector. Political leaders are in powerful positions with rather large megaphones and can advocate for and create favourable conditions for the private sector. Through responsible de-regulation, enlightened government policy and fiscal incentives, public sector leaders can be heroes of the moment by taking the lead on changing how we think and do differently at work, helping the private (and public) sector see the benefit and start to redesign the organization and jobs for the future.

The private sector role

Arguably, the organizations that have the most to gain from PEIP are in the private sector. There is significant untapped people potential, and therefore significant untapped financial value to be had by thinking and doing differently when it comes to the workforce. Most organizations have optimized their processes and back office, and are financially engineered to the point of diminishing returns. There is very little opportunity left to squeeze more blood out of that turnip. The next, and probably final, frontier is people performance. The good news is that although it may be the final frontier, unlike materials, money and manufacturing, the sky is the limit for human potential. Of course, human capital is, in a numeric sense, finite – there is only so much to go around. However, the capacity for human ingenuity, energy and passion has shown no limits throughout human history; we always find a way to make things better and more valuable. So, it seems that we saved the best for last – better late than never, etc (insert your favourite cliché here).

Having said this, then, what is the private sector role in PEIP? The private sector role is to create the 'fly-wheel' that generates ever-increasing value that makes all boats float in the world economy. A fly-wheel is an incredibly powerful tool in the physics of movement. It is, by definition, 'a heavy revolving wheel in a machine which is used to increase the machine's momentum and thereby provide greater stability or a reserve of available power'. The private sector role is to be the one to create and maintain momentum and expand the reserve of available power (value).

The private sector 'fly-wheel' has five key components:

- Know
- Plan

- Engage
- Invest
- Measure

Know

It is beholden on the leadership of private sector organizations to educate themselves continuously on all aspects of the means of production, services and value. They need to understand meticulously all levers they have at their disposal to improve performance and value; to know when (and when not) to pull these levers and in what order. One of the most difficult levers to judge is the people lever. Humans by nature are somewhat random. Always expect the unexpected when it comes to humans. One of the most, if not the most, unpredictable variables in managing a business is people. It should be no surprise that the top-performing organizations have leaderships that have a thorough understanding of their workforce. They are like managers of sports teams who understand the skills, personalities and the foibles of their team and can marshal them to be the best they can be, when it matters most. So, the first requirement, the first role of the private sector organization is to *know* your workforce in as much detail as possible. Stay continually tapped into the pulse of the organization and know when to pull those levers, at the right time, in the right place.

Plan

Another major responsibility of the private sector organization leadership is effective strategic planning to ensure success. As pointed out in previous chapters, the vast majority of change programmes fail to achieve their goals. The private sector cannot contribute to improved societal productivity and prosperity if they cannot execute their own programme of change. Embarking on change to take advantage of PEIP requires a significant amount of planning and communicating to be effective. Implementing PEIP requires a detailed understanding of people priorities, the roadmap to get from here to there and an idea of how to manage people's perceptions of change. The plan needs to have an organizing principle that people buy into and can be built bottom up with a certain level of consensus. It is also the responsibility of leadership to find the right people to drive the programme forward, to give it the best chance of success – a diverse team in skills, background and outlook. This team should have the respect and confidence of the workforce to deliver and to garner full support from the entire organization.

Engage

When executing a major programme of change, it is essential to conduct it as a 360-degree exercise. The most successful change programmes not only engage the workforce, but also engage customers and suppliers. Reaching out to internal and external stakeholders improves the chances of success as it takes into account all aspects of the organization. More importantly, it showcases the organization as a role model for change. External stakeholders appreciate being asked for their input; however, often it motivates them to make change in their own organizations. Individual customers also work in organizations. Seeing another organization do something special, and experiencing the difference it makes, inspires others. This 360-degree engagement creates a virtuous cycle; the workforce seeing customers and suppliers encouraged by change has a motivating impact on them to support the change. Don't be shy about your programme, share it with others. The courage to think and do differently is contagious.

Invest

The discipline of creating a business case for major change programmes is exceptionally important. The two things that every successful change programme has are first, a clear set of organizing principles for why change and how change will be achieved and second, a clear business case that shows the value and return on investment of the change. Shareholders and the workforce alike need to have a clear understanding of the potential value of moving forward. Additionally, a clear understanding of the cost, the investment, that is required to achieve the return, needs to be agreed up front. The other message being sent when the leadership of an organization puts millions into a programme of change is one of confidence in the organization and its future. It's hard to believe, but in 2015 the amount of investment in programmes designed to help the workforce be more productive and engaged had only reached its 2001 level. It took nearly an entire generation to get back to where we were at the beginning of the internet revolution. Demonstrating confidence by making a justifiable investment in people is a winning message, internally and externally, to the market.

Measure

Having a business case for change sets the table for the last component of the role of private sector organizations. It was not long ago that the prevailing view was that measuring outcomes of people programmes was at best 'difficult' and at worst 'impossible'. When my co-authors and I wrote *Calculating Success* (Hoffmann *et al*, 2012), an unsettlingly large majority of organizations that we involved in our research were sceptical that improved people performance could be confidently measured. The good news is that the past eight or nine years have seen a sea change in this thinking. More and more people and finance departments in companies are developing advanced skills and capabilities to accurately measure the investment in people. This is a very welcome and timely development, since the key to driving larger change in the economy and society is to have the ability to prove that an investment in getting right people, right place, right time, with the right skills and motivation has a clear return, encourages and, one could argue, *requires* others to do the same. After all, no one wants to be left behind in their industry.

The key role that the private sector plays in the PEIP story cannot be underestimated. Private sector organizations are the most prominent drivers of change and the ones that can create the fly-wheel that gets everyone going in the right direction. However, even more effective is the partnership of private sector organizations with the public sector, as occurred in the 1990s. The two together can do great things for society if they join forces effectively.

The human sector role

A good friend of mine did me the favour of reading an early version of the beginning of this book. His feedback was very helpful and intriguing as he pointed out a few things that had not occurred to me.

First, the PEIP 'equation' to his mind is not as 'simple' an equation as I had characterized it. He is a senior software architect for a large US bank and in his view, even though his organization is 'world class' as it performs well in the usual sense of generating profits, containing costs and creating shareholder returns, it was seriously letting the workforce down. The bank did not have in place a coherent HR operating model or an integrated set of digital tools and data to help the workforce be more engaged and productive.

They were 'a very long way' from even considering PEIP, and even farther from putting the pieces together to create an integrated human capital lifecycle. In fact, the promise of the PEIP concept, which he thought was very compelling, actually made him 'sick' to think of what they were missing in his organization. So, from his perspective, PEIP seemed a pipe dream; not simple at all.

Second, he found the idea of learning as a tool for retention and for improving people's performance to be very compelling. He described how he and others in his department would probably have left were it not for the investment that was available to further their skills and help them build their resumé. He did say that there was a 'tiresome process' that had to be adhered to, to make the case for the investment of each learning event, however, the funds were usually forthcoming. Having a regular opportunity to build new knowledge and skills was very attractive and motivating for the staff in the IT department. He had no doubt that this focus on learning improved everyone's capabilities and developed greater performance. The only issue is that this is not integrated into the broader human capital lifecycle and even sits outside of HR!

Third, and most intriguing to me, was something he said almost in passing, but it really resonated. He pointed out that the idea of PEIP inspired him personally, but was also a concept where he felt it was important for individuals to do their share in taking the idea forward. So, to this point, this is where *you* come in. We have spent an entire book understanding what organizations need to do to drive change and garner the benefits of this change. However, don't wait for the organization to do these things for you. Take the initiative.

If you are in the leadership of the organization, it is up to *you* to define the way forward, marshal the resources, and communicate a clear plan. This is your time to not only manage the business but to drive the business to a new and better place – one that creates a workplace that allows people to engage with their work and flourish as never before. Be the example of effective and positive change.

If you are in HR, this is *your* time to clasp hold of the strategic agenda of the organization and make it your own; to make clear links between the organization's strategic imperatives and the people strategy to create the workplace where people are invigorated to try new things and have the time and space to grow and prosper; where their mental, physical and fiscal wellbeing is understood and invigorated. A workplace where 'productivity' is improved and measured not just by inputs and outputs, but by how much more engaged the workforce becomes, and how much innovation is developed; new ways of working, new products and services. The place where the organization knows that 'everyone has been made for some particular work and the desire for that work has been put in every heart' and organizes work to achieve this goal.

Lastly, and most importantly, *you*, the employee, you need to *ask*, dare I say *demand*, change and be part of the solution. Or even better, go from being a part of the solution to taking responsibility for it, to help deliver it and do so effectively. And, once you arrive at PEIP, it is *your* responsibility to take control of your career, your life and how you live it, to take full advantage of being the right people in the right place at the right time with the right skills and right motivation. It's not going to be automatic; you will have to work at it to make it work for you!

Optimist or pessimist? Your choice

Now we arrive at the final question. Who are you? Are you an Optimist or are you in the Pessimist camp? There is no judging here. I have tried to put forward a case for a new way of thinking and working (it's actually not that new, it has been around a while, as we have seen) that gives reason for optimism. You are free to accept or reject the principles and concepts outlined. Even if you choose *not* to choose, you still have made a choice. You may not be sure – which is completely fair. You may want more information, or simply want to ponder a bit more in the context of your daily work. All of these options are completely valid. Either way, when a choice has been made, things become clearer on which path we will take. Regardless of the choice, this is progress. However, bear with me as I make one last pitch for the Optimists' point of view.

The one downside of our always-connected 24/7 digital world is that the negatives of everything get a great big megaphone. It is human nature to spot threats and react to them quickly. In fact, we would not be here on Earth and at the top of the food chain if we were not exceptionally good at this. The problem is we were not designed to deal with the speed and volume of the perceived threats and challenges that the internet can serve up to our devices. The constant stream of worrying news tends to put a downward pressure on our view of current affairs; to be unduly pessimistic about the future when, overall, things have never been better here on planet Earth. It would be easy to counter this assertion immediately by pointing out that we are potentially on the verge of ruining our planet's climate through the overburning of fossil fuels. True, we are at an inflection point on this existential threat. However, the flipside of this argument is that the world's population has never been more aware of the threat; creating a raging debate on the causes and the solutions means there is political will to, at minimum, engage on the subject. That is progress.

Pulitzer Prize-winning author Jared Diamond wrote an article for the *Guardian*, 'Reasons to be cheerful', wherein he acknowledges that there are reasons to be gloomy about the future, but that these reasons are somewhat overblown (Diamond, 2005). As he points out, the green shoots of hope are all around us. He sees three main trends that we should be optimistic about:

- the rapid and widespread increase in political awareness of the world's problems;
- an increase in big business getting involved in helping to solve the problems;
- the measurable progress already being made on fixing these problems.

On the first reason to be positive, for example, he notes that despite the current Trump Administration position that man-made climate change is 'fake news', at the State level there has never been more consensus, more belief and more activity on addressing the issue. The activity at the State level is effectively cancelling out the federal government's position and contributing positively to solving the problem. Adding to this, Diamond contends that the energy and commitment of young people all around the world in addressing this challenge is starting to have a real impact on older generations. He equates the current situation, where young people are marching to demand change, to that of the 1960s and the protests against the Vietnam War. Take, for example, the Swedish teen Greta Thunberg calling on schoolchildren to skip school to protest climate change. Greta has captured the media's attention using social media and good old-fashioned town square protests to bring attention to the problem. Diamond contends that governments that are blind to climate change are already losing the battle to sweep the problem under the rug.

Second, Diamond is encouraged by the fact that big business is increasingly recognizing that it is good business to be environmentally aware and prochange when it comes to addressing the world's challenges. Diamond serves on the boards of the World Wildlife Fund and Conservation International and, through his experiences with other boards' members (mainly very senior executives of the world's largest companies), has learned they are not all 'evil' self-interested beings. Sure, he has found it is a mixed bag when working with these executives, but overall, he has been pleasantly surprised at the commitment of many in these organizations to being a major part of solving problems. For example, in working with Chevron, Diamond found that they had far more rigorous environmental standards for their oilfields than many national parks organizations looking after park habitats. Also, company scientists and engineers are highly educated people with highly marketable skills, who can work anywhere. Working in an oilfield is a difficult and dangerous lifestyle usually lived far away from family and friends. Oil companies have found that if their employees cannot be proud of what they are doing, they will very often go elsewhere. Behave responsibly, and even more responsibly than conservation organizations, is actually a good talent retention strategy. This, in Diamond's experience, is creating an environment where many companies are very conscious of doing more good than bad – a very positive trend, driven by the need to engage their workforces.

Lastly, another reason Diamond remains positive about the future is that he can see measurable progress in tackling global challenges through bilateral and multilateral work on creating agreement and solutions among nations. He outlines an excellent example of two enemies working together to solve a problem that impacts them mutually: recently Lebanon and Israel, mortal enemies, negotiated an agreement to deal with a major problem that their mutual airspace encounters twice a year. Eagles and other large migrating birds fly south from Lebanon through Israel every autumn then turn around and do the same in the opposite direction in the spring. Unfortunately, these large birds are flying in such numbers that they regularly collide with aeroplanes, with disastrous results for the birds and the aeroplanes. Such collisions are the leading cause of fatal plane crashes in the region. Despite their enmity, the two nations came together, rapidly, to agree an early warning system on each side of the border, whenever bird activity increases in local airspace. Diamond argues that 10 years ago deep suspicion between enemies would mean this type of agreement would have been almost impossible, but today there is more openness to tackling these problems for mutual benefit.

Another reason for optimism about the future is emerging rapidly: 'responsible capitalism'. The idea is that capitalism, done well and fairly, makes everyone richer, not just the primary owners of the enterprise. Over the past 10 years or so, more and more private sector organizations are recognizing the power of giving employees a share of ownership. There are few things more motivating than having skin in the game. When employees have a real and meaningful financial stake in the outcomes of the business, they, unsurprisingly, behave differently. They behave like owners. They maximize their own performance as well as that of those around them, and they focus on the costs the organization incurs, as this has a direct impact on their own wealth.

The idea of 'employee ownership trusts' (EOTs) and 'employee share ownership programmes' (ESOPs) are rapidly gaining in presence and popularity because data shows that these types of businesses see a measurable increase in people engagement and productivity. As we have seen, overall productivity is stagnating or falling in organizations globally. However, those organizations that have significant employee ownership are seeing the opposite. A recent meta-analysis of existing studies, with 102 samples covering 56,984 firms, finds that employee ownership has a significant positive relationship, on average, to company performance. This exists across all firm sizes, and has increased over time, possibly because firms are learning to implement employee ownership more effectively (O'Boyle *et al*, 2016). The Employee Ownership Association (EOA) has measured improvements in people productivity of 4 to 5 per cent in the first year of an EOT/ESOP, with continued increases year on year. Additionally, the EOA has measured 10-year job growth in EOT/ESOPs of over 25 per cent relative to non-EOT/ESOP organizations. EOT/ESOP organizations also achieve higher wages and net wealth for employees: 33 per cent and 92 per cent respectively (Employee Ownership Association, 2017). With these results, it is not surprising that these programmes are gaining in number and popularity.

Now to bring home the Optimists' point of view. It is hopefully becoming clearer that there are currently a number of momentous trends all breaking in the right direction at just the right time. Organizations are developing a much deeper understanding and putting into action plans to improve performance through a focus on getting right people, right place, right time, with the right skills and motivations. They are investing in programmes that align people to the latest digital technology that makes work look more like home, giving people the tools to do more and work smarter. Organizations are much more in tune to workforce well-being, as well as finding previously untapped talent in the world of neurodiverse individuals. They are finding new ways of organizing work, and structures are being put in place within the organization to take advantage of this new thinking and smart technology, to make people better and make work more engaging. When you combine these people-performance trends with the more global macro trends described above, there are myriad reasons to be more optimistic and less pessimistic about the future. No doubt we face formidable challenges on planet Earth; however, when looked at in the arc of human history, the challenges we face today are all in the context of the fact that, so far, in the 21st century we are faced with less war, less poverty, less disease and less crime than at any time in known human history. Our challenges are 'first world, first class' problems that are not only eminently solvable (and being solved), they present us with the opportunity to drive unprecedented levels of people engagement, innovation and performance which will in turn drive unprecedented levels of prosperity and, indeed, human happiness. A world where we organize around the principle that *everyone has been made for some particular work and the desire for that work has been put in every heart.*

References

Aga, G, Francis, D C and Meza, J R (2015) SMEs, Age, and jobs: a review of the literature, metrics, and evidence, Policy Research Working Paper 7493, World Bank Group. Available from: http://documents.vsemirnyjbank.org/curated/ru/451231468000937192/SMEs-age-and-jobs-a-review-of-the-literature-metrics-and-evidence (archived at https://perma.cc/YDD5-NQRR)

Bond, D (2019) Inside GCHQ: The art of spying in the digital age, *FT Magazine*, May. Available from: https://www.ft.com/content/ccc68ffc-7c1e-11e9-81d2-f785092ab560 (archived at https://perma.cc/YNN3-XBRG)

Diamond, J (2005) Reasons to be cheerful, *Guardian*, 13 January. Available from: https://www.theguardian.com/society/2005/jan/13/environment.science (archived at https://perma.cc/27ZE-Z7R3)

Employee Ownership Association (2017) Employee Ownership Association Annual Conference 2017: Where employee ownership meets, National Center for Employee Ownership, Oakland, CA. Available from: https://employeeownership.co.uk/wp-content/uploads/DAY-1-14.45-15.45-EO-Sector-Update.pdf (archived at https://perma.cc/G794-49G8)

Hoffmann, C, Lesser, E and Ringo, T (2012) *Calculating Success: How the new workplace analytics will revitalize your organization*, Harvard Business Review Press, Boston, MA

O'Boyle, E, Patel, P C and Gonzalez-Mulé, E (2016) Employee ownership and firm performance: A meta-analysis, *Human Resource Management Journal*, **26** (4), pp 425–48. Available from: https://doi.org/10.1111/1748-8583.12115 (archived at https://perma.cc/5SVT-BXNU)

OECD (2016) Chile. In: *Financing SMEs and Entrepreneurs 2016: An OECD scoreboard*, pp 155–73, OECD Publishing, Paris

Rijkers, R, Arouri, H, Freund, C and Nucifora, A (2014) Which firms create the most jobs in developing countries? Evidence from Tunisia, *Labour Economics*, **31**, pp 84–102. Available from: https://doi.org/ 10.1016/j.labeco.2014.10.003 (archived at https://perma.cc/FN3X-H3P9)

SBAA (2015) *An introduction to FTAs (free trade agreements)*, Small Business Association of Australia, Nerang, QLD

INDEX

NB: page numbers in *italic* indicate figures or tables

9/11 terror attacks 32, 84, 107–08, 170

AARP 18
ABC 112
absenteeism 21, 70
Accenture 102
  9/11, impact of 108
  autonomy 53–54
  change management services 84
  flotation 65
  performance management 24
  Woods, Tiger 57
  see also Andersen Consulting
Aetna 90
Aflac 69
ageing workforce, the 18–19, 146, 147–51
  baby boomers 147
  biomedicine 149–50
  'pro-tirement' 150
  'senescence' 149
  'silent generation' 147–48
  working later in life, impact of 148
Agro Food 55
Amazon 116, 176, 210
  Echo 168
American Productivity & Quality Center (APQC) 133–34
Andersen Consulting 82, 106, 169
  'Androids' 85
  digital technology 168
  employer-employee relationships 138, 139
  performance management 24
  see also Accenture
Apollo 11 15
Apple
  Mac 169, 170
  Music 38, 39
  productivity in 38
  purpose 59–60
  recruitment 210
  stores 61
apps, value of 41
Attenborough, David 148
attention deficit hyperactivity disorder (ADHD) 146, 155

autistic spectrum disorder 5, 16, 19–20, 146, 155
automation, impact of 28–31
  agile, becoming 30
  data collection 29
  Great Decoupling, the 30, 165
  of repetitive tasks 29
autonomy 51, 52–56
  and company culture 53–54
  and employee well-being 68
  empowering leadership, impact of 55–56
  and job crafting 54–55
  principles of 53
  and remote working 54

Balanced Scorecard 199
Barnes, Andrew 87
Bellon, Sophie 153
Berkshire Hathaway 1
Bertolini, Mark 90
big data 27, 90, 189
Blau 154
Bloomberg 107
Blue Planet 148
Blue Vision Labs 163
Bono 6
Brannan, Charles 71
Brantley, Bill 74
Bregman, Peter 137
British Telecom (BT) 84, 106–07
Brynjolfsson, E and McAfee, A 164–66
Buffett, Warren 1–2, 148
Bureau of Labor Statistics 18
burnout 89

Calculating Success 28, 218
case for change, making the 183–97
  benefits of 187–97, *188*
    engagement 190
    insights 189
    process efficiency 189–90
    simplification 188
    total workforce management 190

case for change, making the (*continued*)
  business case 186, 190–97, *193*
    financial benefits 195, *196, 197*
    operational optimization 194
    people experience 195
    risk management 194
    strategy enablement 194–95
  'cost of doing nothing' 186–87
  economic viability 184
  human element 184
  outcomes 185
  pros and cons 185
  roadmap for change 187, 198–200, *201*
  stakeholders 186
  success factors 202–03
  technology, as an enabler of change 184
  timing 184–85
  vision and mission 184–85
CEDEFOP (European Centre for the Development of Vocational Training) 118–19, 120, 124, 127
  Skills Anticipation and Matching (SA&M) 119–24
    foresight 120–22
    skills forecast 122–24
Centre for Economics and Business Research 70
Chanute, Octave 158
Chevron 222
climate change 221
Clinton administration 213
cloud computing 82, 101, 171, 176
CNN 112
Compaq 169
'computer productivity paradox' 83
Congressional Budget Office (CBO) 40, 83
Conservation International 221
Consumer Financial Protection Bureau 70
contingency planning 93
Curtis, John 88

Darwin, Charles 87
data revolution, the 27–28
  'big data', value of 27
  data processing speed 27
  data protection 28
Davies, Sally 19
Da Vinci, Leonardo 158
Dell 38
Deloitte 169
Delphi method 123
depression 21

Diamond, Jared 221–22
digital transformation 17–18
  success factors 202–03
dot.com bubble 84, 105, 107
Dow Jones Index 83
Drive 23–24, 51
driverless cars 163
Drucker, Peter 17
Dweck, Carol 57
dyscalculia 146
dyslexia 146
dyspraxia 146

E&Y 60, 169
economic 'pie', growing the 44–45
Ek, Daniel 38–39
e-learning *see* online learning
Employee Ownership Association (EOA) 223
employee shares 65
  employee ownership trusts (EOTs) 223
  employee share ownership programmes (ESOPs) 223
employee well-being 66–71
  financial 68, 69–71
  mental 68, 71
  physical 68–69
  well-being programmes, benefits of 67
employer brand, your 14, 111–14
  employer brand team 113–14
  internal use of 112–13
  steps to creating 111–12
EnableNow 116
engagement, business impact of 49–51, *50*, 81–82
Enterprise Resource Planning (ERP) 169, 172, 174
Ernst & Young 156
European Job Mobility Portal (EURES) 114

Facebook 104, 112, 168
Farm Service Agency (USDA) 134
'federated' HR 11
Fiennes, Ranulph 49
Fleming, Jeremy 210–11
flexible working 68, 71, 182
FluidSurveys 132
Ford Motor Company 156
Ford, Henry 89
Freddie Mac 156

Gallup 49, 73
gender balance, in the workforce 5, 19, 146, 151–54
  local culture, impact of 154

team dynamics 152–53
women in executive roles 151
General Electric (GE) 52, 116
genome, human 145
Geological Survey (US) 134
Gerstner, Lou 99
Glassdoor 154
Godfrey, Arthur 150
Google
  Home 168
  Maps 162
  productivity 38
  recruitment 156, 210
Gore, Al 213
Gothenburg 88
Government Communications Headquarters (GCHQ) 16, 210–11
GPS 162–63
'Great Decoupling' 30, 165
Great Recession of 2008 28, 108
  and financial well-being 70
  IBM performance levels 110
  and investment in people 84
  and rate of productivity increases 32
  and regulatory compliance 194
  and slowed economic growth 45
  workload management 68
gross domestic product (GDP)
  projected growth in 46, 47–48
  US vs Europe, 1995 to 2006 83
Grove, Andy 74
GuideMe 116

Hemingway, Ernest 206
'hire and fire binges' 26, 105–08
Hitch, Patricia 96
Holbrooke, Richard 42–43
holidays, taking 86
Horne, Lena 85
HR value model 8, 9
Huffington, Ariana 69, 90
Human Capital Institute 125
human capital lifecycle, integrated 40, 92, 92–97, 139, 182
  CEO perspective 93–94, 95
  employee perspective 94–95
  at PEMCO 95–97
human resource information systems (HRISs) 172–77, 173
  actionable insights 189
  future of HR, the 176
  HR on demand 176, 182
  'HR service centres' 174
  people analytics 177
Huntsman, Jon 87

IBM 133, 169
  AI Skills Academy 117
  autonomy 53, 54
  behaviours and mindset 108–10
  Global Business Services 99
  HR operating model 99–101
  'JAM' sessions 72
  tools and technology 102–03, 104
  Watson 166
  Workforce Management Initiative 103, 109–10
Industrial Revolution 2, 15, 28, 206
innovation 71–76
  and engagement 72–73
  'jam sessions' 72
  'organizational drag' 38–39, 73, 74, 182
  'organizational thrust' 74–75
    energy 75
    talent 75
    time 75
  Social Exchange Theory (SET) 73
Instagram 112
Intel 74
Internet of Things (IoT) 16
Investopedia 43

Jive 116
Jobs, Steve 59, 60
Johnson, Lyndon 40

Kaiser Permanente 133
'Knowledge, The' 161–62, 163
Krugman, Paul 37, 82

labour market and skills intelligence (LMSI) 119
Landel, Michel 153
Langley, Samuel 158
Lehman Brothers 110
LG 42
'Life 3.0' 150–51
Lilienthal, Otto 158
LinkedIn 94, 104
  and NPR 112
  and recruitment 2, 26
  Talent Brand Index (TBI) 112
  workplace learning research 116
living wage, a 64
Luddites 28, 161
Lyft 163

MacDonald, Randy 99, 104
Maslow's Hierarchy 63
Massachusetts Institute of Technology (MIT) 28

230 INDEX

massive open online courses (MOOCs) 22
mastery 51, 56–59
   and job satisfaction 58
   'laws' of 57
McAfee, Andrew 28
McDermott, Bill 66
McKinsey Global Institute 9
McKinsey Transformation Change survey 81
McNaughton, Stan 97
Microsoft
   dot.com crash 107
   recruitment 156
   Windows 170
   Office 169
'mission-critical' cultures 39
MITRE 133–34
motivation 23–24, 49, 136–39
   employee role 138–39
   intrinsic vs extrinsic 51
   management role 137–38
   performance reviews 52
   in the public sector 210
Musk, Elon 60, 62

NASA 170
National Public Radio (NPR) 112
Netflix 38, 116
Netscape Communications Corporation 106
neurodiversity, harnessing 146, 154–60
   attention deficit hyperactivity disorder (ADHD) 146, 155
   autistic spectrum disorder 5, 16, 19–20, 146, 155
   dyscalculia 146
   dyslexia 146
   dyspraxia 146
   recruitment programmes 155–56
   Wright Brothers, the 156–60

Octel 168
office perks 64
O'Leary, Michael 25
Open University 66
Optunli 134–35
Oracle 169, 171, 176
   Oracle Fusion 104
Organization for Economic Co-operation and Development (OECD)
   country populations 18
   key economic trends and policy 45, 47, 48, 183
   lifespan projections 148
   skills trends 114, 115, 118

'organizational bulimia' 26
'organizational drag' 38–39, 73, 74, 182
'organizational thrust' 74–75
   energy 75
   talent 75
   time 75

Palmisano, Sam 99, 104, 109
Pang, Alex Soojung-Kim 87
Parkinson's Law 88
PayPal 20
PEMCO 95–97
people engagement, innovation and performance (PEIP) 3–4, *4*, 9
   ageing workforce, the 151
   as an aspirational goal 49
   behaviours and mindset 104–10
      IBM case study 109–10
   case for change, making the 183–97
      benefits of 187–97, *188*
      business case 186, 190–97, *193*
      'cost of doing nothing' 186–87
      economic viability 184
      human element 184
      outcomes 185
      pros and cons 185
      roadmap for change 187, 198–200, *201*
      stakeholders 186
      success factors 202–03
      technology, as an enabler of change 184
      timing 184–85
      vision and mission 184–85
   case for change, making the 183
   components of 5
   gender balance, in the workforce 152, 154
   'hire and fire binges' 26, 105–08
   HR operating model 97–101
      IBM case study 99–101
   'human sector', role of 218–20
   and innovation 75–76
   neurodiversity, harnessing 155, 160
   private sector, role of 215–18
      engage 217
      invest 218
      know 216
      measure 217
      plan 216–17
   public sector, role of 209–15
      fiscal pressure on 209–10
      'long runways' 212–13
      purpose and motivation 210

right motivation 136–39
　employee role 138–39
　management role 137–38
right people 110–14
　employer brand, your 111–14
right skills 114–24
　employees, training existing 115–17
　skills forecasting 117–24
　skills gap, the 114–15
Rumi 92, 136
SMEs, role of 206–09
　hands-on knowledge 207–08
　legacy tech and processes 208–09
　as majority employers 206–07
strategic workforce planning (SWP) 124–36
　action planning 132–33
　American Productivity & Quality Center (APQC) 133–34
　benefits of 136
　demand analysis 128–29
　gap analysis 131
　Optunli 134–35
　principles of 126
　segmentation of jobs 127–28
　supply analysis 129–30
　SWP charter 126–27
　three dimensions of 126–27
　trends, historical 127
　workforce engagement analysis 132
struggle to deliver 43
success factors 202–03
technology, harnessing 4, 4, 101–04, 146–47, 160–78
　automation, impact of 28–31
　cloud computing 82, 101, 171, 176
　creativity 166
　data revolution, the 27–28
　dexterity 167
　driverless cars 163
　emotion 167
　Enterprise Resource Planning (ERP) 169, 172, 174
　in the home 168, 171
　human resource information systems (HRISs) 172–77, 173
　IBM case study 102–03
　Luddites 28, 161
　PCs 169
　satnavs 163
　'second machine age' 165
　software as a service 171

Technology Tsunami, the 17–18
technology, as an enabler of change 184
Uber 162
uber-efficiencies 166
Y2K 170
turbo-charging 139
PeopleSoft 101, 102, 104, 174, 176, 177
　customization of 188
Perpetual Guardian 87
Pets.com 107
Phillips 133
　mastery 57
Pink, Daniel 23–24
　Motivation 3.0 51, 53
pivotal jobs 40
Poincaré, Henri 87
'Power Law' distribution 52
presenteeism 70
Price Waterhouse 169
productivity
　defining 37
　　components of 38
　'productivity paradox' 31–33
　　contributing factors 32
　　solving the 33
Provo 88
purpose 51, 59–62
　in Apple 59–60
　benefits of 60
　in the public sector 210
　'purpose-driven' cultures 59, 39
　in Tesla 60–62
PWC Consulting 99

Qualtrics 132

Race Against the Machine 164
RACI model 134
'rank and yank' 52
'responsible capitalism' 222–23
Rest 87
retirement, cost of 18–19
Revieweal 198
rewards programmes 62–66
　employee shares 65
　living wage, a 64
　office perks 64
　paid study 66
　in the public sector 214
　recognition 64
　sabbaticals 66
　'soft benefits' 63

Rometty, Ginny 99
Rumi 3, 4, 92, 136
Ryanair 25

sabbaticals 66
Samsung 42
SAP 171, 176
   autonomy 53, 54
   employee well-being 66
   Enterprise Resource Planning (ERP)
      software 169, 174
   'JAM' sessions 72
   recruitment 156
   SAP HR 104, 174, 188
      in IBM 101, 102–03, 109
   SAP SuccessFactors 82, 103, 104, 177–78
   skills and learning 116
satnavs 163
Schramm, Jen 18
'second machine age' 165
Second Machine Age, The 28, 164
Sines, Edward 157
Singer, Judy 155
skills 114–24
   employees, training existing 115–17
   Skills Anticipation and Matching (SA&M) 119–24
      foresight 120–22
      skills forecast 122–24
   skills development 21–22
      online learning 21–22
      and retention 22, 23
   skills forecasting 117–24
   skills gap, the 114–15
Slack 116
sleep deprivation 69, 89–90
Social Exchange Theory (SET) 73
Society for Human Resource Management (SHRM) 18
Sodexo 152–53
'soft benefits' 63
software as a service 171
Solow, Robert 31
South Korea 42–43
Spotify 38–39, 116
strategic workforce planning (SWP) 124–36
   action planning 132–33
   American Productivity & Quality Center (APQC) 133–34
   benefits of 136
   demand analysis 128–29
   gap analysis 131
   Optunli 134–35
   principles of 126
   segmentation of jobs 127–28
   supply analysis 129–30
   SWP charter 126–27
   three dimensions of 126–27
   trends, historical 127
   workforce engagement analysis 132
stress, at work 20–21, 68
SurveyMonkey 132
SWOT analysis 123–24

technology, harnessing 146–47, 160–78
   automation, impact of 28–31
      agile, becoming 30
      data collection 29
      Great Decoupling, the 30, 165
      of repetitive tasks 29
   cloud computing 82, 101, 171, 176
   creativity 166
   data revolution, the 27–28
      'big data', value of 27
      data processing speed 27
      data protection 28
   dexterity 167
   driverless cars 163
   emotion 167
   Enterprise Resource Planning (ERP) 169, 172, 174
   in the home 168, 171
   human resource information systems (HRISs) 172–77, *173*
      actionable insights 189
      future of HR, the 176
      HR on demand 176, 182
      'HR service centres' 174
      people analytics 177
   Luddites 28, 161
   PCs 169
   satnavs 163
   'second machine age' 165
   software as a service 171
   Technology Tsunami, the 17–18
   technology, as an enabler of change 184
   Uber 162
   uber-efficiencies 166
   Y2K 170
Tesla 60, 62
Thiel, Peter 20
Thrive Global 69
Thunberg, Greta 221
Transport for London (TfL) 68
Trump administration 221
Turing, Alan 16
Twitter 112, 210

Ulrich, Dave 175, 176

'value agendas' of HR 9
van Dyke, Dick 148
ViaWriting 198
von Braun, Wernher 160

Walgreens 156
WalkMe 116
Walmart 29
Washington Post 112
Welch, Jack 52
Who Says Elephants Can't Dance? 99
women, in the workforce *see* gender balance, in the workforce
Woods, Tiger 56–57
Workday 82, 103, 104, 176
WorkForce Europe 21
workforce planning 25–27, 93
    degree programmes on 27
    'hire and fire binges' 26, 105–08
    strategic workforce planning (SWP) 124–36
        action planning 132–33
        American Productivity & Quality Center (APQC) 133–34
        benefits of 136
        demand analysis 128–29
        gap analysis 131
        Optunli 134–35
        principles of 126
        segmentation of jobs 127–28
        supply analysis 129–30
        SWP charter 126–27
        three dimensions of 126–27
        trends, historical 127
        workforce engagement analysis 132
    talent shortfalls 25, 26
working smarter, not harder 85–92
    big data 90
    burnout 89
    concentration period, maximum 87
    deadlines 89
    holidays, taking 86
    metrics vs analytics 91
    shorter working days/weeks 87–88
World Wildlife Fund 221
Wright, Orville and Wilbur 156–60

Y2K 170
Yahoo! 106
YouGov 71

Zero to One 20